Whispers From Heaven

DAILY DEVOTIONS
REVEALING GOD'S GREAT LOVE FOR US

As it is in the natural, so is it in the spiritual...

DEBORAH L. WOODARD
©2019 ALL RIGHTS RESERVED

Whispers From Heaven

Author's Note

The photo on the cover of this book is one of many I have taken over the years. I am always in awe of God's beautiful handiwork, and I love to snap photos of his exhilarating nature scenes! My favorite time to write is morning, which is why I chose this photo. The sun rises each morning in a unique and different way to greet each of us where ever we are and whatever we might be going through. As it is in the natural, so is it in the spiritual! God's mercies are new every morning! As Lamentations 3 proclaims: "22 The LORD's unfailing love and mercy still continue, 23 Fresh as the morning, as sure as the sunrise. (GNT).

Copyright © 2019
Deborah L. Woodard

ALL RIGHTS RESERVED.

No part of this publication may be reproduced, stored in a retrieval system, or transmitted in any form or by any means, electronic, mechanical, photocopy, recording, or any other, except for brief quotations in printed reviews, without the prior permission of the author.

Whispers From Heaven Revealing God's Great Love For Us
was proudly published by
Thumb Printing Professionals • Palms, Michigan • 2019

MY SPIRITUAL JOURNEY

I never recall a time when my parents did not take us to Sunday School and church. They taught us to give thanks for our meals and obey the ten commandments. They believed in God and they taught us that the Holy Bible was God's word. Their faith was just a simple fact of life, and they passed it down to me. I am so grateful for this inheritance.

My Grandma and Grandpa Kirkpatrick lived next door, attended church with us, and also impacted my life in a big way. I would often catch Grandma praying or reading her bible in her front living room, and they always read the daily bread over breakfast. Even though I wasn't that devoted on my own as a youngster, those morning devotions became a daily habit as I grew (train up a child…).

When I was about eight or nine years old, an evangelist spoke one Sunday at our little Methodist church. I don't remember the message, but I do remember the altar call. He invited anyone who wanted to come to the altar and invite Jesus into their heart. I sat there with my heart pounding as he read Revelation 3:20, "Behold, I stand at the door, and knock: if any man hear my voice, and open the door, I will come in to him, and will sup with him, and he with me"(KJV). My grandma had a picture of this very scene hanging on her dining room wall, and it now became so very real to me. I went forward and gave my heart to the Lord that day, and I promise you that through all of the trials and troubles of my life, through all the darkness and losses, mistakes and regrets, Jesus has never left me. Though I may have turned my back on Him in my darkest days, he was always waiting patiently and lovingly to welcome me with open arms and no criticism, no chastisement, no rebuke, no guilt. Any negativity came from my own doubts, fears and sins, which He continually washes away with a single prayer!

I have been in many different assemblies, different religions, and different churches through the years, but I do not esteem myself as an expert on religion. I only know this: I am so grateful for my faith. I am so thankful that He rescues me. I am so amazed at his unmerited mercy, unearned grace and unfathomable LOVE no matter what!

INTRODUCTION

It's five A.M. on a chilly morning in January, 2010. The Lord awakens me to get up and write early this morning. As I tiptoe down stairs and brew my coffee, I anticipate the time alone in prayer with only me and the Lord and my laptop. I am one of those people who have spurts of creativity to write, be it poems, or random ramblings or pages out of my memory bank.

That morning, as I scanned through my files, I glanced at a document I had written in a few times entitled, "Metaphors and insights." I scrolled past it and then hesitated. Something inside me caused me to click on it and as I did, I glanced out the window and whispered a prayer for the Lord to open my heart to whatever he had for me that morning. From that day onward, whenever I sat down with my coffee, early in the morning, I whispered a similar prayer and I can attest to you my friends, His promise in Matthew 7:7 is true! "Ask, and it shall be given you; seek, and ye shall find; knock, and it shall be opened unto you: 8 For every one that asketh receiveth; and he that seeketh findeth; and to him that knocketh it shall be opened." Indeed! The Lord is so faithful! I cannot recall one single time where I was denied when I carved out moments to pray for wisdom, guidance and nuggets of truth. I kept notes at the end of my document throughout this journey and this scripture pretty much says it all:

Thine, O LORD, is the greatness, and the power,
and the glory, and the victory, and the majesty:
for all that is in the heaven and in the earth is thine;
thine is the kingdom, O LORD,
and thou art exalted as head above all.
1 Chronicles 29:11 (KJV)

DEDICATION

A number of years ago, I began writing as the Lord saw fit to drop these thoughts and metaphors into my heart. My darling husband suggested that I turn them into a devotional. As I soon discovered, it truly takes a lot of time, energy, and attention to write a book, and he has supported and encouraged me every single step of the way. He has packed lunches, washed dishes, folded laundry and helped me develop ideas throughout this process. Thank you Honey! I love you so very much, and I could not have done this without your constant support, love, and encouragement!

I would like to dedicate this labor of love to the loves of my life: To my husband who is my rock and number one fan; to my children and their spouses, thank you for your love and continual encouragement. I hope you know how much I love each of you! To my precious grandchildren, who I pray will know the Love of Jesus as I do. To my mom (and dad who I miss dearly), thank you for your faith and for taking me to church to learn about the unmatchable love of Jesus. To my Sissy, it means so much that you have shared my excitement through this venture! To my publisher who has become a dear friend, thank you so much for everything! This would not be happening without you! To my hubby's mom, dad and sister who have always shown me the love of Jesus! To each of my beloved family and friends who have supported, encouraged and prayed for me, I am truly grateful. If you know me, you know that the Lord Jesus is my light, my salvation, and my rescuer. It is my great honor to give him all the glory for every good thing in my life. May these 'Whispers from God' inspire you to look at our incredible world and see His amazing love in each precious moment we are granted!

A PRAYER FOR MY READERS

Heavenly Father:
Each devotion written by my hand
has been a work of Your Holy Spirit.

Each metaphor has been graciously whispered into my heart
in a moment, so that I can better understand
how much YOU love me.

Each one is meant to encourage and help me
so that I, in turn, can encourage whomever is reading this book.

Lord I thank you for each of these devotions
and for allowing me to be an instrument
in bringing the message of Your Love,
Your Compassion,
Your Power, and Your Glory
to anyone who might listen.

I pray that each person who picks up this book
might catch a glimpse
of your great and marvelous LOVE for each of us!
Amen!

JANUARY 1

As the New Year marches in, we may be in the process of purging our closets, cleaning our homes, gathering our financial statements for taxes, and making budget goals and plans for the future. In doing so, we are forced to look back over the past year and review our failures and successes in an attempt to see where we have been and where we want to be emotionally, mentally, financially, physically, socially and spiritually. Until we take inventory on our past, we cannot make changes for our future. This process can be at once painful and fulfilling. Thinking about this, the Lord whispered to me...

As it is in the natural, so is it in the spiritual...

In the same way we need to keep tabs on our home organization and finances and see what we ought to keep and what we ought to purge, so too ought we do the same for our spiritual being. We live in a world which continually claims "There is no right or wrong," and "Everything is acceptable" and "Moderation is the key" and "Don't judge others" and "Take it easy, don't be so hard on yourself" and "You deserve a break." These attitudes have a very enticing pull on the mind and soul and we are lulled into a false sense of security by these notions. However, as Christians, we are actually called to examine our actions. Galatians 6:4 tells us, "Each person must examine his own actions, and then he can boast about his own accomplishments and not about someone else" (ISV). Also, and perhaps more importantly, we need to ask God to examine our hearts: Psalms 26:2 asks, "Examine me, O LORD, and try me; Test my mind and my heart." Psalms 139:3 also asks, "Search me, O God, and know my heart: try me, and know my thoughts...." We are exhorted to examine ourselves throughout God's word.

When we allow God to examine our hearts and follow his word in order to listen to truth and allow him to show us our human condition, it should ring true to what we already know about ourselves. Lord, I know that I am either listening to you or listening to my flesh or listening to the world. I ask you to please reveal anything that is disrupting my walk with You, that I might gain victory over it through the power of your Holy Spirit. In Jesus' name, Amen!

JANUARY 2

The New Year is here, and the weather outside is cold and barren. There is very little sunlight, and the weather has not been warm enough to go out unless you are fully and heavily clothed from top to bottom. To top it off, this year we have yet to have much snow, which for me personally is not appealing. I believe if it's this cold, we should have something beautiful to look at! As I take note of the lack of snow and depressing mood that this dry, bitter weather is creating in me, I suddenly realize…

As it is in the natural, so is it in the spiritual…

Just as the dry, bitterly cold wind and brown colorless landscape can leave a person feeling empty and longing for a change, so too does a dry and apathetic spirit. Today as I look out over the dawning morning and see only grayness and bitterness, my prayer is that the Lord would continue to work in my heart and my husband's heart so that we can live our lives in such a way that we bring light, joy, peace and fulfillment to this life we live and to others. We want the landscape of our hearts to be full of life and the richness of the Lord. Only God can take a dull, dry, apathetic heart and turn it into one flowing with beauty and color beyond our own comprehension. Isaiah V 61:1-3 says it well, "The Spirit of the Lord God is upon me; because the Lord hath anointed me to preach good tidings unto the meek; he hath sent me to bind up the brokenhearted, to proclaim liberty to the captives, and the opening of the prison to them that are bound; 2 To proclaim the acceptable year of the Lord, and the day of vengeance of our God; to comfort all that mourn; 3 To appoint unto them that mourn in Zion, to give unto them beauty for ashes, the oil of joy for mourning, the garment of praise for the spirit of heaviness;

that they might be called trees of righteousness, the planting of the Lord, that he might be glorified" (KJV). Lord, help each of us know our role in this Christian walk...that we are the ones who are to carry the good news to others and proclaim the gospel of hope, peace, joy and unfathomable love to those who are just existing in this world today! AMEN

JANUARY 3

As a teacher, I love a perfectly white board upon which to write. If there is residue from previous markings, it is distracting and just plain annoying to me. At the end of each lesson, I take the time to spray it and wipe it completely clean so the board is fresh and white and so the new markings may be clearly seen. As I thought about this, on this last day of this month, the Lord pointed out...

As it is in the natural, so is it in the spiritual...

Millions of people around the world have celebrated this new year, making resolutions, wiping the proverbial slate clean, out with the old, in with the new. In the same way that I take time at the end my lesson to clean my whiteboard, so too can we take this opportunity to wipe off the smudges and residue from our spirit to start afresh as we walk through this New Year. As David prayed in Psalms 51:10, "Create in me a clean heart, O God; and renew a right spirit within me" (KJV). We can truly take our smudged hearts to the Lord Jesus Christ, and he will cleanse us and make us new! 2 Corinthians 5:17 tells us, "Therefore if any man be in Christ, he is a new creature: old things are passed away; behold, all things are become new" (KJV). Dear Lord, thank you for shedding your blood, which covers my sins each day! Lead me in the paths of righteousness and cleanse me each day! In Jesus' name, Amen!

JANUARY 4

A new snowfall is one of the most beautiful sights to me. It covers all of the bleak, dirtiness of yesterday, it provides protection for the earth from the damaging winds and erosion, and it glistens and sparkles in the light of the sun. As I thought about this, the Lord nudged me and whispered:

As it is in the natural, so is it in the spiritual...

Just as the snow covers up the dirt and stubble of yesterday's unappealing landscape, so too does the love of Jesus Christ cover up my sinful yesterday. His love is like the snow; it turns what was once ugly and unappealing into something breathtaking and beautiful to behold. It blankets me with beauty and gives me a new and fresh beginning. It protects me from the elements of the world - those cold winds that would blow across my soul to rob me of the goodness He has placed therein. Isaiah 1:18 says: "Come now, and let us reason together, saith the LORD: though your sins be as scarlet, they shall be as white as snow; though they be red like crimson, they shall be as wool" (KJV). Thank you Lord for cleansing me and washing me and covering me with your blanket of goodness and love! In Jesus' name, Amen!

JANUARY 5

As I lay awake at 4 a.m. this morning, listening to the wind, I wondered what the roads would be like. The fluffy snow that fell this week would still be fluffy because the temperatures have been so bitter cold. Snow can be so beautiful and yet, so fierce. It sparkles and glistens and provides a playground for the young at heart and yet, it can be deadly to those who must get through it to a destination. To us teachers and our students, it sometimes means a day off from work, while to other people, it means they must trudge through it and travel in perilous conditions. It truly is all a matter of perspective. As I write this, I am awakened to the fact that...

As it is in the natural, so is it in the spiritual...

While some people anticipate each new day in their Christian faith and exude excitement over the beauty and blessings that fall upon them, others view it as if it were a tiresome and perilous journey that they must somehow get through by their own strength and resources. They grudgingly trudge through the day as if it is a chore to live for God. Philippians 4:4 reminds us to "Rejoice in the Lord always. I will say it again: Rejoice!" (KJV). Lord, I want to live with a joyful thankful heart, like a child on a snow day, I want to view each day as a gift from you. Help me not to grumble and trudge through my day, but rather, embrace it with glee and the knowledge that you are ever before me! In Jesus' name, Amen!

JANUARY 6

As I sit in my toasty, comfy home watching the snow swirling in its majestic, winter waltz, I truly find myself relishing in the fact that we are "snowed in." There is something nostalgically magical about a winter storm so great and terrible that it immobilizes us – even if it's only for a day or so. Yes, it is true that we are just coming out of our Christmas break, and while I had envisioned myself spending days and days of relaxing and snuggling up with a cup of hot coco and a good book during this break, I honestly have not carved out one single day to do just that. There must be something in my DNA or heritage or Type A personality that doesn't allow me to 'be still' for an entire day unless I am recovering from surgery or in the throes of illness. Even today, despite the fact that we are going nowhere due to this wonderful, awful weather, (and the fact that we do NOT have a snowmobile) I find myself formulating my 'to do' list and enlisting my hubby to assist me in an effort to feel somewhat accomplished. I understand, intellectually, that it is OKAY to give myself and my hubby time off from chores and tasks but it is difficult to do. As I thought on this the Lord reminded me...

As it is in the natural, so is it in the spiritual...

Luke 10 recounts how when Jesus came to a certain village, a woman named Martha opened her home to him, and her sister Mary sat at the Lord's feet while Martha bustled about distracted with her 'to do' list. Martha complained to Jesus about Mary's lack of assistance and asked Him to tell Mary to help her! His reply is an important statement for anyone who is task oriented: Luke 10:41-42 "And Jesus answered and said unto her, Martha, Martha, thou art careful and troubled about many things: 42 But one thing is needful: and Mary hath chosen that good part, which shall not be taken away from her." We need to follow Jesus' biblical exhortation to choose the better way. Lord, thank you for this day of respite! I am going to make a strenuous effort to brew that cup of hot coco, curl up with my bible and my laptop, and thoroughly ENJOY my day inside my own personal snow globe! Amen!

JANUARY 7

The last few days we have been hit with one of the biggest snowstorms we've seen in years with several days of snowfall and now temperatures plummeting below zero with wind chills reaching as low as minus 35 degrees! Yikes! As a school teacher I appreciate (and yes… celebrate) the snow days that have extended our Christmas vacation by a total of three additional days during this much needed break! The blizzard conditions are so ferocious that the two by three feet deep path my husband shoveled out to our wood stove several hours earlier was almost completely filled in this evening. I had walked outside earlier and in less than an hour, my footprints were untraceable! As I thought about this, the Lord allowed me to see…

As it is in the natural, so is it in the spiritual…

It seems that my life is somewhat like a trek in a snowstorm. I have spent a great deal of time and effort breaking a trail in my spiritual path; I've had to shovel a lot of stuff off my path in order to make my walk possible. Although it was a lot of work, it was rewarding and I was ever so thankful to my heavenly Father for giving me the strength and determination to forge that path. But, just as in a snowstorm, as long as we continue walking our path, it remains clear and unobstructed. However, as soon as we stop walking, the elements rush in, cluttering our path and making it difficult to navigate. Soon enough, the path will not be visible, and we will find ourselves standing in the doorway wondering how on earth we will ever find our path again. But God is good and he is able and he gives us strength to shovel the stuff out of our life, clearing our path towards Him. Psalms 16:11 says it well, "Thou wilt shew me the path of life: in thy presence is fulness of joy; at thy right hand there are pleasures for evermore" (KJV). In Jesus' name, Amen!

JANUARY 8

The snowy winter weather sweeps across the land and covers everything over like a frozen tundra. On one hand, it is harsh and cold, but on the other hand, the snow and ice provide protection from the damaging cold and bitter winds that are yet to come. Underneath the icy surface lies a field, waiting to be tilled and planted with good seed so that it can produce good things. As I thought about this, the Lord revealed…

As it is in the natural, so is it in the spiritual…

The struggles and problems of this life can sweep across our hearts like a snowstorm, covering it like a frozen tundra and producing an icy, coldness in a person. On one hand, it seems like these people are harsh and cold, but on the other hand, perhaps this chilly layer of coldness provides protection from the damaging cold and bitter winds that life may send their way. Disappointments, sorrows, trials and tragedies can be tough, and we need to allow God's love and protection and joy to cover them and soften that surface! Psalms 5:11 says, "But let all who take refuge in you be glad; let them ever sing for joy. Spread your protection over them, that those who love your name may rejoice in you"

(NIV). Lord, let me be a guide to those who are in search of your love and know it not. Let me point those who are hopeless to the hope of the world! In Jesus' name, Amen!

JANUARY 9

Driving along the snow-covered roads on our way home today, we encountered a car embedded sideways in a deep, snow-filled ditch. The driver's side was damaged because the young girl had hit a road sign on the way into the ditch, but other than being shook up, she was fine. We got her into our warm vehicle and she told us that she had been just driving along straight ahead when suddenly the car began to slide sideways, and before she knew it, she was in the ditch. Her lack of experience and wisdom in driving on icy roads were factors that contributed to her ending up in a snowy ditch. This experience reminds me that…

As it is in the natural, so is it in the spiritual…

Just as we must be careful and use wisdom when driving on the road, we must also be careful on our spiritual path lest we end up on a slippery slope and find ourselves sitting in a ditch, stuck and unable to get out. Ephesians 5:15-17 says, "Therefore be careful how you walk, not as unwise men but as wise, making the most of your time, because the days are evil. So then do not be foolish, but understand what the will of the Lord is" (NASB). Dear Lord, please help me to be ever mindful of each step I take and each word I speak; I do not want to find myself stuck in a ditch because of carelessness. In Jesus' name, Amen!

JANUARY 10

The wind is ferocious this January morning and the weather bureau has issued winter storm advisories for extreme wind chill and limited visibility with more snow to come. Looks like we will hunker down and stay put on this Sunday morning, even though we always plan on being in church. Better to be safe than sorry and end up in a ditch! As I thought about this, the Lord revealed to my heart…

As it is in the natural, so is it in the spiritual…

As the years pass, I find myself leaning toward the "better safe than sorry" motto more and more. I do not know what lies ahead. The winds of this day and age can be shockingly bitter to someone who grew up in a different era. My visibility is limited to the moment in which I live. I can make all the plans I want, but I have no guarantee that they will come to pass. The Lord has reminded me this morning that he has my future in his hands and that I can rest assured that no matter what "weather" I face, he will be my guide and protection. My heart is filled with praise in knowing this. Psalms 25: 4-5 reflect my heart, "Show me your ways, LORD, teach me your paths. 5 Guide me in your truth and teach me, for you are God my Savior, and my hope is in you all day long" (NIV). Thank you Lord Jesus, for your guidance and protection through all of life's bitter storms. Amen!

JANUARY 11

Today has been a bitter cold day with 20-30 mile per hour winds creating a sub-zero dangerous white out. As we sat snuggled in blankets inside our nice warm house, I noticed a red-headed woodpecker clinging to the south side of our walnut tree. Since the wind was blowing from the north, it was trying to take refuge on the less windy side. A short time later, I saw a fat squirrel in the exact same spot as the woodpecker had been…It was on its way down the tree but had stopped in what must have been that small place of protection from the harsh winds. As I watched the squirrel, the Lord whispered to me…

As it is in the natural, so is it in the spiritual…

Just as that bird and that squirrel sought a place of refuge and safety from the violent wind, so too do we need to seek refuge from the harshness that blows into our lives. Whatever the situation, be it financial, health, family, relationships, habits, hopelessness or problems with sin, God can provide a safe place where we can find rest and healing. II Samuel 22:3 says it so well, "My God, my rock, in him will I take refuge; My shield, and the horn of my salvation, my high tower, and my refuge; My saviour, thou savest me from violence" (ASV). Dear Lord, thank you for your promises. I know that You are my refuge and strength. A very present help in trouble! (Psalms 46:1 KJV). Help me to get on the right side of the tree and find my shelter in YOU! In Jesus' name, Amen!

JANUARY 12

Yesterday my hubby got stuck in the snow because he was looking across a field for a coyote and simultaneously glancing at his phone. He drove right into a snowbank. Needless to say, he had me bring a shovel and the digging began, but he soon found that it wasn't going to be easy to dig himself out. I suggested that he call my brother, who has a truck and a tow rope and lives right down the road, but my darling didn't want to 'inconvenience' anyone (and if he is honest, it was a little bit about pride too!) so he sweated and worked and sweated and worked and still wasn't getting anywhere so we ended up going for help anyway! As this was going on, it occurred to me that…

As it is in the natural, so is it in the spiritual…

How often do we get ourselves into a bind and just pick up our own shovel in an attempt to dig ourselves out without calling on the Lord God Almighty, who has all power to rescue us from any situation?! If only we would call on him FIRST, we could save ourselves a lot of agony and stress and work! Psalms 50:15 exhorts us, "Call on me in the day of trouble and I will deliver thee and you shall glorify me" (KJV). Lord, help me to humble myself and call on you in my times of need for I know that you are my ever-present help in times of trouble! Amen!

JANUARY 13

It is a twenty-degree day which began with mixed precipitation, including heavy snow, ice and strong winds. I checked the weather early and saw some schools west of here closing, but since I hadn't received a text, I went through the daily motions and got ready. I drove down my back road, through heavy snow and winds, got out onto the pavement, just a short bit of my thirty-mile work trek, and I turned around. I must admit, my decision to retreat was a mixture of cautiousness and indignance. I was a bit annoyed that the school had not cancelled or at least delayed. Hadn't they watched the weather report? Was no one out checking conditions? They were treacherous! And I, for one, was not willing to risk my life on this day! As I thought about this, the Lord revealed to me…

As it is in the natural, so is it in the spiritual…

Our spiritual journey can be likened to my drive this morning. We may be going through the motions, following the routines of our life, and suddenly in the middle of our expedition, we realize that we are putting ourselves at risk for danger. Looking back, I can see many foolish road trips in my journey. I have found myself heading down the same road again and again, braving the elements of life, ignoring treacherous roads and forging ahead into the unknown. Today, the Lord is showing me that I can make a decision to choose the safety of HIS arms, and turn around and head back to where I began. Lamentations 3:40 urges, "Let us test and examine our ways, and let us return to the Lord!" (NIV). Joel 2:13 also urges us with a promise, "Return to the LORD your God, for he is merciful and compassionate, slow to anger and boundless in loyal love often relenting from calamitous punishment" (NET). Lord, thank you for turning me around in the midst of my storm. Help me to stay on this path of righteousness which you have set before me. Lord, I need not fear the storms of tomorrow, for you will direct my path each day. In Jesus' name, Amen!

JANUARY 14

As the sun slowly edges above the eastern horizon on this below-zero January morning, it sends splashes of an extravagant, gaudy, electric pinkish-orange so beautiful that I must take time to just sit and watch the beautiful masterpiece develop. I relish in the beauty of God's creation. I give praise to my heavenly Father for the beauty of his hand and the wonder of this world in which we exist. As I sit reading my morning devotions and watching out the window, the scene continues to change and within minutes, the beauty of the sunrise is completely erased by the dark gray foreboding clouds that invade the eastern skyline. As I watch the changing scene unfold before me, I am somehow saddened as the Lord quietly reveals to me …

As it is in the natural, so is it in the spiritual…

Life is like the sky…ever changing and continually presenting new and wondrous treasures for us to behold. Unfortunately, along with the beauty, there is also darkness and storm clouds to be encountered. Light and darkness are biblical metaphors used to teach us about sin and the entanglements of this world that seek to overcome and destroy the light of the world. Christians are called 'The light of the world' set here to shine the glory of God into the hearts of others. However, if we are not careful, clouds of doubt and sin can quickly hide any light that the Lord wants us to display and we are suddenly just another gray cloud, blending in with all the rest of the world. Lord, please help me to fight against the clouds that seek to cover my light. Help me to be unashamed of the radiant light that you have put inside me and help me to be a beacon of help and love to those who are in need. In the mighty name of Jesus Christ, my Lord and Savior, Amen.

JANUARY 15

The forecast for this weekend here in Michigan is something extraordinary. We all know that basically, temperatures are derived from either a cold front or a warm front. We are obviously in the midst of a very strong cold front! This week, our temperatures have remained at a bone-chilling minus 30 degrees with wind chills, but 4 days from now it's supposed to be 50 degrees Fahrenheit! Such a drastic change in temperature in just a few days is almost unbelievable. Interestingly, when researching this phenomenon, I discovered that the larger the temperature variance, the stronger the front would be. Logically, the closer proximity you have to this weather front, the stronger it will affect you. As I thought about this dichotomy of degrees, the Lord whispered to me...

As it is in the natural, so is it in the spiritual...

In the same way that great and mighty fronts create drastic changes in temperatures, so too does our great and mighty God bring tremendously drastic changes in the heart and mind of the believer. Additionally, the closer we come to this powerful source of change, the more we will be affected! When we allow the Lord to move in our lives and situations, we will experience drastic change to our spiritual condition. How? Romans 12:2 tells us, "Do not conform yourselves to the standards of this world, but let God transform you inwardly by a complete change of your mind. Then you will be able to know the will of God--what is good and is pleasing to him and is perfect" (GNT). Lord we thank you for the drastic ways you bring change to our hearts if we only allow you to get close to us! Help me to seek you daily and draw close to your power! Amen!

JANUARY 16

Today is our granddaughter, Evie's birthday. She is an absolutely gorgeous little girl. Her giant blue eyes are surrounded by the most luscious lashes, and her cherub face is angelically surrounded by her golden halo of blonde hair. She is a child that everyone gazes at and "Ooohhhs" and "Ahhhhs" over. The most adorable part is when she is talking to me in all seriousness and expressing her ideas with the sweet innocence of a three-year old. As her grandma, I wish I could protect her from the pains and heartaches of living this human experience. It occurs to me that our children have no idea what realities may be ahead because they trust in their parents and grandparents to take care of them. As I thought about this, I realized…

As it is in the natural, so is it in the spiritual…

In the same way we love our babies and want to protect them, and our children and grandchildren have that childlike trust in us, so too does our God love us and wants us to trust him through all of the troubles of this life. Many passages in the bible tell of God's mighty hand of protection over us. Psalms 91:1-2 has many promises, "He that dwelleth in the secret place of the most-High shall abide under the shadow of the Almighty. 2 I will say of the Lord, He is my refuge and my fortress: my God; in him will I trust." Psalms 91:4 is a beautiful picture, "He shall cover thee with his feathers, and under his wings shalt thou trust: his truth shall be thy shield and buckler." Psalms 91:10-12: "There shall no evil befall thee, neither shall any plague come nigh thy dwelling. 11 For he shall give his angels charge over thee, to keep thee in all thy ways. 12 They shall bear thee up in their hands, lest thou dash thy foot against a stone." Dear Lord, I am so thankful that you have created us to be not only physical beings, but also spiritual beings, and you have made a way for that spiritual part of us to be forever safe within your shelter. Help us to grasp these beautiful promises and teach them to our little ones that they might feel safe no matter where they are or what they are going through. In Jesus' name, Amen!

JANUARY 17

Wintertime provides the most beautiful canvas of God's handiwork. One particular picture was illuminated to me this morning as I gazed out my window at the heavy snow covering the boughs of my spruce trees. These trees are laden down with the burden of bearing the heavy snow that falls each winter, and yet they accept this task with such majestic grace. The resulting scene is spectacular. "Soon," I thought, "the snow will melt and the branches will no longer be laden down with this task." The beauty of this burden the branches bear will not be visible for several seasons. This thought somehow saddened me. As I pondered this, the Lord whispered to me...

As it is in the natural, so is it in the spiritual...

Each of us experience spiritual 'seasons' in which we must bear our burdens, as well as, those of others. We can choose to bear those burdens God has allowed into our lives with grace and beauty with the knowledge that we can cast our cares upon Him. Jesus reminds us in Matthew 11:28 to "Come to me, all you who labor and are heavy laden, and I will give you rest" (KJV). Verse 30, "For my yoke is easy and my burden is light." Lord help me to remember when my burden is heavy that I am not supposed to bear it alone. Thank you Lord, for your promises are true! In Jesus' name, Amen!

JANUARY 18

Wintertime is a magnificent showcase of beautiful scenery and landscapes. Many people tend to prefer enjoying winter scenery from the warmth of their cozy homes rather than actually stepping outdoors to enjoy it. The beauty of the pristine, sparkling, white landscape usually does eventually tempt us to step outside, but unless we are properly attired with protective clothing, we will suffer consequences very quickly. As I pondered this, the Lord whispered...

As it is in the natural, so is it in the spiritual...

We are all subject to temptations that appear very alluring and attractive. Humanity faces three major categories of temptation according to lust of the flesh, lust of the eyes, and pride of life, and these encompass a multitude of sins that people battle every day. If we are not properly clothed in the spiritual sense, we will find ourselves quickly affected by the harsh elements hidden behind their own attractive guise. Romans 13:14 tells us, "But put ye on the Lord Jesus Christ, and make not provision for the flesh, to fulfil the lusts thereof." Lord help us to cover ourselves with Christ Jesus - our protector - as we venture into the elements of this world so that you may keep us safe in your presence through bitter cold times this life may bring. In Jesus' Name, Amen!

JANUARY 19

Wintertime inevitably requires a bit of extra physical exertion from those who do not live in warm, sunny climates. We have to draw upon our physical strength to clear off sidewalks, driveways, and vehicles when the snow falls and leaves its sparkling blanket. If we are not physically fit, we will find ourselves quickly exhausted. This can be frustrating and even dangerous to our bodies. Many people suffer heart attacks each year while shoveling snow and they find themselves facing eternity because they were unprepared to handle the physical exertion they put upon themselves. We often perceive ourselves as stronger and more fit than we actually are, and this deception can be deadly. Thinking on this, the Lord dropped this thought into my heart...

As it is in the natural, so is it in the spiritual...

We often put ourselves in treacherous situations filled with potential dangers to our soul, and we do so without proper preparation. We have failed to build ourselves up spiritually through prayer, fasting and seeking God's will for the day and yet we step into situations that exceed our spiritual strength. We must understand that we are in a battle for our soul and begin each day by exercising not only our physical self, but also our spiritual self so we may face our daily situations with God's strength and power. My pastor teaches us how to get strong: "The Joy of the Lord is your strength" Nehemiah 8:10; you might ask, "How do I get joy?" Psalms 16:11 says,

"Thou wilt shew me the path of life: in thy presence is fulness of joy; at thy right hand there are pleasures for evermore" (KJV). You may ask, "How do I get in the presence of God?" Many bible verses tell us that thanksgiving and praise is the way into God's presence! Psalms 100:4 says, "Enter into his gates with thanksgiving, and into his courts with praise: be thankful unto him, and bless his name" (KJV). Thank you Lord for your word which teaches us that being thankful and giving you praise brings us into your presence where we find joy and strength for such a time as this! Amen!

JANUARY 20

Our neighbor has been stuck in his driveway three times in the past three days. He has come knocking on our door two times after ten o'clock in the evening. Both my husband and I found ourselves grumbling at the situation (to each other) for our neighbor's lack of preparation (he should have shoveled first!) and for his lack of good sense in being out in these ridiculously cold and snowy nights. Last night, after he knocked and as my husband was dressing to go help dig our neighbor out, the Lord quickened something to me...

As it is in the natural, so is it in the spiritual...

As our young neighbor knocked, the Lord revealed to me that this was actually opportunity knocking. It was a test, asking us to show Love for our neighbor. I said this to my hubby, and he agreed and continued on his trek in a different frame of mind. The job was done quickly and he returned happy to have been able to help the young man. He was actually getting his truck out so he could go to work in the morning. It turns out that what we had perceived as foolishness, was actually him trying to be prepared. God often sends us his opportunities in disguise but we often miss out because we are too busy counting the costs that it might require of us. In Matthew 22:36-39, a rich young ruler asked Jesus, 36 "Master, which [is] the great commandment in the law? 37 Jesus said unto him,

Thou shalt love the Lord thy God with all thy heart, and with all thy soul, and with all thy mind. 38 This is the first and great commandment. 39 And the second [is] like unto it, Thou shalt love thy neighbor as thyself" (KJV). 1 John 3:17 says, "If anyone with earthly possessions sees his brother in need, but withholds his compassion from him, how can the love of God abide in him?" (BSB). Dear Lord, please remind us that when we see someone in need whether they need tangible things or just a helping hand, this is an opportunity to obey you and show that your love abides in my heart! In Jesus' name, Amen!

JANUARY 21

We seldom think about what lies beneath the snow in the winter. Underneath the white covering, the frozen ground contains a world within itself. This world houses the hope of countless seeds that died as the frost covered the earth. The snow is not only beautiful to look upon, but is also a protective cover for the seed, providing a barrier to the harsh elements until it comes to life in the spring. As I pondered this truth, God illuminated something to me...

As it is in the natural, so is it in the spiritual...

He has sprinkled His seed into our heart through his Holy Word and His Holy Spirit. We must cover that seed and protect it with all that we have, so that the harsh elements do not destroy that tender plant that is yet to be born, and the fruit that will come forth as a result. Matthew 13:23 explains that good soil is an obedient heart, "But the seed sown on good soil is the one who hears the word and understands it. He indeed bears fruit and produces a crop--a hundredfold, sixtyfold, or thirtyfold" (BSB). Dear Father in Heaven, please protect the seed of your word and your Spirit that you have placed in my heart. Please cover this seed with your mighty hand so that it may grow into a strong plant that will bear much fruit to nourish souls for your kingdom. In Jesus' name, Amen!

JANUARY 22

The sunshine on the snow in the winter creates a brilliant effect. Although the snow does not change in regard to its brightness, the reflection from the sun creates the allusion that the snow is somehow much whiter and brighter than it appears when the sun is behind the clouds. The clouds remain until the wind blows them away and the sun is once again revealed. As I pondered this weather-related phenomenon, the Lord was showing me...

As it is in the natural, so is it in the spiritual...

The Lord is so kind to reveal to me a spiritual parallel to the effect that the sun has upon the snow. Jesus said in Matthew 5:14, "Ye are the light of the world..." and then instructs us in, 16. "Let your light so shine before men, that they may see your good works, and glorify your Father which is in heaven" (KJV). The Lord was showing me that when the SON is visible and working in our life, we are illuminated brightly to those who are looking at us; however, if we keep Him hidden behind the clouds of our life, the world won't see His light shining from us. It takes the wind of the Holy Spirit to blow those clouds away so our light may shine brightly. Heavenly Father, please help me to recognize when the clouds roll in that I need the wind of Your Spirit to blow them away, so that Your light will shine brilliantly through my life. In Jesus' name, Amen!

JANUARY 23

This morning while writing the accounts of so many years ago, about a very painful time in my life, the sun was peeking over the horizon. We all know that each morning's sunrise ushers in a brand-new day, filled with various weather and elements such as sunshine, clouds, rain or snow that will be recorded for all time as the weather of that day. It's in the books once the sun sets upon a day. The Lord graciously helped me to understand that...

As it is in the natural, so is it in the spiritual…

Just as the sun rises each morning and is a brand-new day, so is the Lord is there ready and willing to extend to us a brand-new clean slate upon which we can write our own personal weather for each day. Lamentations 3:23 remind us, "It is of the LORD'S mercies that we are not consumed, because his compassions fail not. They are new every morning. Great is his faithfulness!" (NLT). Lord help me remember that with your help, we can rewrite our own legacy and replace the cold cloudy, rain filled seasons of our life with sunshine and warmth. In Jesus' name, Amen!

JANUARY 24

As I was cleaning my home this late wintery morning the sun was shining and I could clearly see the dust that had accumulated. I thought about how odd it is that although it is closed up during the winter months and no dust is coming in through screen doors and windows, it still becomes very dusty and dirty very quickly. It seems that not a week goes by without dust collecting in the corners and under the beds and if this is not removed the home can be unhealthy to live in. It can be a monotonous task to keep it spotless but the reward comes when I finally put the vacuum and duster away and I can enjoy the beauty of a clean home free of dirt and dust! As I thought about this, the Lord pointed out that…

As it is in the natural, so is it in the spiritual…

Just as our earthly homes need cleaning on a very regular basis if we want it to be spotless, so too must our spiritual house (our heart) be cleaned on a very regular basis to remove dust, dirt and cobwebs that can accumulate over the course of a very few days. We live in a fallen world full of contaminants that can infiltrate our spirit without enough light shining on our hearts. Much like the dust and cobwebs can infiltrate our homes when we live in darkness. We must allow God to shine his light and cleanse our heart to remove these undesirable elements or before we know it, our spirit can become polluted and unhealthy! 1 John 1:7, "But if we walk in the light, as he is in the light, we have fellowship one with another, and the blood of Jesus Christ his Son cleanseth us from all sin." Thank you Lord for your light that shines to the deepest corners of my heart. Help me cleanse it daily! In Jesus' name, Amen!

JANUARY 25

We lost power due to a snow storm yesterday. Thankfully, we have a generator to keep our furnace and lights going in this sub-freezing weather. The snow will wreak havoc on electric lines and trees when it is heavy and wet like this snowfall was. Now, it is freezing so the ice will remain solid and firmly holding onto whatever it is attached to until the weather warms up. As I thought on this, the Lord pointed out that...

As it is in the natural, so is it in the spiritual...

Just as the snow and ice can cause us to lose power, so too can the bitter storms of life wrap its frigid hands around us and cause us to lose the power of the Holy Spirit inside of us. We may feel that sins and temptations, anger, bitterness, jealousy or hatred have the power over us now. The Lord reminded me of His promises in Romans 6, "that if we have been buried with Jesus Christ in baptism, sin's power is broken." Verse 4 explains this mysterious transformation, "Therefore we have been buried with Him through baptism into death, so that as Christ was raised from the dead through the glory of the Father, so we too might walk in newness of life" (NAS). We have died to sin and have risen in new life with Christ. His power flows through us so that the icy precipitation of this life will not cling to me! Lord, please help me stay plugged into Your Holy Spirit! My source of power! In Jesus' name, Amen!

JANUARY 26

Yesterday as I went to leave for town, my windshield was covered with several inches of snow. I grabbed the brush and went to swipe it off, but much to my amazement, it was frozen all the way through! Rather than simply brushing off soft snow, I ended up chipping chunks of ice off of my windshield for a good twenty minutes! What had been soft and fluffy when it fell from the sky, had turned into a brick like material with the colder temps. If only I had brushed it off last night while it was still soft! As I was chipping away the Lord whispered to me...

As it is in the natural, so is it in the spiritual...

Just as snow becomes very rigid with icy temperatures, so too can our hearts turn to ice when we encounter life's difficulties, be it situations or people. Our hearts become icy when we fail to remove those first layers when they fall upon us. Just like snow, it's much easier to deal with troubles of life when they are still soft and fresh. Ezekiel 36:26 is a prophecy and promise from God to His people, "And I will give you a new heart, and a new spirit I will put within you. And I will remove the heart of stone from your flesh and give you a heart of flesh. And I will put my Spirit within you and cause you to walk in my statutes and be careful to obey my rules" (ESV). Dear Lord, when I harbor hurts and pains of life, the cumulative result is a stone-cold heart that is hardened with layers of resentment, unforgiveness or hatred. Help me to turn to you and allow you to remove any hardness, that I may receive what you have for me this day. In Jesus' name, Amen!

JANUARY 27

Wind direction is a big factor when you are outdoors braving the elements. Especially in cold weather, you are seriously impacted by wind in your face versus wind at your back. If you're attempting to get to a particular place and must face a frigid wind, you will definitely want protection for your exposed skin. As I thought about this, the Lord dropped this thought into my heart...

As it is in the natural, so is it in the spiritual...

Just as a freezing wind can be extremely dangerous to our exposed skin if we forge ahead into it, so too can the effects of this sometimes cold and evil world wreak havoc on our spirit if we march onward without proper protection. Many bible passages talk of the Lord's protection. One I like in particular is II Samuel 22:3, which says, "My God is my protection, and with him I am safe. He protects me like a shield; he defends me and keeps me safe. He is my savior; he protects me and saves me from violence" (GNT). Proverbs 18:10 puts it this way, "The name of the Lord is a strong tower, the righteous run into it and are safe" (BSB). Lord Jesus, your name IS indeed a strong tower, my protection, my shelter, my safe harbor and in you is where I find refuge from the storms of this life. I thank you and give your glory for your strength, your love, your power, your grace, your forgiveness and your protection! In your mighty name I pray! Amen!

JANUARY 28

Winter wonderland is such a beautiful sight! When it falls from the sky it is soft and beautiful, but a slight change in temperature can cause the precipitation to become a glaze of ice that grips every single molecule in sight. The once beautiful soft, fluffy, snow is now rigid and seemingly unmovable as long as the temperature is below freezing. As I thought about this the Lord revealed to me that...

As it is in the natural, so is it in the spiritual...

In the same manner as snow turning to ice, so too can our hearts be frozen in sin's icy grip if we allow external elements to affect us. Life can be brutally cold and soon, it seems there is no way to release ourselves. Thankfully, the Lord has a way to soften and warm the temperature of our heart. We have access to the One who can break us free from any situation or sin. He can melt the icy grip of sin in a heartbeat, freeing us from certain spiritual death. When we trust in Jesus Christ, we no longer are frozen in our situation or our sins. Galatians 5:1 confirms this, "Christ has set us free in freedom; stand fast therefore, and be not held again in a yoke of bondage" (DBT). Thank you Lord that your promises are true! With one prayer, I can feel your presence and be freed from the sin that has had me bound so I may live and serve you with joy! In Jesus' name, Amen!

JANUARY 29

This morning with the temperatures below zero, I let my sweet doggie out to go potty. Within 30 seconds, she had done her business and then started to come back towards the door. Suddenly she lifted one paw and held it up, and then while looking pitifully at me, she gingerly lifted another paw up and held it up. I called to her and she attempted to take a couple of steps toward me, but then she just stopped. I called to her again, but she just glared at me, frozen in her steps with one paw held up. I ran and got boots and went out and picked her up, wrapped her in a blanket and snuggled her closely as I warmed her up. In the midst of this moment, the Lord pointed out...

As it is in the natural, so is it in the spiritual...

In the same way that I ran to rescue my little sweet Jewel, my Lord Jesus has run to me so many times to rescue me from my place of frozenness. He has plucked me up and out of impossible situations I could not extricate myself from, and he has wrapped me in his warm embrace, holding me closely as I recovered from the bitter situation, I was stuck in. Psalms 57:3 proclaims, "He reaches down from heaven and saves me, challenging the one who tramples me. Selah. God sends His faithful love and truth" (HCSB). Yes, the Lord has done this for me and for you! What a Loving Heavenly Father we have who reaches into any situation to rescue us! Thank you Lord for your faithfulness and your love for me! Amen!

JANUARY 30

As I waited for my coffee to brew this morning, I looked outside to a beautiful snow-covered world. I opened my sliding door and noticed immediately how amazingly quiet it was outside. It was as if the snow created some type of protective shelter to the noise of the world around me. I stood and gazed at the beautiful scene, then I closed my eyes and relished in the peaceful moment. As I whispered a prayer of thanks for that quiet moment, the Lord reminded me...

As it is in the natural, so is it in the spiritual...

That moment, surrounded by the beauty and quiet of the snow was very similar to the way I feel when I kneel to pray. The world and its sounds are silenced as I fix my mind on the Lord for those precious moments. These times of prayer create a shelter from the thoughts and noises of the world. It is in this place where I can bow before the ONE who created all things to inquire of Him and find rest, refreshing, wisdom and peace from the chaos of this world we live in. Psalms 91:1 reminds me, "Whoever dwells in the shelter of the Most High will rest in the shadow of the Almighty" (NIV). Lord, I am so grateful to have access to your peace at any time in the midst of the noise that clamors for our attention. Let me daily turn to you for moments of quiet rest in your Presence. In Jesus' name, Amen!

JANUARY 31

As I lay awake in the middle of the night, the snow is swirling just outside my window, blanketing the lifeless, gray, colorless world with such beauty and freshness. When I awake, I will discover a whole new world covered in crystal whiteness and I anticipate the beauty of the next morning. As I drift off to sleep, I hear the Lord whisper...

As it is in the natural, so it is in the spiritual...

When we come to Jesus, we become brand new! We replace our drab and lifeless spirit for His beautiful Spirit; our human failures into His glorious victories; our human needs for His bountiful supplies. II Corinthians 5:17 says, "Therefore, if anyone is in Christ, he is a new creation. The old has passed away; behold, the new has come" (ESV). Oh Lord Jesus, thank you for covering me and cleansing me and making me a new creation! Amen!

FEBRUARY 1

Two days ago, our road was muddy and the ugly brown grass on our yard was beginning to poke through the sad, stained snow. Yesterday a snowstorm covered it all up again and it is a thing of beauty. Huge swirling drifts and waves of snow stretch for miles here in the open country. It is truly a sight to behold. All of the ugliness is covered up once again by beautiful, white, sparkling snow. As I thought about this the Lord whispered…

*** As it is in the natural, so is it in the spiritual… ***

Just as the winds here in Michigan brought snow to cover our ugly mud and brown grass, so too, the Wind of the Holy Spirit blows across our spirit to refresh us and make us clean and beautiful. The wicked parts of us disappear and what is left is something to behold. Proverbs 10:25 says, "When the whirlwind passes by, the wicked is no more, But the righteous has an everlasting foundation" (KJV). Lord, I pray this day that the wind of your Spirit will blow all wickedness away from my heart. I ask that your righteousness and holiness will be my covering, and that this covering will remain intact so that my ugliness doesn't poke through to reveal itself. In Jesus' name, Amen!

FEBRUARY 2

Well, it is another single digit morning here in mid-Michigan. The air is so still your breath is frozen into a shape as it leaves your mouth.

Yesterday the snow and wind created havoc. Schools closed, people were stranded, and accidents were reported. Today it is serene, and still. Not even the tiniest hint of a breeze. It truly is the calm after the storm. As I looked out the window at the peaceful scene, the Lord revealed to me...

As it is in the natural, so is it in the spiritual...

When we face trials and troubles in this world, we need to take refuge in Jesus, who has the power to calm the storm and bring peace to any situation. Without Him, we are tossed about at the will of the storm around us. With him, we are covered and protected and safe from the storm. It brings to mind the story of Jesus and His disciples taking a boat several miles across the small sea of Galilee. It was right after he had taught great multitudes and then shared with his disciples the truths behind his amazing parables. Jesus was asleep in the boat when the storm came up and the disciples cried out in fear, asking if he cared not that they perish! Mark 4:39 says, "And he arose, and rebuked the wind, and said unto the sea, Peace, be still. And the wind ceased, and there was a great calm. 40 And he said unto them, Why are ye so fearful? how is it that ye have no faith? 41 And they feared exceedingly, and said one to another, What manner of man is this, that even the wind and the sea obey him?" (KJV). My prayer is that I will trust that Jesus is awake at all times during any storm I might encounter. I know what kind of Savior I serve...he is the One who is in control of everything! Hallelujah! Amen!

FEBRUARY 3

"It's a blustery ole day," said Winnie the Pooh. This morning I woke to one of those days. The wind is blowing, the windows are rattling, it's cold and dark outside. It's the kind of day I wish I could just stay snuggled in front of my fire, reading and writing and sipping hot coco. But I must shake off those thoughts and prepare for another day at school. As I thought on this, the Lord nudged me...

As it is in the natural, so is it in the spiritual…

We all have days when we want to just curl up and stay home, but God's word encourages us to keep going. Galatians 6:9 encourages, "And let us not be weary in well doing, for in due season we shall reap if we faint not" (KJV). We are warned about idleness in II Thessalonians Chapter 3 and told to avoid those who are idle and disruptive and unwilling to work for food. He closes with encouragement, "And as for you, brothers and sisters, never tire of doing what is good" (NIV). Dear Lord, help me to follow your will and your purpose for my life each day, even when I am weary, for I know that my rest is found in you. In Jesus' name, Amen!

FEBRUARY 4

Today, while driving my husband's pickup to get out of our snow, drifted roads and go to school, the temperature of the air blowing out of the heater suddenly turned cold. I stopped and called him and he said to watch the temperature gauge and if it started overheating to stop driving so the engine didn't blow. Well, I got about three or four more miles down the road when it did exactly that. The warning light came on and I began to smell something warm so I pulled off the road and turned it off. We had to call a tow truck to take it to the shop. It will probably need a new radiator because the plug keeps coming out of this one and the fluid then drains out and causes engine failure. As I thought about this, the Lord showed me that…

As it is in the natural, so is it in the spiritual…

When we allow our spiritual self to run low on fluid (Holy Spirit anointing) that is so essential to keep ourselves in operating condition, we, too, need to take a time out for repair. We need to pull ourselves into the Church or prayer closet and allow the world's greatest mechanic to repair our heart, mind, soul, and spirit. He alone can fix the leaks and fill us up with the "oil" of His Holy Spirit so that we can continue on our mission for HIS purpose. Matthew 25 tells the parable of the ten virgins carrying their lamps out to meet the bridegroom; The five wise virgins had extra oil with them, so they were brought into the wedding banquet while the foolish and unprepared were shut out. The harsh reality of being unprepared is seen here in verse 11 and 12: "Afterward came also the other virgins, saying, Lord, Lord, open to us. But he answered and said, Verily I say unto you, I know you not" (KJV). Oh Lord, please help me be in tune to the warning lights that you send into my life, urging me to take care of my spiritual self so that I do not run out of oil! Help me daily be filled with your Spirit so that I can be effective and prepared to do your good will at all times. In Jesus' name, Amen!

FEBRUARY 5

This winter has been brutal. Lots of snow and very cold temperatures have taken a toll on the wood supply that we use to heat our home. We thought we had cut plenty of wood to last through the winter but alas, this winter has required much more that we had planned for. Now, we are unable to go back into the woods to cut because of the snow and my husband is concerned about running out of this most important fuel. As I thought about our dilemma, the Lord whispered to me that...

As it is in the natural, so is it in the spiritual...

When we study the Word of God and fast and pray, we are building up our spiritual fuel supply. This is the fuel that will keep us going when we face the cold winds that will inevitably come at us in this world. Fire and flames are a representation of God's Spirit throughout the bible. The Lord instructed Aaron in Leviticus 6 to keep the fire burning continually; it must not go out. We are instructed in the new testament "Quench not the Spirit" (I Thessalonians 5:19, KJV). If we have taken time each day to do the things we know we need to do to keep our spiritual fire burning for the Lord, our flame will not die out, even during the coldest, bleakest times. Have you been building up your fuel supply? Lord, help me to remember that I need spiritual food to fuel my fire for you each and every day. AMEN!

FEBRUARY 6

Our beautiful snow-covered fields suffered the ravages of a ferocious windstorm yesterday. What had been a 5 or 6 inch blanket of protection and beauty is now stubble and dirt due to the winds. Every farmer hopes the snow will stay during the winds to protect the topsoil from erosion. However, despite our fervent wishes, it doesn't take long for the beautiful landscape to be stripped down to a bleak and ugly scene. As I thought of this natural truth, the Lord revealed to me…

As it is in the natural, so is it in the spiritual…

Just as the wind strips the snow off the field leaving it bare and exposed, each day, the wind of life blows through our world bringing all sorts of problems and trials, and if we are not securely covered by the blanket of God's love and protection, this life can strip away the beauty of our spirit life, leaving us bleakly exposed to all of the harsh elements this world brings into our lives. Psalms 91:4 promises: "He will cover you with His feathers; you will take refuge under His wings. His faithfulness will be a protective shield" (HCSB). Lord, please help me to cover myself with your Spirit so your protection and covering will never leave me exposed to the harsh elements this world brings to me. Thank you for your promises! Amen!

FEBRUARY 7

Another snowy day looms ahead, and as the frigid winds blow outside my window, I ponder how people in the old days ever kept warm in these sub-zero temperatures in cabins without the pink insulation we now use in our walls. The main item necessary for survival was their fire. Much time and energy was spent gathering wood in order to keep the home fire burning and they used rags and even snow to plug the cracks in the log homes to retain the precious warmth from escaping. They huddled close to the source of heat for warmth, not straying too far for too long. As I thought on this the Lord, gave me this thought...

As it is in the natural, so is it in the spiritual...

The Lord wanted to let me know that just as those folks depended on fire for their very life, so too ought we depend on Him for our spiritual survival. We ought to spend much time and energy feeding our spirit with good kindling, such as bible study, prayer and worship in order to keep that fire burning. We ought to use whatever is at hand to plug up and repair the cracks in our spiritual armor to retain the precious knowledge from escaping. We ought to huddle close to the Lord each day and not stray from Him as we go about our tasks. Psalms 73:28 says, "But it is good for me to draw near to God: I have put my trust in the Lord GOD, that I may declare all thy works" (KJV). Dear Lord, I know that you are my source of strength and life. I must draw near to you each day that I might continue to trust in you and tell of your mighty works! Amen!

FEBRUARY 8

Awakening this morning to a light snowfall, I am wondering how this day will unfold. The weatherman predicted last night that we could see as much as nine inches of snow today, however, this could change quickly depending on the direction the storm takes. Although the weather is something we try to predict, even the weather man sometimes gets it wrong. Systems can veer off or veer back in certain direction without permission and surprise us with precipitation we weren't prepared for. While thinking about this, the Lord opened my thoughts to the reality that...

As it is in the natural, so is it in the spiritual…

We are unable to accurately predict our future. Period. There is no forecast available to tell us what events may come storming into our life today. No matter how prepared we might be for the weather, there is only one way we can prepare for the spiritual attacks and negative effects of "life" that might arrive on our doorstep today. Prayer and feeding on God's word are the only things that we can do to even begin to help us face the difficulties that each day could potentially bring. Sickness, disease, death, tragedies, and life altering news affect each of our lives at one time or another. The only thing we can cling to is God's eternal promises. Proverbs 27:1 warns, "Do not boast about tomorrow, for you do not know what a day may bring forth" (NAS). Isaiah 46:10 says, "I distinguish the end from the beginning, and ancient times from what is still to come, saying: 'My purpose will be established, and I will accomplish all My good pleasure" (BSB). Lord when I trust in YOU to guide me, I can find comfort in knowing I am in the hands of my creator who knows all things. For this, I am ever grateful! In Jesus' name, Amen!

FEBRUARY 9

Today is my Father's birthday. Dad was a farmer and you really never had to wonder what he was thinking because he verbalized his thoughts quite well. He kept a journal of the weather, the farming details as well as his day-to-day health situation and some of his feelings, fears and thoughts about life. Dad suffered from COPD in his last 10 years and had some very rough days and some days that were decent. He passed away in 2009 and to-date, I have not read his diaries, but I have a strong desire to know my father's thoughts especially when it's his birthday. As I thought about this, it became clear …

As it is in the natural, so is it in the spiritual…

Just as I want to read my earthly father's thoughts so that I might know him a little better, I also have a strong desire to read my Heavenly Father's words so that I might know HIM better each and every day. Psalms 119:105 reminds me that "Thy word is a lamp unto my feet and a light unto my path" (KJV). Let me study YOUR words, oh Heavenly Father so that I might know you better and continually abide in your light. Thank-you Lord for your word. It is filled with your truth, direction, exhortation and wisdom. It provides examples for every conceivable issues of this life and it is alive even today. AMEN!

FEBRUARY 10

Snow and wind produce interesting effects. We walk across a snowy yard and in a very short time, our tracks are not visible. The wind has blown the snow so that it has completely covered them. No one could ever know those tracks were there an hour ago! Everything is clean and new and untouched! As I think about this, the Lord quickens to me that...

As it is in the natural, so is it in the spiritual...

For a person who lives in relationship with the Lord Jesus Christ, regrets are like those footprints in the snow; as soon as we whisper our prayer asking for forgiveness, we are covered. Our tracks disappear in God's sight. We have a fresh, new path each and every day and a brand-new opportunity to walk with Christ in newness of life. Lamentations 3:22 tells us, "It is of the Lord's mercies that we are not consumed, because his compassions fail not. 23 They are new every morning: great is thy faithfulness" (KJV). I am so thankful for his mercies and compassions toward me, his child. In Christ Jesus I pray, Amen!

FEBRUARY 11

The beautiful snow we've accumulated over the past month or so has been viewed with distain by some who do not like the cold weather and the precipitation that comes with it. On the other hand, there are those of us who love the crystal, white, pristine wonder of a snow-covered landscape. I happen to associate with the latter group, I love a good snowstorm and, as a teacher, I celebrate snow days! (Sorry not sorry!) Unfortunately, even in the dead of winter, snow is sometimes followed by rain, which makes a HUGE mess. The worst part of all is the dreary landscape a winter rain leaves behind. As the snow is washed away, we are left with a vision much less appealing to the eye. Thinking about this, the Lord pointed out...

As it is in the natural, so is it in the spiritual...

As I was thinking about our recent snow-followed-by-rain today, God quickened this truth to me: Our hearts can be as pristine and white as the snow one day, but if we allow sinful things to rain upon our heart, the beauty and cleanness can be suddenly washed away and the ugliness inside all of humanity is revealed. The same feeling of dreariness and sadness can take over. In order to maintain our clean heart, we must guard it against things that strive to erase the beauty that lies therein. Heavenly Father, please help me to maintain my heart through your cleansing hand! As David pleaded in Psalms 51:7, "...Wash me and I shall be whiter than snow" (KJV). In Jesus' name, Amen!

FEBRUARY 12

Yesterday we had a blizzard here. We barely made it down our road with our four-wheel drive pick-up at two in the afternoon. When the snowstorms hit and the winds blow, we are snowed in until the snow plow comes. Honestly, I sort of enjoy being stuck at home, unable to go anywhere. It provides an opportunity for me to relax a little and have some much needed peace and quiet where I can write, read and rest. Thinking about this it occurred to me that...

As it is in the natural, so is it in the spiritual...

We all face storms in our spiritual life as well…and in the midst of those storms, we need that peaceful time in meditation and prayer where we can allow the Lord to speak to us and direct our paths. Hebrews 46:10 says to "Be still and know that I am God." When the winds of trouble enter our life, we often do not take time to just "Be still" and we end up getting blown off track, unable to find our path back to a peaceful place. The Lord tells us to take time and commune with him in that peaceful place away from the storms of our world. He calls us to meditate on him each day so that the cold winds of this world do not overwhelm us. Lord, help me to carve out those precious quiet times each day where I can "Be still and know" that You are my source of peace even amidst the storm. Amen!

FEBRUARY 13

Valentine's Day is tomorrow. It's the day when children trade "Be My Valentine" cards, men buy heart shaped boxes of chocolates for their sweethearts, and people express their love to one another with gifts, dinner dates and romance. The story behind this "holiday" is not so pretty. In the second century, the church was being persecuted and the emperor had prohibited young people from marrying in order to keep soldiers' minds on the battle at hand. A priest named, Valentine, was secretly marrying couples and upon being discovered, he was sentenced to torture and death. One of these Roman judges had actually converted to Christianity because Valentine had miraculously healed his blind daughter. As the story goes, he sent his final letter from his prison cell to this child, signed, "From Your Valentine." Thinking about his willingness to sacrifice his life for the sake of love, led me to understand…

As it is in the natural, so is it in the spiritual…

This patron saint was willing to give his life for the sake of marrying couples in the church, and likewise, there comes a time where we must be willing to lay our life down for the sake of our faith. Through the power of the Holy Spirit, we are able to die daily to our own desires and live for the Lord. This may be as simple as exercising self-control, forgiveness, generosity, patience, or kindness in our daily life. Or, it might literally require us to take a stand for our faith in a world seemingly filled with apathy, cynicism, and unbelief. Jesus taught in Matthew 16:25, "For whoever might desire to save his life will lose it; but whoever might lose his life on account of Me will find it. 26 What will it profit a man if he gains the whole world, yet forfeits his soul? Or what can a man give in exchange for his soul?" (BSB). Even today, around the world, many are being martyred for their faith in Jesus. Dear Lord, you have clearly taught us in your word that true love requires sacrifice. Help me to lay aside my own selfish desires and follow your voice daily as you guide me in the way I should go. Help me be like Saint Valentine, who gave his very life for the cause of love. In Jesus' name, Amen!

FEBRUARY 14

Valentine's Day is a very special day. It used to mean something a bit different and then in the year 2003, a very special blessing arrived into our lives. Our first grandchild, Caleb, was born. During my daughter's labor the baby went into distress so they performed an emergency cesarean. They were concerned that Caleb may have some serious problem so they shipped him to a children's hospital about an hour away. Of course, this was very disturbing and to make matters worse, Melissa had to stay put! A new mama wants nothing more than to hold her baby and be there for him every minute possible! We all felt pretty helpless. We truly had no control over this situation. In an attempt to do something helpful, we would go to see Caleb and video tape him and bring the video back to mama. Other than that, we couldn't do much except pray! Thankfully, after a few days we were able to bring him home. He is a healthy teenager now and we are so thankful to have him in our lives.

Thinking of all of this, the Lord reminds me...
As it is in the natural, so is it in the spiritual...
In the same way we were truly powerless over the life of our grandson, so too must we recognize that we are powerless over our spiritual battles until we relinquish them to the Lord God Almighty, the creator of Heaven and Earth. The One who is in control. The sooner we realize this, and humble ourselves under His mighty hand, the more peace we will have on this earth. I Chronicles 29:11 proclaims, "Thine, O LORD, is the greatness, and the power, and the glory, and the victory, and the majesty: for all that is in the heaven and in the earth is thine; thine is the kingdom, O LORD, and thou art exalted as head above all" (KJV). Dear Lord, I am so thankful for this faith you have given me and your peace which passes all understanding. I thank you for being in control of things I am not! I thank you for my amazing grandson, Caleb! I ask that you impart it to all who read these words that they may be filled with the knowledge of Your power and Your glory...In Jesus' precious name! Amen!

FEBRUARY 15

As I looked out my frosty window early this morning, I noticed some deer out in the field. They have been out each morning for the past few weeks, digging and pawing through the thick snow to forage for food. The poor things are starving, even though just beneath the snow lies plenty of left-over sugar beets, and corn stalks. The problem is that just below the surface is a layer of ice that they must fight and dig and work to break through for just one morsel of food. As I thought about this, the Lord quickened to me that...

As it is in the natural, so is it in the spiritual...
So many people are starving for that which they know not lies right under their noses...they are searching desperately to satisfy a hunger that

burns within but yet, they cannot seem to fill that void with what they find in this world. If only they would be willing to dig a little deeper to find the great storehouse that God has prepared for us. If only they knew that by turning to Jesus for our daily bread, we would never hunger for the things of this world again. We could stop digging and pawing in our futile attempt to satisfy a hunger that can only be satisfied by the Lord. Matthew 5:6 says, "Blessed are they which do hunger and thirst after righteousness, for they shall be filled. Lord, please help me to hunger after you and not the things of this world. I no longer want to fret and dig and scrape for the things that will never, ever, satisfy my soul. Amen.

FEBRUARY 16

We are thinking of driving toward the city to go thrift shopping today, however, some of the weathermen are predicting snow. One weather forecast says we could see 4-6 inches today, while the other says it won't arrive until this evening. Perhaps we should wait until tomorrow? If only we could truly know what will happen! As I think about this, I am reminded...

As it is in the natural, so is it in the spiritual...

We never know what a day may hold or what plans the Lord might have for us. James 4 says, "13 Come now, you who say, 'Today or tomorrow we will go to this or that city...'" He reminds them: "14 You do not even know what will happen tomorrow! What is your life? You are a mist that appears for a little while and then vanishes. 15 Instead, you ought to say, 'If the Lord is willing, we will live and do this or that'" (BSB). Indeed, we should look to the one who can give us divine guidance each and every day. Lord, help me to look to you each day rather than make my own plans! Help me to hear your voice and seek your will for this moment and trust that you will protect me through all kinds of weather. Amen!

FEBRUARY 17

Today, I read a Facebook post by a friend who said they hoped there was beer in the fridge when they reached their destination because they'd had a stressful ride in the snowy weather. I thought of my own response to life's stressors, and how I too, have a tendency to try and 'fix' it myself. We all tend to turn to our own favorite remedy to alleviate stress. As I thought on this, the Lord whispered...

As it is in the natural, so is it in the spiritual...

It occurred to me that rather than turning to prayer as we are called to through God's word, we often attempt to deal with life's problems and stresses in our human ways. Rather than try to use our human methods for stress relief, the bible teaches us to hit our knees and lift our problems to the Lord. He tells us in 1 Peter 5:6-7 to "Humble yourselves therefore under the mighty hand of God, that he may exalt you in due time: 7 Casting all your care upon him; for he careth for you" (KJV). This spoke to me today because it does require humility to ask for help of the Lord. Lord, help me first recognize my utter need for you each and every day and help me remember that your remedies for stress are much better than mine! In Jesus' name, Amen!

FEBRUARY 18

Snowed in...again. While I will admit that I do enjoy having a snow day break from school, this year has been especially snowy, and we've already had many days where we cannot get out until the snow plow goes by. So, as I sit here writing, I am once again, waiting for the snow plow to arrive so we can be...well, NOT snowed in. This was my thought as I finished my bible study for the morning. Suddenly the Lord quickened to me that...

As it is in the natural, so is it in the spiritual...

Just as we are at times forced to stay put because of circumstances beyond our control such as a snow storm, so too the Lord may exercise his divine will in our spiritual lives to allow us to recognize that we have been snowed in, in a spiritual sense. He may allow us to be stranded on what seems like a deserted island of loneliness, grief, illness, or even stagnation. We may feel as though we just cannot make progress in our walk of faith. We take two steps forward and two steps back and find ourselves right back where we started. We make vows to make changes and then we are too weak to withstand temptation or we allow our own fleshly desires to drive us back to the things we swore off just a few days ago. During these times, we may feel like giving up the fight of faith but we must remember that even the apostles felt like this. A trip to the book of Hebrews reminds us that, "Faith is the substance of things hoped for; the evidence of things not seen" (11:1). This verse reminds us that we do not always see God's hand upon our lives but we are called to "Walk by faith, not by sight" (II Cor. 5:7). Hebrews 12:1 reminds us that we are "Surrounded by so great a cloud of witnesses (who have borne testimony to the Truth)" and to "throw off every weight, and the sin which doth so easily beset us and let us run with patience the race that is set before us." As we study our bibles, we are quickly reminded that others have faced the same challenges that we face and yet have found a way to fight through it all and make progress. Paul said it so eloquently in II Timothy 4:7; "I have fought a good fight, I have finished my course, I have kept the faith: 8 Henceforth there is laid up for me a crown of righteousness, which the Lord, the righteous judge, shall give me at that day: and not to me only, but unto all them also that love his appearing" (KJV).

    Lord, help me to fight the good fight and keep my faith. Help me to realize that you may have me "stuck" here so that I recognize how desperately I want to move forward. Give me the strength to move forward upon the path you have set before me. Amen.

FEBRUARY 19

Driving through deep snow on our way home, we found ourselves stuck in a drift. The deep snow on the surface was the obvious culprit to blame for not being able to move, or so we thought. However, when my hubby got out to check things out, he found that it was not the snow, but rather the unseen ice underneath the snow that impeded us from moving forward. As I pondered this, the Lord whispered...

As it is in the natural, so is it in the spiritual...

Just as the unseen ice was to blame for our physical progress that day, so too are the unseen slippery elements in our spiritual walk to blame for our lack of progress. We may blame those things easily seen such as busyness, daily problems, illness, our past, or other typical 'life' issues for our inability to move forward on the path God has set before us, but in reality, it is what is under the surface is to blame. The unseen ice keeps the wheels from gripping dirt and likewise the unseen issues of our hearts are what keeps us from moving forward spiritually. Doubts and fear may keep us from stepping out of our "stuck" situation and onto God's path and if we do dare step onto it, we are immediately met with obstacles and challenges to throw us off that path and back onto the ice where we continue to spin our wheels. How do we resolve this slippery situation? Paul writes to the Philippians in chapter 3 verse 13, "Brethren, I count not myself to have apprehended: but this one thing I do, forgetting those things which are behind, and reaching forth unto those things which are before, 14. I press toward the mark for the prize of the high calling of God in Christ Jesus (KJV). We must ever be mindful of the path that God has set us on; Psalms 40:2 reminds us that "He lifted me out of an horrible pit, out of the miry (or icy) clay; he set my feet on a rock, and established my goings" (KJV). Lord, help me to remember that when my wheels are spinning, and I feel as if I am going nowhere, that I must look underneath the surface of the daily toils of life and address the underlying issues that are the real culprit. Help me to break through the icy layer that impedes and reach forward so I may get back on the path you have set my feet on. Amen.

FEBRUARY 20

One day long ago when I was about 10 years old, my brother and I were riding our snowmobile throughout woods when we came across a dog who had cornered a cat up a tree. The poor kitty was obviously afraid of the dog so we shooed the mutt away and my brother had me rescue the cat. Well that was a silly thing to do because before I knew it that cat had turned and bit me! Its fangs went right through my snowmobile mittens and almost through my hand! YEEOOWWCH! My brother raced me to my grandma, who was a nurse, and she fixed up my hand but my brother had to get the cat so it could be tested for rabies. It was a traumatic time in a little girl's life, waiting for two weeks to find out if I had to get rabies treatment, but the question I ask myself today is, "Would I save that cat again?" As I think about this, the Lord reminds me...

As it is in the natural, so is it in the spiritual...

Forgiveness is a miraculous spiritual fruit that is not easy to produce at times. If we've been 'bitten' by someone or some situation in the past, it takes a willing heart and a humble soul to forgive. One of the most impactful bible verses about forgiveness - and there are many - is Mark 11:25 when Jesus says, "And when you stand praying, if you hold anything against anyone, forgive them, so that your Father in heaven may forgive you your sins" (NIV). Matthew 18:21-22 clearly shows Jesus' expectations for us regarding forgiveness when Peter asks how many times he must forgive his brother who has sinned against him. "Jesus said to him, "I do not say to you, up to seven times, but up to seventy times seven" (NAS). It seems that forgiveness is a vital part of our relationship with the Lord. If we hold unforgiveness in our hearts it is a detriment to our salvation! Lord, search my heart and reveal to me any bit of unforgiveness. Help me to truly forgive that I may gain peace and forgiveness from you! In Jesus' name, Amen!

FEBRUARY 21

In the winter season, it is difficult at first glance to determine which trees are alive and which ones have died. My husband pointed out to me that those with very few twigs are most likely dead. They were apparently not receiving nutrients during the growing season, so they became dry and brittle. The ravages of winds and rains and snow took a toll on these feeble twigs and they were easily broken off. The trees that still have all of their twigs when the leaves are long gone, signify that they are still receiving nourishment from the root system. Therefore, they are firmly attached to the tree. As I thought on this...the Lord pointed out that...

As it is in the natural, so is it in the spiritual...

Just as branches must be connected to a living tree in order to remain vital and fruitful, so too must we remain connected to the living God in order to remain vital and fruitful! How is this accomplished? We must stay plugged in through daily worship, prayer and Bible study as well as being in fellowship with other believers. If we are detached from the source of our spiritual nourishment, our spirit will weaken and eventually die. Jesus taught in John 15:5, "I am the vine; you are the branches. If you remain in me and I in you, you will bear much fruit; apart from me you can do nothing. 6. If you do not remain in me, you are like a branch that is thrown away and withers; such branches are picked up, thrown into the fire and burned" (NIV). Dear Lord, help me to remain in you daily to receive life-giving nourishment from a source that never dies! You are the everlasting, life giving, living God and it is my desire to cling to you and remain alive and productive. In Jesus' name, Amen!

FEBRUARY 22

The temperatures are going to be so cold this week that the governor of Michigan has issued a state of emergency. I can't remember this ever happening before due to the cold. Today is our third day off from school, and tomorrow isn't looking any better. The county offices are even shut down. People are urged to stay inside unless they absolutely have to be outside due to the risk of frostbite, which can occur in as little as ten minutes in this weather. I went from house to car a couple of times and the cold literally took my breath away. I whispered a prayer for the homeless who are searching for a warm place to sleep in this weather, while I sleep in my beautiful warm house. As I think about those who are out there with no hope and no direction, the Lord whispers...

As it is in the natural, so is it in the spiritual...

In the same way that many are living in extremely unfortunate conditions, outside with no shelter in this physical world, so too are there many who are living in extremely unfortunate conditions, outside of My shelter. Many are living their lives with no hope, no peace, no direction in a very cold world. We need to spread the good news that "God is our refuge and strength, a very present help in time of trouble" (Psalms 46:1, KJV). Psalms 91 is another favorite of mine: "He that dwelleth in the secret place of the most High shall abide under the shadow of the Almighty" (KJV). Dear Lord Jesus, help me to reach out to those who are broken and lost, cold and hungry, defeated and without direction. Help me to have compassion and give not only toward physical needs, but to give them hope beyond anything this world can offer, which can only be found in You. In Jesus' name, Amen!

FEBRUARY 23

The thermometer reads -17 degrees on this wintery morning. I am thankful for a warm house and hot cup of coffee. If I were simply looking out my window, I really wouldn't be able to truly tell how frigid it is out there without the aid of my thermometer with the beautiful pink and orange sunrise streaking through the clouds. I would actually have to gather up my courage, open the door and step out into the weather before I would be able to truly experience and feel that this is a bitterly cold day. As I thought about this, the Lord gave me some insight that...

As it is in the natural, so is it in the spiritual...

Just as we must literally step outside of the comfort zone of our home to truly experience the weather that comes into our world, so too we must step outside of our spiritual comfort zone in order to experience the things that God has prepared for us! Matthew 16:24 says, "Then said Jesus unto his disciples, If any man will come after me, let him deny himself, and take up his cross, and follow me" (KJV). If we are to do anything for the kingdom of God, we must be courageous and step out of our comfort zone and be willing to take up our cross; translation: take on the spiritual weather that will rain down on you because of your faith. Only then will you be stepping out of your spiritual comfort zone and only then will you be able to truly experience and know his strength, his joy, his peace in your life.

FEBRUARY 24

While driving in the snow at dark, have you ever noticed that the snowflakes appear to be bombarding you from every direction? They seem to be magnetized toward the light of the headlamp creating a whirlwind of swirling white that blinds you and yet mesmerizes and compels you to look at it. This scenario can be extremely dangerous as it causes us to take our eyes off of the road and focus on the swirling stow! As I thought about this it occurred to me that...

As it is in the natural, so is it in the spiritual...

In the same way that this wonderful, mesmerizing, visual trickery of snow in the headlights can be dizzying and dangerously compelling, so too can we become drawn to the visual trickery and attractions and distractions of this world, which can cause us to get our eye off the road we are supposed to be on…that path that God has put us on! Proverbs 4:24 says, "Keep your eyes straight ahead; ignore all sideshow distractions" (MSG). Dear Lord, help me each day to look to you and trust in you to lead me down the right road. Help me to not lose focus or be distracted by the spectacular things that would steer me into a ditch! In Jesus' name, Amen!

FEBRUARY 25

This morning it is so cold outside that our porch on the back of our house is making loud cracking noises. I am thankful that our home is built on a strong foundation that is resistant against shifting or cracking. This bitter weather can havoc with buildings when the foundation is not done properly. Our shed is a prime example. The floor is cement, but it wasn't firmed up properly underneath the cement so there are huge areas that have heaved during cold winter months and spring thaws and now the floor is useless in those places. As I thought about this, the Lord spoke to me and said…

As it is in the natural, so is it in the spiritual…

Just as the cement floor without a proper foundation will be moved and thereby it is not functional or useful, so too will the believer be moved if their faith and life is not built upon the firm foundation of Jesus Christ. We must place all of our trust in HIM alone and then we can be solid as a rock so that we may be used of God to fulfill our purpose. Jesus teaches in Luke 6:47 I will show you what he is like who comes to Me and hears My words and acts on them: 48 He is like a man building a house, who dug down deep and laid his foundation on the rock. When the flood came, the torrent crashed against that house but could not shake it, because it was well built 49 But the one who hears My words and does not act on them is like a man who built his house on ground without a foundation. The torrent crashed against that house, and immediately it fell - and great was its destruction" (BSB). Dear Lord, please help me to put my trust in you, for you are the firm foundation that cannot be moved or shaken. When all else in this world is unstable, you are my rock! In Jesus' name, Amen!

FEBRUARY 26

Driving through the fog on my way to work one day, my vision was so impeded in places I could barely see beyond the front bumper of my car. I had hit a deer the week before and was a bit fearful that another might be lurking behind the thick curtain I could not see beyond. There were patches where the fog had lifted and I could see a bit further but the fog still thwarted my vision beyond a certain point. As I came into town, the fog seemed to lift completely so I could see beyond the horizon once again. On that drive, God whispered to me...

As it is in the natural, so is it in the spiritual...

In our walk with the Lord, we need to operate as if we were in thick fog, holding his hand each step of the way, fully concentrating on the place directly in front of us where we are about to take our next step. In doing so, we are relying on his eternal vision, rather than our earthly vision, which is limited even when we think we can 'see' beyond the horizon. The truth of the matter is, even when it seems clear to us, we never really do know what lies beyond the hood of our front bumper! Proverbs 19:21 reminds us, "Many plans are in a man's heart, but the purpose of the LORD will prevail" (BSB). Lord, help me to always look to you for guidance in my steps, for no matter what my plans are, you are in charge of my tomorrows! In Jesus' name, Amen!

FEBRUARY 27

Today is the birthday of my darling blond-haired blue-eyed girl. She arrived on a cold, snowy day in 1982. She had a glint of strawberry blonde on top of her head for a short time, but it soon became apparent she'd be a blondie. She was quite the opposite of her dark-haired dark-eyed sister in many ways. This baby girl of mine liked to be held, rocked and bounced and she let you know it if you slacked off on that job! She began walking at eight and a half months! No doubt to keep up with big sister. At the age of about eighteen months when she had conquered enough words to communicate with us, she became the most joyful little sweetheart. She was, and still is so beautiful inside and out. I still marvel at how each child from the same parents can be so unique in their own special ways… as I thought on this the Lord whispered…

As it is in the natural, so is it in the spiritual…

Just as each child has their own unique DNA which makes up their own unique person, with our own unique hair color, eye color, dimples, and freckles, so too are we each created to fulfill our own unique spiritual purpose! Ephesians 2:10 reminds us, "For we are his workmanship, created in Christ Jesus unto good works, which God hath before ordained that we should walk in them" (KJV). I am so blessed to have my daughter in my life (and each of my children and grandchildren!). I hope she knows that she fulfills a unique calling specifically designed by the Lord to be that special daughter, granddaughter, wife, mother, sister, aunt, that only she can be! Lord, help us to remember that you have gifted us for special works and we need to ask you what these are so that we can live our lives in a way that is pleasing to you! In Jesus' name, Amen!

FEBRUARY 28

Every now and then I see a lone oak tree in the middle of the field. Actually, there are a couple right near my house. Something about this just stirs me. It makes me think that this majestic tree must have impacted the farmer, for instead of cutting it down, he carefully navigates around it each year as he works, plants, harvests and plows the field. As I think about this, the Lord whispers...

As it is in the natural, so is it in the spiritual...

In the same way this tree is special to this farmer, and to those of us who notice it, so also are each of us special. Yes, we are special to our loved ones, but in Jeremiah 31:3, God says, "I have loved you with an everlasting love; therefore, I have continued my faithfulness to you" (ESV). Even though you might feel that you are standing all alone at times, in reality you are right where you are because the Lord has been faithful to preserve you, so that you can impact others with your beautiful self. Dear Lord, thank you for creating each of us in a very special way and giving us each a beautiful purpose here on this earth. Amen!

MARCH 1

A preacher went to visit an elderly farmer who had been missing from church for the past few weeks. The old man invited his pastor into his sitting room where they sat in front of a nice warm fireplace. Not much was said but after a spell, the preacher took the fireplace tongs and reached into the flames drawing out a flaming hot coal and set it on the hearth. It wasn't long before the coal lost its heat and turned black and cold. "Well, I guess I'll be going," said the preacher.
"Yep, thanks for the sermon," said the farmer.

As it is in the natural, so is it in the spiritual...

In the same way that lump of burning coal loses its fire after being separated from the rest of the wood, so too can we lose our fervor for the things of the Lord if we are too long separated from other believers. The body of Christ was instituted by God for the purpose of building each other up to do good works for His kingdom. Hebrews chapter 10 instructs church members in this matter: "24 And let us consider how to stir up one another to love and good works, 25 not neglecting to meet together, as is the habit of some, but encouraging one another, and all the more as you see the Day drawing near" (ESV). Indeed, if we want to be 'on fire' for the things of the Lord, we need to spend time with others who have the fire of the Holy Spirit burning in their hearts. Thank you Lord for showing me the importance of staying close to the source of fire which burns brightly in your church. Help me to stay close to the fire that I may continue to burn brightly for your Kingdom! In Jesus' name, Amen!

MARCH 2

We humans are often concerned with the weather. When planning for our day, we want to know if it's going to be hot or cold, snowy or rainy, windy or calm. We want to know if we can put on lighter clothing, or layer up for a chilly day. We want to know whether to dig out rain boots or sandals, a winter coat or a sweater! In many seasons in Michigan, the weather can vary by 30, 40 or 50 degrees or more during one 24-hour period! This morning as I checked the weather on my phone, it occurred to me that...

As it is in the natural, so is it in the spiritual...

The Lord is teaching me that just as we seek to find out our daily weather report, so too, ought we seek a daily spiritual report from the Master of this universe! My heavenly Father is teaching me to rely on his guidance during daily prayer for planning my day, rather than relying on a weather report or my own foolish earthly desires. We need to look outside of ourselves to find HIS will for our day each and every day. Perhaps he will lay someone on your heart to visit with, or send a note or make a call. Psalms 143:8 reminds us to ask God to "Cause me to hear thy loving kindness in the morning: for in thee do I trust: cause me to know the way wherein I should walk; for I lift up my soul unto thee" (KJV). Dear Lord, I know You will guide our every step if only we will ask, listen, and follow Your voice! Help me to check Your plan for my day before anything else! In Jesus' name, Amen!

MARCH 3

As the snow melts, it reveals the stubble of a plowed cornfield outside my window. I am reminded that this season will pass quickly and the farmers will move into the busyness of spring planting. I relish each of the seasons here in Michigan and with the passing of one season, I find myself experiencing a mixture of emotions. I am sad to see one season pass, but at the same time I am happy to embrace the new season. We tend to complain about snowy or rainy seasons but no matter how we feel about it, we can't change the weather nor stop the seasons from coming and going...

As it is in the natural, so is it in the spiritual...

In our walk with God, we find ourselves passing through seasons. Some seasons bring sunshine and rain and a fruitful time filled with joy and spiritual blessings. Another brings harsh weather that is not fit for man nor beast. Yet another season might be dry with no precipitation what-so-ever. Whether or not we understand it, each season has its own purpose. The dry season creates a desire within us to cry out for rain. The rainy season produces fruit that will sustain us through the rough, cold winter season. The harsh season creates a desire within us to draw closer to our source of warmth – our Heavenly Father. Ecclesiastes 3:1 says, "To everything there is a season, and a time to every purpose under the heaven..." (KJV). Dear Lord, please help me to understand the spiritual seasons that may enter into my life and to cherish each one for what it represents. Help me to joyfully embrace each season with and live my life in a way that is pleasing to you.

MARCH 4

March is a month of transition. It occurred to me this morning that when it is cold outside, one degree can make a definite difference. If it is one degree colder, it could mean freezing rain and treacherous roads. One little degree can turn rain into pellets of ice that make the road extremely hazardous. As I thought about this, the Lord prompted me…

As it is in the natural, so is it in the spiritual...

Just as the temperature in nature can determine whether or not we have rain, ice, or snow, so too does the temperature of our spirit determine what our immediate precipitation will be. We all long for the warm and gentle spiritual rain that brings growth, but when we do not cover ourselves with prayer and fasting, we can encounter icy, stormy weather that can be treacherous for our spiritual well-being. Psalms 46:1 says, "God is our refuge and strength, a very present help in trouble. Let us draw near to Him today and receive strength, and protection from the storms of life" (KJV). Thank you Lord for being my refuge! Help me remember this promise in my times of need! Amen!

MARCH 5

This winter has been deemed an "old fashioned winter" by many people. According to some reports this is the snowiest winter here in Michigan for the past forty or so years. The Great Lakes froze over 92.2%, whereas the previous record was set in 1979 at 93.3%. Also, snowfall amounts in the lower-peninsula of Michigan have exceeded the average amounts by 14-22 inches depending on location. Needless to say, this winter has been very cold and very snowy! Some people love the snow and some detest it. However, as with any weather that arrives on our doorstep, we have literally NO control over what falls from the sky. As I thought on this, the Lord reminded me…

As it is in the natural, so is it in the spiritual…

The Lord has control over the weather, just as he has perfect control over each and every area of our life, if only we let him. Job 37:9 reminds us: "Out of the south cometh the whirlwind: and cold out of the north. 10 By the breath of God frost is given: and the breadth of the waters is straitened. 11 Also by watering he wearieth the thick cloud: he scattereth his bright cloud:12 And it is turned round about by his counsels: that they may do whatsoever he commandeth them upon the face of the world in the earth. 13 He causeth it to come, whether for correction, or for his land, or for mercy. 14 Hearken unto this, O Job: stand still, and consider the wondrous works of God" (KJV). Indeed, our God is omnipotent, omnipresent, and in control of everything. Lord help me to remember that you are in control of my life each day, each hour, each moment. In Jesus' name, Amen!

MARCH 6

Today, my school is delayed by two hours due to icy road conditions and fog. These two issues can be dangerous, but often, as the sun rises above the horizon, the fog dissipates and the salt trucks have made their runs. I am sure our decision makers are hoping this will be the case! As I thought on this, the Lord nudged me and whispered...

As it is in the natural, so is it in the spiritual...

Just as the sun melts the ice and abates the fog, so too does the SON of God, Jesus Christ, shine His light to melt the icy hearts of man and drive away the fog, and illuminate our path. When we allow the Son of God, Jesus Christ, to shine into our hearts, our way is made clear and our travels are so much better! Jesus speaks to this in John 8:12 "Then spake Jesus again unto them, saying, I am the light of the world: he that followeth me shall not walk in darkness, but shall have the light of life" (KJV). Dear Lord, please shine daily into my heart and melt away any fog or ice. Help me to clearly see the path upon which I travel so I may make it safely home to you. In Jesus' name, Amen!

MARCH 7

As I got in my vehicle this morning, rushing off to work I remembered that we had not filled it with gas last night. Man! I could just imagine running out of gas, as it's happened before. First the car would sputter then chug, chug, chug, and finally it would run dry and coast to a stop. "Lord!" I prayed, "I just want to get to my destination!" As I whispered this, the Lord spoke to my heart...

As it is in the natural, so is it in the spiritual...

Just as a car must have fuel to travel the many roads it must travel in order to get us to our destination here on earth, so too must we be filled with God's fuel - the Holy Spirit - so that we can travel the roads we must travel in our daily travels. When we are running on fumes, we will sputter and chug and run dry and coast to a stop. We must allow God to fill us daily so that we, through His power, His spirit, can be witnesses to a world who is in desperate need of Jesus Christ. Acts 1:8 says, "but you will receive power when the Holy Spirit has come upon you; and you shall be My witnesses both in Jerusalem, and in all Judea and Samaria, and even to the remotest part of the earth" (KJV). Lord Jesus, thank you for your Holy Spirit! Thank you for sustaining me and giving me the fuel each day that will help me reach my destination! Heaven! In Jesus' name. Amen.

MARCH 8

My pastor was presenting a message on Sunday and began talking about the echo. The echo is an amazing phenomenon of this world. There are canyons and caves and naturally occurring acoustically perfect sites in our world where even a whisper will resonate dozens of times after a noise is made. He went into detail about several of these locations and gave specific details about how long the echo lasted in each locale after someone called their own personal yodel ay hee hooo! As our pastor spoke on this wonder of nature in his sermon, he also pointed out that…

As it is in the natural, so is it in the spiritual…

Just as the echo of a voice continues on even after the person has ceased to speak, so too can the echo of one's life continue on even after we are gone. What we do and say here on earth will not only impact those who are left behind but also our words are heard by the Lord our God. We must be careful to speak words that are uplifting and kind for the Lord is listening to every syllable. Dear Lord, David prays as we ought to in Psalms 19:14, "Let the words of my mouth, and the meditation of my heart, be acceptable in thy sight, O LORD, my strength, and my redeemer" (KJV). AMEN!

MARCH 9

I was reading in Numbers chapter 10 about the children of Israel setting up camps and "raising their standards". This word has certain negative connotations attached to it in the world of Christianity. People tend to dislike any sort of standards being established in a church. They are quick to yell, "Legalism!" whenever standards are mentioned, even when the bible is clear on such matters. I looked up the word Standard in the Strong's Concordance and it means: flag; it is derived from a word that means "to flaunt; to raise a flag; to be conspicuous." Hmmm…as I thought on this the Lord pointed out to me that…

As it is in the natural, so is it in the spiritual…

Just as the Israelites were establishing who they were to anyone who passed by their camp, so ought Christians be encouraged to raise up their standards - their banners - and to flaunt their identity and be peculiar and conspicuous to the rest of the world so that those who come near to us might know that we are of the House of the Lord Jesus Christ and NOT of this world. Romans 12:2 says, "Do not conform yourselves to the standards of this world, but let God transform you inwardly by a complete change of your mind. Then you will be able to know the will of God - what is good and is pleasing to him and is perfect" (GNT). Lord, it is so easy to get caught up the agenda of this world! Please guide and direct my heart to be transformed to raise a standard, a banner, to show others your great love! In Jesus' name! Amen!

MARCH 10

Time is a precious commodity. We are each given 24 hours in a day. Most of us sleep for 1/3 of our day, work for 1/3 of our day, and then we are left with those last eight hours to take care of necessary tasks such as errands, bills, meals, caring for children, and etc. Some days if feels as if the clock is on fast forward, and suddenly we are out of time for the things we wanted to check off our list. While thinking about this, the Lord quickened to me that...

As it is in the natural, so is it in the spiritual…

The Lord has called us into his purpose and given us a daily task to serve him and love him with our whole heart, mind soul and strength. When we find ourselves running to and from trying to accomplish OUR agenda, we often neglect the more important spiritual matters; Paul writes in Ephesians 5:15: "See then that ye walk circumspectly, not as fools, but as wise, 16 Redeeming the time, because the days are evil. 17 Wherefore be ye not unwise, but understanding what the will of the Lord is." Lord, please help me to remember that I must spend my time wisely and invest in your kingdom each day through prayer and seeking your will for my day so that I may bring glory and honor to you and your kingdom. AMEN!

MARCH 11

We were having lunch with friends the other day and talking about our old barn which was already a bit dilapidated 20 years ago when we bought our home. Last spring it gave in and fell. We were discussing how a barn need to be kept up; boards replaced, tin on the roof replaced, and a fresh coat of paint to keep the weather out every so often. They need to be kept in good repair if we want them to survive! As I spoke those words, the Lord reminded me...

As it is in the natural, so is it in the spiritual...

Just as we must examine the structures we want to preserve and keep them in good repair lest they rot and fall apart, so too do we as Christians need to examine our spiritual structure to make sure we are standing on firm foundation with our main beams secure, our broken pieces repaired, our protective coating intact in order to fend off the attacks of the enemy. Life can take its toll on our spiritual condition so we must allow God to restore us. In Joel 2:25, the Lord promises, "And I will restore to you the years that the locust hath eaten, the cankerworm, and the caterpillar, and the palmerworm, my great army which I sent among you" (KJV). I Peter 5:10 promises, "And the God of all grace, the One having called you to His eternal glory in Christ, of you having suffered a little while, He Himself will perfect, will confirm, will strengthen, and will establish you" (BSB). Lord thank you for your promise of restoration. That all of the years of destruction can be repaired by a touch of your hand and a moment in your presence. There is none other like YOU! Hallelujah! Amen!

MARCH 12

I was picking up hundreds of pine cones in my front yard this week and was reveling in the fact that each year, there are hundreds of theses cones and also nuts that fall from the trees onto my lawn. Yes, every year we must clean them up, or else our lawn would be seriously affected. The mower blades would be dull in a few trips around the lawn, and also, it would not be pleasant to walk on or look at. That was when the Lord whispered the thought...

As it is in the natural, so is it in the spiritual…

Just as the nuts, cones and debris must be cleared so our lawn can grow properly, so too must we remove the debris from our hearts before we can grow spiritually. If we fail to allow God to clean our hearts, minds, and souls, we will be seriously afflicted with the cares and worries of this world, and we would not be pleasant to be around! Psalms 51:10 "Create in me a clean heart O God; and renew a right spirit within me" (KJV). Help me to daily ask for a clean heart upon which you can grow a wonderful spiritual lawn so that I may be a blessing to others.

MARCH 13

As I started to bow my head in prayer this morning, an image of a boxer came into my mind. He was coming toward his corner, bloodied and bruised, tired and worn, barely hanging on to make it to the stool. He needs to have his wounds tended, as well as a rest, some water and encouragement and a strategy to help him win. As I pondered this vision, God whispered to me…

As it is in the natural, so is it in the spiritual...

Just as the boxer must seek refuge in his corner, so too must we take time out and seek rest and refuge from our battles in the safety of our "corner" with the Lord. My church and my bible study and prayer time are two places where I receive healing, refreshing, encouragement and strategies for victory, so we can fight the good fight of faith and live a victorious life for Christ. I Timothy 6:12 tells us to "Fight the good fight of faith, lay hold on eternal life, whereunto thou art also called, and hast professed a good profession before many witnesses" (KJV). Lord I know you are in my corner, ready and desiring to bring healing, refreshing, instruction and encouragement to my day. Help me to seek refuge in you each day! In Jesus' name, Amen!

MARCH 14

As I was in prayer yesterday, I had a thought pop into my mind of a property owner, seeking to locate the property lines which he had neglected to maintain. Over the years, markers had fallen down, and could not be easily found and now it was apparent that the farmer who tilled the adjacent land was infringing on this owner's territory and planting and reaping crops on territory that was not lawfully his. The Lord was showing me that...

As it is in the natural, so is it in the spiritual...

We are the purchased possession of Jesus Christ (Eph. 1:14) yet when life gets busy or when we become careless or weary, we fail to maintain spiritual boundaries that were established and soon there are weeds, thorns, thistles and even trees growing and we can no longer locate the property lines previously established. We must then turn back to the Lord so he can strengthen us as we go in and remove the stubborn weeds and thorns and trees and them drive new stakes into the ground and reestablish the property lines so that we can plant and reap a harvest for the Lord. I promise you that "farmer" who has been tilling your soil will not be happy when he sees you trying to reclaim your lost territory. He will fight to retain this territory so you must be prepared! But as I Cor 6:20 reminds us, "For ye are bought with a price: therefore, glorify God in your body, and in your spirit, which are God's" (KJV). Lord help me to maintain the boundaries you have established in my life so that I might sow and reap a harvest of spiritual victories for your kingdom! Help me to recognize when the enemy seeks to push in to YOUR territory to plant and reap for his purposes! Help me to allow YOU to drive the stakes deep and help me keep sight of those boundary lines! Help me to trust YOU to protect what has been established in my life. In Jesus' name, Amen.

MARCH 15

I was reading one of my favorite authors yesterday, Corrie Ten Boom, and she was talking about when we allow the Holy Spirit to take up residence in our lives. She began talking about a certain lady who had a bible study in her living room and when more people would come, she would have to remove some of the unnecessary furniture to make room. As she wrote, she revealed her point that

As it is in the natural, so is it in the spiritual…

Just as the hostess of the bible study had to remove unnecessary furniture from her living room to make room for her growing bible study, so too must we remove unnecessary things from our lives to make room for the things of God which should be increasing in our lives. We all have superfluous things that we could let go of to give more room to the things of the Lord. Jesus teaches in the parable of the sower in Mark 4:19 where "the cares of this world, the deceitfulness of riches, and the lusts of other things enter in, choke out the word and it becomes unfruitful." (KJV). Clearly, when we clutter our hearts with busyness, worries and aspirations of our own we won't have room for the things of the Lord. Dear Lord, please let us seek you daily to show us what extra clutter and unnecessary furniture is occupying room in our heart where you should reside. Help us to purge our hearts to make room for you that we might fulfill that purpose which you have placed upon us. In Jesus' name! Amen.

MARCH 16

Last night we arrived to visit our pastor and his wife, so this morning, I am waking up in a different house and things look different. The morning light comes in through the Eastern window and is shining through an object, reflecting the shape of that object upon the opposite wall. The object is transformed through its reflection on the wall; the reflection is intricate and beautiful and one would never guess what it actually is. As I looked at this, the Lord spoke to me...

As it is in the natural, so is it in the spiritual...

The Lord whispered to me, "When my light shines through You... you become a reflection of ME. Suddenly, you are changed from what you once were, to become a magnificent image of me when my light is shining through your life. No one would ever guess who actually were before this transformation." Matthew 5:16 tells us to "Let your light so shine before men that they may see your good works and glorify your Father, which is in heaven" (KJV). Oh Lord, on this day and every day let your light shine through me and transform me into something beautiful and magnificent so that I may bring glory to YOU! In Jesus' name, Amen!

MARCH 17

With a maiden name like Kirkpatrick, you can imagine that St. Patrick's Day did not go by unnoticed in our household. My dad used to play Irish songs (Clancy lowered the boom boom boom boom!) and we would all proudly proclaim our Irish heritage on that day. Shamrocks, Leprechauns, and the infamous Pot O' Gold are all St. Patty's Day traditions today. However, truth be told, St Patrick's Day is not about Leprechauns, Shamrocks or Good Luck at all! St. Patrick was actually a spoiled, rich young Roman (side note: he was not actually canonized by the church as a Saint...but I digress). Around the year 405, while living in Britain, Patrick was kidnapped and sold into slavery in Ireland. Though raised by family of faith, Patrick was an atheist when he was kidnapped, but while he was in Ireland, he heard the voice of God speaking to him and drawing him. He was forced to tend sheep for six years, much of which he spent in prayer. A dream from the Lord prompted him to make a perilous escape across Ireland to return home. Upon his homecoming, he was welcomed by his much-relieved family, but he did not stay. He heeded God's call to return to Ireland and share the Gospel so that his former captors could be set free! St. Patrick's story is rich with failures, doubts, fears and perils. But mostly it is a story of transformation. As I thought about all of this, the Lord whispered to me...

As it is in the natural, so is it in the spiritual...

Like St. Patrick, we too must overcome many things in this life. We may have had a drastic tragedy in life, which stole us away from our dreams and plans. We may have endured cruelties of others. Perhaps we are enslaved to drugs or alcohol or imprisoned by our circumstances. But the question is, will we listen for God's voice calling us? Will we answer His call? Acts 17:30 says, "Therefore having overlooked the times of ignorance, God is now declaring to men that all people everywhere should repent, 31 because He has fixed a day in which He will judge the world in righteousness through a Man whom He has appointed, having furnished proof to all men by raising Him from the dead."(NAS). St. Patrick heeded God's call, then traded his riches and freedoms to become a slave of the Lord, so that his former captors could be set free. Paul writes about this in Romans 6, saying "17 But I thank God that with all your heart you followed the example set forth in the teaching you received. 18 Now you are set free from sin and are slaves who please God" (CEV). Lord I am so thankful that You called me out and have come to set me free from things that once held me captive. Help me to be like "Saint" Patrick and share my story of how YOU rescued me to all who will listen. Happy St. Patrick's Day!

MARCH 18

Thinking back on yesterday and trying to count how many times I heard the phrase "Luck of the Irish" or some other phrase containing the word "Luck." Let me preface this by saying I do not mind when someone wishes me "Good Luck!" I simply have found myself adding to the wishes of "Good Luck" with something like "I'll say a prayer for you" or "Praying God's blessings on you" or something like that. It seems that each time I go to speak words of encouragement, the Lord whispers to me...

As it is in the natural, so is it in the spiritual...

The words we speak are so powerful! Even something as subtle as the words described above have totally different connotations. As believers in Christ, we take comfort in God's hand upon us and his divine guidance, providence and protection. Philippians 4:19 encourages us to look to the Lord for every need! "And my God will supply every need of yours according to his riches in glory in Christ Jesus" (ESV). Lord you have gently nudged me to guard my words and be sure that in every word I say, I will purpose to bring glory to YOU! In Jesus' name, Amen!

MARCH 19

For weeks now, I've been driving our 4-wheel drive pickup and it's been shaking and shimmying when I'm driving down the road. I've checked the air in the tires and it is fine. This is very annoying because not only does it shake and shimmy, but it pulls the steering wheel toward the ditch! My husband had mentioned that it might be mud on the rim of the tire, but since he has been taking the car to work, he hasn't been annoyed by it and I kept forgetting to ask him to check it out. Last night, when I got home, I remembered to mention it to him. He crawled under the truck with a screwdriver and sure enough, there was a lump of mud on one rim and mud encasing the entire rim on the other rim. In less than one minute, he knocked the mud off the rims and told me what he'd found. This morning, when I got in the pickup, I immediately thought of the fact that he'd gotten rid of the mud, so off I went hoping the problem had been resolved. Lo and behold... it was awesome! No more shaking, no more shimmying! The truck drove smoothly down the road and even the steering wheel didn't pull to the side!

Immediately, the Lord dropped this thought into my mind...

As it is in the natural, so is it in the spiritual...

How many times do we put up with annoying issues of life that bog us down and stress us out and wreak havoc on our ability to keep our path straight? The really awesome thing is that in an instant, we can lay these issues down at Jesus' feet simply by using the tool God gave us (which is PRAYER) to remove our "mud". Philippians 4:6 says, "Do not be anxious about anything, but in everything by prayer and supplication with thanksgiving let your requests be made known to God." What an awesome God I serve who cares enough for me to teach me a spiritual lesson with something like mud on my tire rims! My prayer is that God will continue to lead me to seek him in prayer so I might know the power of his Holy Spirit in my life! With God's help, all of the burdensome stuff off of my heart can be removed so that my path can be straight. I do not want to waver down this road of faith. Thank you God for teaching me! Amen!

MARCH 20

I am very nearsighted. When I take my glasses, off I am unable to see clearly. I've had nightmares where I am driving without my glasses, and not being able to see past the front of the car is VERY scary! I am so grateful to have glasses to put on, because when I do, everything is easily seen. As I thought on this the Lord clarified to me...

As it is in the natural, so is it in the spiritual...

As I awoke this morning, the Lord wanted to help me to see some things very clearly. A day or two earlier, I was driving and praying, when something that I had been blinded to suddenly became crystal clear. As a divorced mom, I've struggled with many regrets, and also with insecurities that my children might carry resentment. That morning in prayer, however, God put on my spiritual spectacles and let me catch a glimpse of who I am. He helped me see that I am the one my children and grandchildren children and grandchildren can look to and see God's amazing Love, power and truth. He showed me that my faith is not only important today, but for generations to come. 2 Timothy 1:5 emphasizes the importance of a mother's and a grandmother's faith: "I am reminded of your sincere faith, a faith that dwelt first in your grandmother Lois and your mother Eunice and now, I am sure, dwells in you as well" (ESV). We all want our children and grandchildren to look at us with respect, love and admiration, but mostly, I want them to know how much God Loves them. It's my daily prayer! Thank-you Lord, for allowing me to 'see' clearly who I am and how important my role is for my children and grandchildren. Help me to follow you that they might also do the same! In Jesus' name, Amen.

MARCH 21

The days are growing longer! Spring is technically here, but it is slowly making its long-awaited appearance. The transition between Winter and Spring are almost agonizing for us here living in Michigan and other northern states. Slowly but surely, we enjoy more sunshine and less darkness along with slightly warmer temperatures. Oh, how we long for sunshine on our face without the bitter cold and darkness of winter. As I thought about this the Lord revealed to me…

As it is in the natural, so is it in the spiritual…

In the same way that March and April cast off the cloak of cold and darkness in exchange for the sunshine and warmth of Spring, so too can we progress spiritually from one season to another. As we cast off sin, regret, addictions, weaknesses, and bad attitudes, we exchange them for forgiveness, hope, freedom, strength and honor through the power of the Holy Spirit! Ephesians 4:21-24 exhorts us, "21 You were told that your foolish desires will destroy you and that you must give up your old way of life with all its bad habits. 23 Let the Spirit change your way of thinking 24 and make you into a new person. You were created to be like God, and so you must please him and be truly holy" (CEV). Thank you Lord for your Holy Spirit, which renews my mind and thinking each day as I bow before you and ask. In Jesus' name, Amen!

MARCH 22

Today is my birthday! A day of celebration where my family and friends will all send wishes my way, in the form of, "Happy Birthday!" Each of us gets this day, once each year to reflect on our life, the stories from our childhood, our increasing age, our accomplishments, our wants, our favorite meal, and our favorite flavor of cake! We are entitled to be the spoiled one on this special anniversary of our birth day. As I thought about this, the Lord whispered to me…

As it is in the natural, so is it in the spiritual…

The Lord reminded me that there is another occasion even more important than our yearly birthday. Just as we were born into an earthly family. so too must we be born again into God' Spiritual family. The New Birth is an essential event in the life of every believer. Nicodemus, a devout Pharisee and leader of the synagogue, questioned Jesus about being 'born again' and Jesus told him, "Truly, truly, I tell you, no one can enter the kingdom of God unless he is born of water and the Spirit. 6 Flesh is born of flesh, but spirit is born of the Spirit. 7 Do not be amazed that I said, 'You must be born again.' 8 The wind blows where it wishes. You hear its sound, but you do not know where it comes from or where it is going. So it is with everyone born of the Spirit" (BSB). Jesus was very clear that to enter into God's kingdom we must experience a spiritual birth. Notice that Jesus likened the Holy Spirit to the wind that day. On the Day of Pentecost where the twelve disciples were gathered together in prayer waiting for the promise of the Holy Spirit. Acts 2:2 "And suddenly there came a sound from heaven as of a rushing mighty wind, and it filled all the house where they were sitting. 3 And there appeared unto them cloven tongues like as of fire, and it sat upon each of them. 4 And they were all filled with the Holy Ghost, and began to speak with other tongues, as the Spirit gave them utterance" (KJV). When onlookers began mocking this tremendous fulfillment of God's promise, Peter addressed them in Acts 2:14-36 reminding them that this was fulfillment of the words of the prophet Joel (2:28,29). After Peter's explanation, many were at that crucial point in time where we all must arrive, a desire to know God's plan of salvation. Let us continue…verse 37, "Now when they heard this, they were pricked in their heart, and said unto Peter and to the rest of the apostles, Men and brethren, what shall we do? 38 Then Peter said unto them, Repent, and be baptized every one of you in the name of Jesus Christ for the remission of sins, and ye shall receive the gift of the Holy Ghost. 39 For the promise is unto you, and to your children, and to all that are afar off, even as many as the Lord our God shall call" (KJV). As believers, we are exhorted to, "Study to shew thyself approved unto God, a workman that needeth not to be ashamed, rightly dividing the word of truth" (II Timothy 2:15 KJV). We are called to study the bible to search out truth. For more than twenty years, I have been doing just that, and I have honestly never found a way that resonates truth to my heart, mind and soul than this Acts 2:38 message. I prayerfully encourage you to explore this spiritual New Birth as I have done. I promise, it will be the best gift you have ever received! Amen!

MARCH 23

It is the end of winter. It is the beginning of spring. Earlier this week, we had some warm weather and the grass began to turn green. But then we had a snowstorm and everything regressed and returned to hibernation mode. As I was thinking about how impatiently I am awaiting the true arrival of Spring, the Lord reminded me that:

As it is in the natural, so is it in the spiritual…

Just as new growth takes time and patience, so too does our transformation as we grow in Christ. As we stretch and become stronger; as we strive to be more like Christ, there are times of growth and there are times we regress. While God patiently waits and draws us, it is our faith in His love and our acceptance of that Love that will strengthen and grow us! Ephesians 3:16-19 says it so well: "16 That he would grant you, according to the riches of his glory, to be strengthened with might by his Spirit in the inner man; 17 That Christ may dwell in your hearts by faith; that ye, being rooted and grounded in love, 18 May be able to comprehend with all saints what is the breadth, and length, and depth, and height; 19 And to know the love of Christ, which passeth knowledge, that ye might be filled with all the fullness of God" (KJV). Dear Lord, as we watch the trees and grass grow and turn green, may we be reminded of YOUR GREAT Love! It is this which strengthens us and prepares us to be productive workers for Your kingdom. Amen!

MARCH 24

This time of year, the stores are switching holiday items from St. Patrick's Day to Easter. Displays of bunnies, eggs, chicks, and all kinds of candy fill the aisles. From marshmallow peeps to giant chocolate bunnies, it's a land of temptation for young and old alike. Children have been talking about the "Easter Bunny" in my classes. Some debate his existence while others staunchly defend it. Flyers for Easter egg hunts are posted on bulletins and social media. Parents and grandparents search for those 'just right' items for the little ones. Today, I did a google search on how the Easter bunny is connected to Jesus' death burial and resurrection. Various articles came up about the origination of these traditions, but none that I found were connected to Christian beliefs. Now, please note that I am not advocating to boycott the Easter Bunny, but I do feel we need to put this most Holy Holiday in a proper perspective. As I pondered all of this, the Lord whispered...

As it is in the natural, so is it in the spiritual...

The Lord so kindly unveiled a few interesting metaphors to me: The Easter Bunny could be a picture of Jesus: you don't actually see him delivering the goodies, but he brings sweet gifts to His children. The colored eggs are like spiritual gifts; a child of God might need to do a little soul searching to uncover theirs, but each one is uniquely created by our heavenly Father. The Lord wants his children to be blessed with all good gifts but he also does not want us trading the truth for a myth. The scriptures are clear on this matter. James 1:17 tells us, "Every good gift and every perfect gift is from above, and cometh down from the Father of lights, with whom is no variableness, neither shadow of turning" (KJV). In II Timothy 4, Paul encourages Timothy to teach and preach biblical truths in all seasons, "For the time will come when they will not endure sound doctrine; but after their own lusts shall they heap to themselves teachers, having itching ears; 4 And they shall turn away their ears from the truth, and shall be turned unto fables" (KJV). Lord, in our earnest desire to be connected to our world and all of its holiday traditions, please help us remember to teach the biblical truths first and foremost during these times. I thank you for your word which is truth for this life we life! In Jesus' name, Amen!

MARCH 25

We are in Florida for Spring Break! It is amazing to me that one can go from 35 degrees and snow to 80 degrees and sun in just an 18-hour car drive. The minute you drive across the border into Florida, there are palm trees lining the roadway and everything is warmer and sunnier. It is as if you have entered into an entirely new realm of life in this Sunshine state! As I thought on this the Lord clarified to me...

As it is in the natural, so is it in the spiritual...

In the same way I just love Florida and that feeling of being welcomed by palm trees waving you in, so too do I get to experience a brand new realm spiritually the very instant I step into God's presence. By calling on the name of Jesus, I can transport myself directly into His beautiful presence where I am uplifted, and humbled beyond words. Psalms 16:11 echoes this feeling; "Thou wilt show me the path of life: In thy presence is fulness of joy; In thy right hand there are pleasures for evermore" (ASV). Oh Lord your presence truly lifts the lowliest hearts, strengthens the weakest spirits and gives hope to those who have lost hope. Thank you for pouring out Your Holy Spirit into our hearts, that we may glean just a taste of what is yet to come. In Jesus' name, Amen!

MARCH 26

Walking on the beach this beautiful morning here in Florida we saw a bird that had its feathers extremely ruffled. I noticed that while the bird was facing away from the wind, its feathers were completely ruffled and disheveled, but as soon it as mustered up some strength and turned around and pointed its beak into the gusty wind, its feathers were smoothed. I looked at my hubby and said, "The Lord has a metaphor in that for me"...

As it is in the natural, so is it in the spiritual...

Just like that bird, we are so often tempted to go in the direction of the winds of this day and age instead of facing the strong gusts that seem to fight against us. However, when we finally make that brave turn around to face the wind, in the direction we are supposed to be headed, He smooths our ruffled feathers, and our spirits quiet in a peaceful resolve that indeed we are headed the right way once again. John 16:33 tells of this peace, "I have said these things to you, that in me you may have peace. In the world you will have tribulation. But take heart; I have overcome the world" (ESV). Dear Lord, thank you for teaching me that even though it sometimes seems hard to go against the wind, that peace you give me overcomes any winds that might try to ruffle me! In Jesus' name, Amen!

MARCH 27

While driving to work and praying, the Lord impressed a thought on my heart; he gave me a picture of a high jumper and showed me that in order for that jumper to reach a new personal record (PR) they must continually raise the bar. The Lord showed me that...

As it is in the natural, so is it in the spiritual...

Just as that athlete must continually raise the bar to improve their performance, so must a Christian raise their spiritual bar to achieve new levels of holiness. If the bar is not raised, we have nothing to aspire to and we will become apathetic and ineffective. Rather we are to grow; as I Peter 2 tells us: "5 And beside this, giving all diligence, add to your faith virtue; and to virtue knowledge; 6 And to knowledge temperance; and to temperance patience; and to patience godliness; 7 And to godliness brotherly kindness; and to brotherly kindness charity" (KJV). There are many other passages exhorting the Christian to grow lest they diminish; pursue God with all of their might, lest they lose sight of Him; Lord. Help me to continue on the path of growth. Help me to continually raise my spiritual bar to achieve new heights in YOU! AMEN

MARCH 28

The Lord awakened me early this morning and urged me to come and spend an hour with him. I felt a promise arise in my heart that if I would spend this extra time, he would have something special for me. I hesitated and tried to go back to sleep, but the thought of Samuel came to mind, and how the Lord patiently called him several times before he arose and answered the call. As I thought about this, it occurred to me that...

As it is in the natural, so is it in the spiritual...

We Christians all have a call to answer- but have we done so? What is my call? What has the Lord called me to do? II Peter 1:10 says, "Therefore, brothers, be all the more eager to make your calling and election sure. For if you practice these things you will never stumble, 11 and you will receive a lavish reception into the eternal kingdom of our Lord and Savior Jesus Christ..." (BSB). Lord, please remind me of the calling you have issued to me no matter how long ago it was. I want to heed Your calling and do that which I have been purposed to do while here on this Earth. In Jesus' name I pray...Amen!

MARCH 29

The longer we live, the more we acquire. As I look around my 1912 farmhouse, I see many cherished antiques from my grandma's house and other items that I have picked up because I like antiques. These treasures all serve as nostalgic reminders of days gone by. I can look at certain items and suddenly I am in the midst of my grandmother's kitchen while she is preparing a Sunday meal or peeling apples or grinding meat in her hand grinder. I can see her face and smell the oatmeal raison cookies she always had on hand. Despite the warm and fuzzy memories, these lovely antiques and 'treasures' can also create a sense of clutter in one's life. If they are not displayed properly or if there are just too many items sitting around a room it is no longer pleasant, but rather it becomes overwhelming. It is at this point we must de-clutter and weed out those unnecessary items lest we lose the beauty of the few most precious possessions. As I ponder this, the Lord reminds me that...

As it is in the natural, so is it in the spiritual...

When we are stressed in life, it is likely because we have taken on too much. We have overbooked, over planned, over committed or over extended ourselves. We can quickly become overwhelmed by life when this happens so we must learn to simplify life by focusing on what is most precious to us. Jesus said, in Matthew 11:28: "Come unto me, all ye that labour and are heavy laden, and I will give you rest. 29 Take my yoke upon you, and learn of me; for I am meek and lowly in heart: and ye shall find rest unto your souls. 30 For my yoke is easy, and my burden is light" (KJV). Are you heavy laden today? Jesus will give you rest. Lord, help me to turn to you, mentally, spiritually, physically, each day so that life does not overwhelm me. Help me to de-clutter my mind and my spirit by taking your yoke upon me and learning of you and therein, I shall find rest for my soul! AMEN.

MARCH 30

Yesterday's scripture, Matthew 11:28 beckons "Come unto me all ye that labour and are heavy laden, and I will give you rest. 29 Take my yoke upon you and learn of me; for I am meek and lowly in heart; and ye shall find rest unto your souls. 30 For my yoke is easy and my burden is light" (KJV). As I thought about this passage, I wondered what it meant by "Take my yoke upon you" and I wondered how it can be easy to carry any yoke, much less the yoke of Jesus Christ, the Savior of the world! I whispered a prayer that the Lord would illuminate this to me. As I thought of this the picture of an oxen came to mind and of a man placing a yoke around the oxen's powerful neck. The purpose of the yoke in this context is to draw strength from the strongest vantage point of the oxen and in doing so, this task will help man to furrow field so he may plant the seed and produce a crop. The Lord pointed to this picture and said...

As it is in the natural, so is it in the spiritual...

Just as putting the yoke around the oxen's neck allows a person to draw strength from the animal, so too, by putting Christ's yoke upon oneself, we are able to find rest IN HIM because HE has already taken on all of our burdens. He will carry us through all of our struggles. His yoke is easy because HE is in it with you! HE is not transferring the yoke to us; he is in it with us! Dear Lord, please help me to see that your ways are so much easier than mine and by walking with you my burdens will be light.

MARCH 31

I awakened this morning to God whispering, "Arise Daughter." It took me a few moments to obey, because I thought to myself, "Lord, is that really you?" Early morning is when I receive inspiration from the Lord to write something, so out I rolled and slipped downstairs and turned on the coffee pot. As I sit here now, looking out the window, I see a lone bird perched up high in our walnut tree. Suddenly he swoops down and grabs a worm or grub for his breakfast. Ah ha! Tis true! The early bird indeed DOES get the worm!! As I thought about this adage, the Lord showed me that…

As it is in the natural, so is it in the spiritual…

Just as this bird arose early and alone, plucking worms for his nourishment before other birds fly in and disturb his feast, so too am I able and I am willing to come to my Lord early before any other thoughts fly into my mind and disturb my feast of spiritual food. It is during this time when I can pluck my much-needed nourishment from the word and be filled. Psalms 119:147 says, "I rise before dawn and cry for help; I wait for Your words." Thank you Lord for calling me to rise with you and be fed by your hand. In Jesus' name, Amen!

APRIL 1

Today is April first - a day when we always had to be on the look-out for being caught in an "April FOOOOOLS" moment by my trickster dad. He always got us some way or another, whether it was to fool us into thinking it had snowed last night or some elaborate prank that he had been planning for days. While most April fool's pranks are done for harmless fun, there are some very sinister deeds done by those who have evil intentions in our world. As I thought about this, the Lord reminded me...

As it is in the natural, so is it in the spiritual...

When talking about the spiritual world, it would be foolish to think that the enemy, your adversary, is a harmless prankster trying to pull a fast one on you. No, indeed. He is an evil foe whose entire purpose is to kill, steal and destroy all that God is trying to do in your life. Being mindful of this is key but also knowing how to beat him at his game is equally important! Ephesians 6:11 give us the strategy, "Put on the whole Armor of God, that ye may be able to stand against the wiles of the devil" (BSB). Lord, I thank you for providing a way to nullify the tricks and schemes of the devil. Thank you for the Belt of Truth, the Breastplate of Righteousness, the Gospel of Peace, the Shield of Faith, the knowledge of my Salvation and the Sword of the Spirit! With these pieces in place, we will NEVER be foiled by his little schemes! Amen!

APRIL 2

Walking through the grocery story one day, I was suddenly face to face with a young man and young woman who were obviously making a statement to the world. I know many will say I was being judgmental, but don't we all look at a person and make assumptions? I was a bit in awe of the passion and obvious commitment they had for their lifestyle. They were dressed in black clothing, complete with chains and leather and t-shirts that depicted satanic symbols. The sported jet-black spiked hairstyles and black eye make-up heavily applied. They both had large gages in their ear-lobes, which had obviously taken years of commitment to achieve, and they had tattoos of snakes and demons and dragons covering their exposed arms, bellies, necks and legs. As I walked on down the aisle, the Lord nudged my spirit and asked... "If those two can walk into a public place and proclaim visible allegiance to their way of life, why is it so difficult for my people to proclaim their allegiance to my ways." He went on…

As it is in the natural, so is it in the spiritual…

Human beings are unique in creation because we can choose to adorn ourselves in many ways. Our outward appearance is a reflection of our lifestyle and belief system. We can promote allegiance to our beliefs with our very appearance. Many will cite I Samuel 16:7 where it says "man looks on the outward appearance, but the Lord looks at the heart." Indeed this is true! However, I Thessalonians 5:22 tells us to "Abstain from all appearance of evil." Also, The Lord commanded modesty throughout the bible from the establishment of the old covenant and all the way through the new testament. Paul wrote in I Timothy 2:9, "Also, the women are to dress themselves in modest clothing, with decency and good sense…10 but with good works, as is proper for women who profess to worship God" (CSB). Whether we want to admit it or not, we do look at others and what they wear and make judgements, so let each of us prayerfully consider what modesty means in our own life and honor God with our attire! Amen!

APRIL 3

Springtime is very slow to arrive this year. It seems that we all are longing for warmer days and lower heating bills. The winter was long and harsh with record snowfalls all over Michigan, so even the hardiest of us is willing summer to get here and soon! As I pondered this, the Lord opened my mind and showed me that…

As it is in the natural, so is it in the spiritual…

We all need warmth to survive this life. Not only do we need to be physically warm, but we need the warmth that comes from other humans. A warm smile goes a long way to melt the iciness of the cold, impersonal world in which we live. Often, we hesitate to approach people when they are having a bad day, but usually, what they truly need is warmth from another human to help them along their way. Instead of avoiding or giving the cold shoulder to that grouchy person we all know, let us add a little warmth to their soul today. You might just be melting their personal ice cube into living water that will warm their very heart and soul. A good reminder is Proverbs 15:1, "A soft answer turneth away wrath: but grievous words stir up anger" (KJV). Lord help me to remember that if someone shows anger or wrath towards me, the best remedy is kindness. In Jesus' name, Amen!

APRIL 4

They say a horse can sense your fear. I grew up being obsessed with horses and I owned several while living at home on my parents' farm. I was never 'afraid' of my horses but I had a healthy respect for their strength, and I knew they had the ability to cause me great harm! I learned at a young age to exercise my authority over the animal but also to avoid dangerous situations as well. A small distraction can cause me to let my guard down and ...WHAM! I am hurt. As I thought about this today, the Lord sparked this thought...

As it is in the natural, so is it in the spiritual...

My experiences with horses can be a good lesson on how to avoid dangerous spiritual situations. In the same way that a horse can bring pleasure but also danger, so too will a life of sin. Many passages in the bible clearly teach that through Jesus' name, and his power, we are to take authority over the enemy, while continually being wise enough to avoid dangerous situations. As we navigate through this life, we are surrounded with so many distractions, and dangers! We must be aware of these and therefore embrace our authority through Jesus Christ. In Luke 10:19, Jesus, says, "Look, I have given you authority over all the power of the enemy, and you can walk among snakes and scorpions and crush them. Nothing will injure you" (NLT). Dear Lord, help me to have a healthy awareness of the power of the enemy, and likewise help me to have a keen awareness of my authority over the enemy, which you have granted through your Holy Spirit, which dwells in me! In Jesus' name! Amen!

APRIL 5

This morning, I got up from reading and writing and tripped over and almost stepped on my little dog, who was lying at my feet. She is usually either trying to sit on my lap or at the very least, snuggling right up tight next to me. Last week my husband got his gun out to shoot a groundhog. Well, our puppy hates guns and she shakes uncontrollably whenever he gets one out, so she always clings to me for comfort and refuge. If I am leaving her, she jumps and jumps to try to gain entrance into my arms. When I do return, she greets me with exceeding joy and affection. She loves to frolic in my presence and when I respond, her excitement is intensified and she runs circles around me with wild abandonment. She truly relies on me for EVERYTHING. This morning, during my near catastrophe the Lord immediately caused me to think...

As it is in the natural, so is it in the spiritual...

God wants us to be with him; how he would have us to sit at his feet and cling to him at all times and through all things. It reminded me of how the Lord desires for me to worship him and live for him with total abandonment and how I need to rely on HIM for EVERYTHING. We could really learn a lesson from our pup. As we love, adore and cling to God the way she does with me, He cannot help but to respond to us with mercy, compassion and love. Deuteronomy 6:5 commands us, "Love the LORD your God with all your heart and with all your soul and with all your strength (NIV). Lord help me to adore you as my puppy adores me. Help me to show affection, love, obedience and adoration to you at all times, trusting in you for all of my needs! In Jesus' name, Amen!

APRIL 6

Driving to work last week, I was praying as I normally do and when I stopped and prepared to turn left onto M-19, my normal route, something urged me to go straight. Since I normally don't like going through Snover on that straight option, I started to turn, but then the urge came at me again in the middle of my turn. Thinking it might be God's voice I whipped a u-turn and went straight as I asked "Lord is that you?" I thought to myself that perhaps he was protecting me from an accident or something so I continued in prayer and when I got to Snover, I was going to turn but the strong thought of "Go straight" came to me again. I obeyed it. As I approached Germania Road I thought I would go straight again but the voice said "turn here" so I did. As I made that turn, I asked out loud, "God is that your voice? Are you protecting me from something? What is this about?" Suddenly like a rush of wind the answer was downloaded into my spirit, mind and soul.

As it is in the natural, so is it in the spiritual…

The Lord impressed upon me, "There are many paths to your destination." I was about to question the Lord on this but he continued, "When you try to reach your destination without listening to my voice, you will encounter rough roads, pot holes, and detours. When you follow my path, life is better." I was astounded. Indeed, life with the Lord is so much better! Is it without pain or problems? No! But as Psalms 16:11 affirms, "You make known to me the path of life; you will fill me with joy in your presence, with eternal pleasures at your right hand" (NIV). Thank you Lord for teaching me to listen as you direct me along life's road! Amen!

APRIL 7

Communication technologies have brought us into a brand-new era. We can now talk face to face at the touch of a button to anyone in the world who has a smart phone or computer. This technology has been developed through many trials and failures. It didn't happen overnight but now we can communicate face to face with loved ones and experience more intimacy and a more 'real' connection. Thinking about this the Lord nudged me... ***As it is in the natural, so is it in the spiritual...***

The Lord revealed to me that He has created a way for us to communicate with him through prayer, but often, our prayers are more like long distance conversations over static filled phone lines. Instead, we need to get with the times and get to a place where we can meet Him face to face. His word says in II Chronicles 7:14: "If my people, which are called by my name, shall humble themselves, and pray, and seek my face, and turn from their wicked ways; then will I hear from heaven, and will forgive their sin, and will heal their land" (KJV). When we seek his face, we are then involving ourselves in true communication with our Heavenly Father, but we must also be willing to obey his voice when he asks us to turn from our own ways so that we may hear from Him. Oh Lord, please help me to communicate with you in a Face-to-Face mode on a daily basis so that I can know and understand you in a more intimate way. In Jesus' name, Amen!

APRIL 8

Each spring brings new life. While driving along I notice budding trees, just waiting for springs first breath of warmth. A long winter finally recedes and warm sunshine beckons the trees to respond. Suddenly bursting forth with green, the tiny new leaves appear, clinging to the source of their life. As long as the light is strong and the days are long, these leaves are given the strength to remain firmly held by that which gives them life. As I was thinking of this miracle of life, the Lord impressed upon me:

As it is in the natural, so is it in the spiritual...

Just as the leaf receives life from its source, so too do we. We receive NEW LIFE, through the Spirit of Christ! As long as we walk in the light as He is in the light; as we cling to him as the leaf clings to the branch, we partake of this new life! II Corinthians 5:17 promises: "This means that anyone who belongs to Christ has become a new person. The old life is gone; a new life has begun!" (NLT). Jesus is our source of life and as we cling to him, we receive his strength. Thank you Lord for New Life! I will daily cling to you for strength.

APRIL 9

Many people spend lots of time, energy and money on physical fitness, from personal trainers to treadmills to elaborate weight machines. When we want to get strong physically, we must put forth a great deal of effort and exercise those muscles over and over again to build up our strength. As I thought about this, the Lord spoke to me...

As it is in the natural, so is it in the spiritual...

In order to get strong spiritually and conquer sin and break strongholds the enemy has over us we must hire a personal trainer. However, the good news is, we need not sweat and suffer! Ephesians 6:10 tells us if we want to be spiritually strong, we must 'put on' the Lord: "Finally brethren, be strong in the Lord, and the power of HIS might" (KJV). Paul goes on to describe how we should put on the whole armor of God so we can withstand the wiles of the devil (vs 11). He explains, I will write about these various components in the days following, but let us begin with the acknowledgement that we alone cannot develop our own spiritual muscles. We must have Jesus as our personal trainer! Just as we have to follow a plan in the natural, so too must we be willing to follow God's plan. We must listen to him, obey him, and go through a training process where we re-train our minds as we learn how to avoid unhealthy things that can set us back. The first step is turning our life over to Him and begin to ask for His guidance. This is done through daily prayer. Lord, help me to set aside time each day in prayer and put on YOUR armor, for it is In Jesus' name, Amen!

APRIL 10

Soldiers in the first centuries were careful to put on their armor before going into battle. Each piece was vital to their survival. A very important piece of armor was a heavy belt made of bronze plates and leather which were connected together and held in place with a buckle. The belt had one purpose; to hold both the soldier's weapons and his protection. It was where he secured his sword and dagger, his two main weapons of warfare, as well as his apron, which protected his vital organs. As I read about this, the Lord made it clear…

As it is in the natural, so is it in the spiritual…

The first piece of armor Paul mentions is the belt: Ephesians 6:14 says, "So stand ready, with truth as a belt tight around your waist…" (GNT). As I studied the purpose of the soldier's belt, God revealed to me that the 'Truth' is Jesus Christ, who is the foundation for all spiritual battles. Much like the soldier's belt, Jesus is what holds all things together! (Colossians 1:17) He, himself said, "I am the way the TRUTH and the life. No one comes to the Father except through me" (John 14:6 BSB). Jesus Christ is the ONE we must attach to ourselves in order to win our spiritual battles. Dear Lord Jesus, I am so thankful that you are the like the belt of truth, securing all of the weapons of our warfare. Without You, we would be hopeless in the battle for our soul. All praise and glory for every battle won is Yours! Amen!

APRIL 11

The second piece of the armor of God we find in Ephesians 6 is the Breastplate of Righteousness. The Breastplate was and still is a very important part of a soldier's armor. A blow to the heart can end in fatality very quickly. The enemy knows the key areas to attack so he is continually taking aim at the heart, trying his best to destroy his opponent. As I thought about this, the Lord wants us to understand…

As it is in the natural, so is it in the spiritual...

Just as one's heart must be protected from physical attacks in a battle, so too must we protect our heart (soul, mind) from the attacks of the devil. The Breastplate of Righteousness covers and protects us from the attacks of Satan. He takes aim at our thoughts and the intents of our heart in order to wipe us out from the battle. However, when we reject sin and choose to obey God, we are putting on the Breastplate of Righteousness, and we thereby render the enemy powerless over our actions. Lord, help me to daily remember to protect my heart, mind and soul by putting on the Breastplate of Righteousness. One translation says, "With righteousness as your breastplate" (GNT) and another says, "Righteousness like armor on your chest" (HCSB). Help me to obey you in my daily walk and be victorious over sin. In Jesus' name, Amen!

APRIL 12

A soldier's feet are of vital importance on the battle field. If the feet are injured, the inability to walk or run can jeopardize their life and the lives of those around them. Footwear is a key piece of the soldier's armor to not only protect the feet, but also to keep them from slipping during battle. As I thought about this, the Lord was showing me...

As it is in the natural, so is it in the spiritual...

Ephesians 6 instructs the Christian to have their feet "shod with the preparation of the gospel of peace." The Gospel is the message of Christ's Victory over death and the grave, and it is what our Christian faith is built upon. Like footwear for a soldier, the Gospel is an essential necessity, for it is the message of God's plan of salvation to those who are lost. The Gospel will keep us moving forward, so that His glorious message of hope can be carried to the world. Dear Lord, thank you for your amazing plan of redemption. By following Jesus Christ our Lord in death (repentance), burial (baptism in Jesus name) and resurrection (be filled with His Spirit), we are carrying your gospel to a lost world. Help me to daily have my feet shod with preparation of Your gospel of peace, so I am able to march into the world and proclaim victory through You! In Jesus' name, Amen!

APRIL 13

We recently watched a movie set back in a time when the most deadly weapon was the bow and arrow. An arrow is stealthy quiet so you may not ever know it's coming until it has mortally wounded you. The only protection you had was your shield, AND, you must have your shield in place at all times if you want to live to see another day. As I thought about this, the Lord pointed out that...

As it is in the natural, so is it in the spiritual...

An extremely vital part of the armor of God is the Shield of faith. Our faith is such a vital part of the armor of God! When we hold onto our shield of faith, the arrows of the enemy cannot destroy us. Ephesians 6:16 instructs us, "Above all, taking the shield of faith, wherewith ye shall be able to quench all the fiery darts of the wicked" (KJV). We must remember not to lay aside our faith when times get difficult or when we are in the midst of a battle! It is especially important to cling to faith when everything around us causes us to doubt. Dear Lord, thank you for the gift of faith. Help me to always hold this shield closely that I may extinguish the fiery attacks of my enemy. In Jesus' name, Amen!

APRIL 14

The Roman soldier's helmet protected the brain, the eyes, the face, and the ears and neck from assault by his enemy. The brain is where our thoughts, senses, sight, and hearing are housed. If this vital organ were injured, the soldier would have no ability to function, for all other body parts are run by the brain! Thinking of this, the Lord pointed out that...

As it is in the natural, so is it in the spiritual...

Paul instructs the Ephesians to "Put on (embrace) salvation as your helmet..." (6:17 NLT emphasis mine). Likewise, we must protect our 'head' from attack by the enemy, for therein lies our thoughts, our sight, our hearing, the center of all of our senses. The enemy's battle plan is to destroy our hope, our peace, our faith and the assurance of our salvation. The Helmet is essential in protecting us from attacks of the enemy on our thought life. Dear Lord, I thank you for this piece of armor, the helmet of salvation, that blessed assurance that I am yours, which no one can destroy. Help me to always remember to protect my thoughts, so that I may remain in the battle for your kingdom. In Jesus' name, Amen!

APRIL 15

Wrestling has become a very big industry in our world today. Participants of this sport have spent a great deal of time in the gym building muscle, practicing their wrestling skills and developing their alter ego. Their stage persona is who they are outside of their private home life. When they step into the public eye, they must relinquish their own identity and 'put on' that character's behavior, personality and attire for all the world to see. As I think about this, the Lord whispers...

As it is in the natural, so is it in the spiritual...

If we Christians want to become strong in the Lord, we must relinquish our own identity and 'put on' the Lord Jesus Christ for all the world to see. Paul doesn't mince words about our conduct and persona, but rather, gives this instruction in Romans 13:13: "Let us behave properly as in the day, not in carousing and drunkenness, not in sexual promiscuity and sensuality, not in strife and jealousy. 14 But put on the Lord Jesus Christ, and make no provision for the flesh in regard to its lusts" (NAS). Dear Lord, help me to purpose in my life each morning as I awake to put on the Lord Jesus before my feet hit the floor. But unlike the wrestler, let my transformation be authentic and not a stage performance! Help me to put on your righteousness in a world searching for their identity. I am so thankful I have found my identity in YOU! Amen!

APRIL 16

While reaching for a drink of water I pondered why I am always so thirsty in the evening. I wondered if might have something to do with what I had eaten throughout the day. Salty food tends to create thirst so I presumed that perhaps this was the cause of my thirst. We put salt in foods to preserve them. The salt draws the water out of the food, helping to keep it fresh longer. Thus, when we eat salty foods, we become thirsty. As I thought about this, the Lord wanted me to see...

As it is in the natural, so is it in the spiritual...

In Matthew 5:13, Jesus tells the multitudes who gathered to hear him: "Ye are the salt of the earth; but if the salt have lost his savour, wherewith shall it be salted? It is thenceforth good for nothing, but to be cast out, and to be trodden under foot of men" (KJV). These are strong words! When we - the salt- are effective, we create a thirst in others for the Living Water - Jesus Christ. Conversely, if we lose our flavor, we are no longer effective, and we no longer have the ability to draw others to Christ. I looked up an interesting study on veins of salt and found that those exposed to the sun, wind and rain may look like salt, but have actually lost their savor; Only the salt veins that are still connected to the rock retains their flavor. Therefore, if we are to retain the ability to affect the world around us, we must stay close to the Rock of our salvation, Jesus Christ. Lord, help me to cling to you, my rock and my salvation, that I may retain my saltiness to draw others to your kingdom. In Jesus' name, Amen!

APRIL 17

Yesterday, we explored Matthew 5:13 where Jesus tells us: "Ye are the salt of the earth: but if the salt have lost his savour, wherewith shall it be salted? It is thenceforth good for nothing, but to be cast out, and to be trodden under foot of men." The point is...there is a specific purpose for salt. Flavor and preservation. We put salt in our food to make it taste better and we add salt to certain foods to preserve them. When pondering this God illuminated to me that...

As it is in the natural, so is it in the spiritual...

We were created for a specific purpose with specific callings and gifts given to us by our Heavenly Father. If we are fulfilling our purpose and are called to be salt in this world, we ought to bring flavor to the world around us by our presence and we need to preserve the truth of God's word by living it out on a daily basis. Dear Lord, please help me to live out the purpose for which you created me. Help me to bring your divine flavor to those in this world, so desperate to find something good. Through Jesus' name I ask, Amen!

APRIL 18

Every now and then, I feel led to share the Lord's message of love, forgiveness and salvation in the form of an excerpt from this devotional. I always feel a little nervous, about posting on social media because I pretty much put myself out there to be rejected and scorned by those who do not share my affinity for "Jesus Culture." Every believer will suffer the challenges of rising above their fears of rejection to be bold in sharing their faith. This can be a very difficult thing to overcome. This week as I shared one excerpt, those thoughts of what others might think arose, so I shared my concern with the Lord, and he reminded me...

As it is in the natural, so is it in the spiritual...

Jesus Christ, God in flesh, came to earth to share His message of love, forgiveness and salvation, but some of his closest friends denied him, rejected him, and even betrayed him. The very people he came to save rejected him, hated him, sold him out, and helped crucify him. Many today still reject those who profess Jesus. When we feel isolated, rejected, scorned, we can take comfort in 1 Peter 4:12-13, "Beloved, do not be surprised at the fiery trial that has come upon you, as though something strange were happening to you. But rejoice that you share in the sufferings of Christ, so that you may be overjoyed at the revelation of His glory" (BSB). Lord, I know that you have called me for a purpose and that is to share the good news of your love, redemption and promises of eternal life in heaven. Help me to remember that although I will experience rejection from others because of my faith, I can be glad and rejoice that I am a daughter of the Most-High God! Amen!

APRIL 19

My grandchildren are quite fickle about eating their meals. As all children do, they prefer junk food and treats to healthy foods. If they have too many snacks, they won't have room in the tummy to be hungry for dinner. Even if the snacks are kept to a minimum, dinner has to be something appealing to them or they will turn their nose up at it and refuse to take a bite. It's up to the parents to prioritize their diet and make sure they receive proper nourishment to become healthy children. As I thought about this, the Lord pointed out…

As it is in the natural, so is it in the spiritual…

Like children who have eaten too many sweets and snacks, when we fill up our lives up with too much junk and too many treats, we don't have room for the things of God. We have so many distractions in our world today that are appealing to our flesh, that we often turn our nose up at the things we truly need. Jesus said, "I am the bread of life. Whoever comes to me will never go hungry, and whoever believes in me will never be thirsty." (John 6:35). Dear Lord, help me to prioritize my 'diet' by taking in Your word and spending time in prayer each day, that I will be filled with proper nourishment for my spirit and soul so that I can become a healthy child of God.

APRIL 20

I have been trying to get inspired to be more active and physically fit but I have yet to establish a habit of daily exercise. With spring break approaching it will be doubly challenging. However, I realize that until I establish a daily routine, I will not make much progress in that area of my life and I will grow weaker and less able to complete physical tasks I want to perform. As I think on this, the Lord prompts me to consider...

As it is in the natural, so is it in the spiritual...

Just as daily habits must be established to improve our physical self, it is even more vital that we establish daily habits to build up our spiritual selves. If we neglect our prayer time and bible study, we are going to be weak and useless for the work of God's kingdom. I Timothy 4:8 "For bodily exercise profiteth little; but godliness is profitable unto all things, having promise of the life that now is, and of that which is to come. Lord as I begin each day, help me to carve out the daily habit of exercising my spiritual muscles by spending time in your word and in prayer that I might be stronger and more fit to do work for your kingdom! In Jesus' name, Amen.

APRIL 21

Today we drove my husband's older pickup to church. We were talking about how it looks pretty good except for where one wheel well fell off revealing the rust underneath that area. Apparently, the salt had eaten through underneath where it was not visible. I made the comment that it just proves that even when something looks pretty good on the outside, it might still be dilapidated falling apart on the inside. The Lord immediately quickened to me that...

As it is in the natural, so is it in the spiritual...

Many people work very hard to appear to be very put together. They have the fashion of the moment and not a hair out of place. While it is true that some of these people may seem content and happy, it is also true that many may be frail and falling apart spiritually. Perhaps their polished appearance is a good cover for a rusty, decayed spiritual life. 1 Samuel 16:7 tells us "But the Lord said unto Samuel, Look not on his countenance, or on the height of his stature; because I have refused him: for the Lord seeth not as man seeth; for man looketh on the outward appearance, but the Lord looketh on the heart" (KJV). Lord, help me to be less concerned about appearances and more concerned about keeping my heart free from the corrosion this world can inflict upon me. Help me remain solid in my faith so no rust or decay can destroy me! In Jesus' name, Amen!

APRIL 22

We occasionally watch a show called "American Pickers" where the hosts of the show travel the country searching for treasures in junkyards, basements, garages, barns or where ever the gems might be found. If an item is considered highly desirable, it might bring a surprising amount of money to the seller. Ultimately, however, these gems are only worth whatever someone is willing to pay for it. As we talked about this, it struck my husband and I that...

As it is in the natural, so is it in the spiritual...

Today our pastor asked: "What are you willing to pay to really truly be a servant of Christ?" Are you willing to give more time and energy? Are you willing to sacrifice vacations and retirement plans? Are you willing to walk away from temporal things to gain things that are eternal? He then pointed out that Jesus was willing to pay with his very life to purchase our redemption!! Roman's 5:8 reminds us: "But God proves his own love for us in that while we were still sinners, Christ died for us" (CSB). Jesus did not waver or call upon angels to rescue him from the cruel torture he endured on that cross. If gems and trinkets are worth whatever someone is willing to pay, how much more valuable are each of us to our Lord! Dear Lord Jesus, when I feel unworthy or unloved, I only need to remember how much you were willing to pay for my life! It is through your sacrifice that I can understand the unspeakable love You have for me! Thank you Lord! In Jesus' name, Amen!

APRIL 23

Today is my son-in-law's birthday. When we first met Nick, we knew that he would fit right into our family. He liked to hunt, fish and he was a Michigan fan! Our daughter was also pretty enamored by this guy. His quick humor keeps me on my toes, and he always makes me feel welcome and appreciated. He is an amazing daddy to their three amazing boys and a wonderful provider for their family. This makes my role as 'mom in law' pretty easy because we love him for all of those reasons! As I thought on this, the Lord pointed out...

As it is in the natural, so is it in the spiritual...

We all make choices in life and most often, our feelings and emotions follow those mental assertions. Jesus called us to "Love one another as I have loved you" (John 13:34) The word "Love" in this verse means 'to love' esteem, wish well. These are intentional verbs and not feelings! We can choose to love others as Jesus loved us when we esteem them and wish them well in our heart of hearts. When we have kids and spouses like my husband and I do, this is pretty easy and we are grateful they are in our lives! Lord help us to love with intention in the way you have called us to! Help us esteem others highly and wish them well to reflect your love in all of our relationships! Amen!

APRIL 24

I was talking to teenage girl in church yesterday about her plans to become a masseuse. I inquired as to which type of massage therapy, but she didn't know. Her innocence and unawareness of the variety of massage techniques were not surprising. I had no idea until several years ago, when I went to a new place for a therapeutic massage appointment. The therapist told me she would like to perform a Reiki massage because she needed to help me gain balance in my 'chi' so I could be in a state of 'zen.' While this sounded innovative and pretty cool, I did not know much about it, so I asked her to please just give me a traditional hands-on massage to loosen some stress knots in my neck and back. I did some studies afterward and discovered that chi technique was developed by a Japanese Buddhist in 1922. It's supposed to encourage the free flow of energy – aka "Chi" throughout the body in order to get that zen experience, which is the Buddhist term for peace. I shared some of this information with my young friend just so that she would be aware of this as she starts looking at training for her certificate and encouraged her to do some research of her own. As I thought about this, the Lord revealed to me...

As it is in the natural, so is it in the spiritual...

In the same way that we must study to learn a trade or skill for a career, so too ought we study and become aware of the spiritual implications of trainings if we are unfamiliar with the meaning behind what we are doing as in massage therapy, yoga, mindfulness and other practices that have a spiritual component. John 4:1-5 teaches us to 'try the spirits' because not all come from God. Philippians 4:6-7 says, "Do not be anxious about anything, but in everything by prayer and supplication with thanksgiving let your requests be made known to God. And the peace of God, which surpasses all understanding, will guard your hearts and your minds in Christ Jesus" (ESV). Dear Lord, help us to be wise as we encounter so many spiritual alternatives to Christianity. Help us to remember that you are our source for peace, love, joy and all good things! Help us look to your word for wisdom in spiritual matters. In Jesus' name I thank you! Amen!

APRIL 25

My eyes are very sensitive to sunlight. I try never to leave home without my prescription sunglasses and I take very good care of them as they are one of my top-four must haves as I leave my house (keys, wallet, phone, sunglasses!). Yes, even on cloudy days, I need them to filter the rays of the sun, otherwise I am squinting and my eyes are watering profusely. I have even had to stop and buy cheap clip-ons to get me safely to my destination! As I thought about this, the Lord shined his light to show me…

As it is in the natural, so is it in the spiritual…

In the same way that I need a filter for my sensitive eyes, so also do we need a filter for our hearts in our world where news and information are right at our fingertips. We are bombarded with stories of tragedy, discouragement and just plain evil. Not to mention, those who loudly voice their opinions about every conceivable topic, and while demanding tolerance of their opinions, some react with hateful, spiteful, pseudo intellectual nonsense when we Christians dare to speak our beliefs! This morning, the Lord has affirmed to me that the best filter ever created is the Word of God. The One who spoke this entire universe into existence is the ONE source I will forever turn to for wisdom. The bible is filled from Genesis to Revelation with every possible human scenario, condition or problem you'll ever hear about on the news or social media. And the awesome part is: you will receive God's counsel on how to filter, translate, understand and decide what to think about this information. Be aware, that if you choose to filter life's input with God's word, you may suffer persecution. That's a promise! II Timothy 3 asserts: "Yes, and all who desire to live godly in Christ Jesus will suffer persecution. 13 But evil men and impostors will grow worse and worse, deceiving and being deceived. 14 But you remain in the things which you have learned and have been assured of, knowing from whom you have learned them. 15 From infancy, you have known the holy Scriptures which are able to make you wise for salvation through faith, which is in Christ Jesus (WEB). Thank you Lord for the world's greatest filter: Your Word! Amen!

APRIL 26

I awoke this morning from a bad dream. In this dream, more like a nightmare, we lived in a different home in a remote location with my mom and brother. My husband and brother were gone away (of course) when a group of what seemed to be rogue soldiers came onto our property and occupied our home. They were drunk and rude and leering and sneering, and I was in fear of my very life. Finally, the menfolk came home and those soldiers' attitudes changed. However, I was still not at peace unless my protectors were present in the room with me. As I thought about this dream, the Lord spoke to me...

As it is in the natural, so is it in the spiritual...

In the same way that the presence of my husband and brother drove away my fears and it also subdued the leering, sneering, glaring evil men, so also does the presence of the Lord provide a blanket of comfort and peace to my soul. Psalms 46:1 says, "God is our refuge and strength, a very present help in trouble." The other bible verse is a song we sing at church from Proverbs 18:10, "The name of the Lord is a strong tower, the righteous run into it and are safe." Where ever I go, even when my husband can't be right next to me, I pray the Lord will be by my side and HE IS! Thank you Lord Jesus for the presence of your Holy Spirit, which comforts me every time I call upon your Name! Amen!

APRIL 27

"You can't control the weather…" is what my grandpa used to say. We are a month into spring and the farmers typically would already have crops peeking up. Thankfully, the weather this year has prevented that. I say 'Thankfully' because we have two inches of ice on the ground right now from an unwelcome, dreadful ice storm that hit our state this weekend. In the midst of what seems like a bad situation, many are counting their hidden blessings. They will take courage in knowing that they are being spared from the agony of watching their precious sprouting plants freeze and die. Knowing that spring will eventually make its way here to the Thumb of Michigan. Knowing that better days are ahead and they will soon be able to plant their crop. As I thought about these things this morning the Lord nudged me…

As it is in the natural, so is it in the spiritual…

Just as we must try to find a positive in the midst of a springtime ice storm, so too must we do the same when life brings unwelcome, dreadful situations. In the midst of our storms, we must remain thankful. We must count our blessings. We must find that hidden blessing. In doing so, we change our perspective and we drive away the dark despair than can accompany dreadful situations. We can take courage in knowing that the Lord has it under control. We dispel the dark dread and we replace it with faith and hope for better days ahead. James 1:12 reminds us: "Blessed is the man who remains steadfast under trial, for when he has stood the test he will receive the crown of life, which God has promised to those who love him" (ESV). Lord, we know that you allow us to go through tests and trials so help us remember that you are in control no matter what. Amen!

APRIL 28

Our power has been out since yesterday afternoon. We are powerless. We are helpless over our situation. We trust that the power company will eventually restore power but until then, we must wait. Thankfully our generator is keeping us warm and keeping the lights on. We are able to cook and use water with minor of showers. As I thought about this, the Lord quickened to me that…

As it is in the natural, so is it in the spiritual...

At times, we feel that we have no power in our lives. We are helpless over our situation. It is these times when we need God's power to intervene and restore our power and our faith that so our light will shine. Acts 1:8 tells us: "But you will receive power when the Holy Spirit has come upon you, and you will be my witnesses in Jerusalem and in all Judea and Samaria, and to the end of the earth" (ESV). Lord, help us to look to you for power to become witnesses of your majesty, greatness and love. Amen!

APRIL 29

I like my coffee at a certain temperature: nice and hot or ice cold. If it's hot coffee, I do not want it scalding hot so that it burns my mount and I definitely don't want it lukewarm. If it's ice coffee, it needs to be, well…ICEY! As I was sipping my lovely HOT coffee this morning the Lord reminded me….

As it is in the natural, so is it in the spiritual…

In Revelation 3, Paul writes to the churches about a vision God gave him: "15. I know your deeds, that you are neither cold nor hot; I wish that you were cold or hot. 16. So because you are lukewarm, and neither hot nor cold, I will spit you out of My mouth." He then tells us why we are lukewarm: "17. 'Because you say, "I am rich, and have become wealthy, and have need of nothing," and you do not know that you are wretched and miserable and poor and blind and naked…" How true this is in our world today! He continues with the remedy: "18. I advise you to buy from Me gold refined by fire so that you may become rich, and white garments so that you may clothe yourself, and that the shame of your nakedness will not be revealed; and eye salve to anoint your eyes so that you may see. 19.Those whom I love, I reprove and discipline; therefore be zealous and repent." This passage finishes up by reminding us that he is there waiting: 'Behold, I stand at the door and knock; if anyone hears My voice and opens the door, I will come in to him and will dine with him, and he with Me. 21. 'He who overcomes, I will grant to him to sit down with Me on My throne, as I also overcame and sat down with My Father on His throne. 22. 'He who has an ear, let him hear what the Spirit says to the churches." Thank you Lord, for your word is truth! May I think of this each time I sip my coffee! Amen!

APRIL 30

Yesterday, I went to the ER with chest pains. This is the second time in two years I have been there for this reason. The nurses quickly hooked me up to the EKG machine, put a pick line in and drew blood to send to the lab. I have learned that the EKG would show if I had already had a heart attack or if I was having one at the time. The bloodwork confirms whether a certain protein, troponin, is present in my system which would indicate an MI (myocardial infarction). The tests came back clear, so I had to wait three hours to see if the levels in my blood had changed. Once that came back the doctor let me know, but since my pain was still present, he said that he would have to advise me to stay. I was a bit confused. I inquired as to why should I stay if the tests came back clear? The answer was because the pain was still there. Of course, I was free to leave, but if I left, I needed to sigh an AMA form (against medical advice). He was following protocol. As I thought about this, the Lord pointed out...

As it is in the natural, so is it in the spiritual...

The bible has certain protocols which the believer is urged to follow. These instructions are given to us for our benefit to help us make decisions in the wake of a spiritual attack. When we are in the midst of an attack, or when we are in pain from life's many trials and troubles, we may not know the best decisions to make so we can turn to God's word for guidance in every situation! He provides clear instructions for every situation! James 1:5 tells us, "If any of you lacks wisdom, let him ask God, who gives generously to all without reproach, and it will be given him" (ESV). Lord I am so thankful for your word. Each time I open it to read, I find Your protocol, Your truth that resonates with my innermost being. I find direction, wisdom and peace in knowing that by following these eternal truths, I am following the advice and prescription of my Lord, my creator, the one who knows each thought and fear and inkling of my heart. Thank you! Amen!

MAY 1

A current Netflix series called "Tidying Up" is all the buzz lately. The hostess shows us how to let go of things that don't bring joy to us and de-clutter our lives. Looking around my home I take note of the plethora of items I have collected over the years. Many are antique pieces and things passed down from my grandma which I have on display. Some of the items are useful, but many are just nostalgic mementos of days gone by. The truth is, I have to be in the right mood in order to embrace this whole purging trend. As I think about this and my collection of treasures, the Lord nudges me...

As it is in the natural, so it is in the spiritual...

Spiritually speaking, we all have some clutter that we need to let go of and give to the Lord. In the same way that we go about de-cluttering our home, so too should we take our cluttered hearts to the expert on de-cluttering our soul. Perhaps you are carrying around antiquated feelings of anger, bitterness or jealousy. Perhaps you inherited an addiction or obsession for something harmful. Letting go of things we have long held onto can be extremely difficult but absolutely freeing. The Lord Jesus talks about this in Matthew 6, saying, "Do not lay up for yourselves treasures on earth, where moth and rust destroy and where thieves break in and steal, but lay up for yourselves treasures in heaven, where neither moth nor rust destroys and where thieves do not break in and steal. For where your treasure is, there your heart will be also" (ESV). Lord, help me clear the sin out of my life. Remove any apathy, anger, hatred, lust, greed, cynicism, jealousy or whatever it is that has cluttered my heart and soul. Please redecorate it with Your love, peace, joy and purpose. In Jesus' name, Amen!

MAY 2

My husband has an affinity for sharpening knives. He has several different tools that he uses, including a couple of different stones, but the one he prefers is an apparatus made with steel or some type of iron discs through which the knife is dragged in order to sharpen the blade. As I thought about this the Lord reminded me...

As it is in the natural, so is it in the spiritual...

I recently heard a great message where the preacher talked about that Proverbs 27:17 which says "Iron sharpeneth iron so a man sharpeneth the countenance of his friend" (KJV). He made the point that you would not use paper or wood to sharpen iron, but rather you would use something as hard at least as hard as the material you wanted to sharpen. Likewise we ought to put ourselves in contact with friends who "sharpeneth" us. Looking up "sharpeneth" in Strong's Concordance, one of the meanings says to be fierce. Just as we reach for the best tools when we want to make our knives more useful and effective, so too ought we reach for those friends of ours who sharpen us and make us into effective, fierce warriors for the Kingdom of God. Thank you Lord for friends who help to hone us into the Godly individual you would have us to be. Amen!

MAY 3

Today was the Kentucky Derby and when thinking about the past winners I recalled that many times, the most unlikely horse wins. It seems not to matter what the bloodline is when these horses bust out of the gate and begin the competition, but instead, it is the horse that maintains a good pace, stays in a good position and runs the race with gusto and endurance that wins. When mud flies in their face or they get bumped off pace, they scramble to regain their position. When thinking about this, it became clear that there is a spiritual application here too!

As it is in the natural, so is it in the spiritual...

It matters not who our father and mother are, or whether we were brought up on the right 'farm', but rather it matters how well we run the race when we enter in. We must maintain a good pace with the Lord, keep ourselves in a good position and endure the mud that life slings at us and then maintain our position in Christ. Hebrews 12:1 says we must "lay aside every weight and the sin which doth so easily beset us, and let us run with patience the race that is set before us" (KJV). The word patience here means cheerful (or hopeful) endurance, constancy: - enduring, patience, patient continuance (waiting). Am I running this race cheerfully, hopefully, and enduring the bumps and mud in the face that come through life's trials? Lord, help me to run this race in such a way that I will be a winner in your kingdom!

MAY 4

As a young girl, I was the designated kitten tamer. Our mama cats would have a batch of babies in the barn behind the hay mow ladder where loose hay had fallen. The expectant mama would dig out a spot in that nook and create a sort of covered nest. Once the babies arrived, I would lay down next to the nest and blindly reach in to extract one kitten at a time to pet them and tame them. You never knew which kitten you were getting until you pulled your hand out. As they got older, many times you would reach in and hear a chorus of hisses and spitting and it was then that you put on the glove and proceeded with caution! I found this out the hard way! As I thought about this, the Lord nudged me…

As it is in the natural, so is it in the spiritual…

Each day is like reaching into that kitten nest. You never know what you are going to pull out. Your adventures could be all soft, warm and fuzzy or they could be harsh and hazardous. One thing is for certain, we do not know what a day will bring. Proverbs 27:1 says, "Do not talk much about tomorrow, for you do not know what a day will bring" (NLV). It is so true! As the old saying goes: "When we tell God our plans he laughs." But we can rest assured that if we put our trust in the Lord, he will direct us! Lord I am so grateful that you know what is in the 'nest' each day. Help me remember that as I reach into the unknown of today, you are there to guide me. In Jesus' name, Amen!

MAY 5

My dog is highly sensitive to noises especially when the house is quiet. This morning, she and I were up early, and the house was very quiet as I was writing. A while later, I heard my hubby moving around upstairs. Jewell heard him too and without raising her head, she began to growl. With each creak of the floor, she uttered another growling protest. It was as if she was complaining about someone disturbing her peace! As I smiled about this the Lord whispered…

As it is in the natural, so is it in the spiritual…

We humans are spiritual beings who were created with great sensitivity to our environment and obviously, our expectations vary depending on where we are. If we go to a football game, we expect boisterous noise. If we go to church, we expect times of prayerful quiet as well as times of joyful noise! If we are alone in a quiet place, we expect a time of peaceful contemplation. I find these times to be of utmost importance to my spiritual well-being. Just as my dog reacts to noise in a quiet room, so too does my spirit react to an unexpected disturbance. It is inevitable that we will experience things on a daily basis that may disrupt our peaceful reverie, so in order to prepare for this, we must keep in mind that the Lord is in charge of all of my daily happenings. Isaiah 26:3 reminds me: "Thou wilt keep him in perfect peace, whose mind is stayed on thee: because he trusteth in thee" (KJV). If we look to the Lord for all of our peace, we can get through any kind of annoyance in our life today. Thank you Lord for being my peace and for helping me to maintain that peace even when life gets noisy! In Jesus' name, Amen!

MAY 6

This week my husband helped me clean all of the antiques I have displayed on top of my kitchen cupboards. These items are mostly from my grandma's home. There are choppers, grinders, egg beaters, rolling pins, seed strainers, food mills, flour sifters and more! Most of them are actually in working order and could be used once again if I would just make them more available to me, somewhere handy in my kitchen cupboard. But there they sit, out of reach and unused. As I thought about this, the Lord clearly spoke…

As it is in the natural, so is it in the spiritual…

Many of us want to be used of God. We are fully convinced that we are called to work in His kingdom. Many have useful skills given to us by our Creator. However, for some reason, we have been sitting on a shelf not doing what we were created to do. The parable of the talents teaches us that we need to use what we are given. The servant who buried his talent was called wicked and lazy. Roman's 12:11 says, "Do not lack diligence; be fervent in spirit; serve the Lord" (HCSB). If we truly want the Lord to USE us, we must make ourselves available.

Most churches have many opportunities where we could give of our time and our talents. And our Master will be glad to see us using them rather than sitting them on a shelf to collect dust. Lord, help me to be a willing servant as I use my talents for Your kingdom. In Jesus' name, Amen!

MAY 7

Sitting in my living room early this morning, I notice that it is extremely dark outside. Clouds have blocked the moon and stars which are not able to shed one bit of light. A person could not safely walk in this kind of darkness! As dawn begins to break, and light appears as a glowing line on the eastern horizon, it becomes slightly easier to see shapes and objects. As the sun makes its entrance, more light spreads across the earth and I am now able to identify what those shapes are. Once the sun is fully in sight, I can clearly see, despite the clouds. If I were outside, I would easily be able to see and avoid any obstacles in my path. As I watched the light dominate the darkness the Lord reminded me...

As it is in the natural, so is it in the spiritual...

Just as the light from the sun overcomes the darkness of night, so too does the Light Of The World - Jesus Christ - rule and reign over spiritual darkness in this world. Even a tiny ray of light helps us see and just as more sunlight brings more clarity of vision, so too does spending more time with Jesus bring illumination and clarity to our hearts and minds. In John 8:12 Jesus spoke to the people once more and said, "I am the light of the world. If you follow me, you won't have to walk in darkness, because you will have the light that leads to life" (NLT). Lord, I thank you for bringing light into my heart that I might see more clearly the way you would have me go. Help me to avoid walking in darkness where obstacles impede me from following you. In Jesus' name, Amen!

MAY 8

I burned my thumb on my curling iron the other day. Despite the fact that I plunged it into cold water right away, it still burned and left a mark. I was frustrated with myself for being so careless in that moment and I kept thinking how easily it could have been avoided if I was paying attention. Yes, my skin will heal! This is a very small example of how human mistakes or mishaps can cause harm. As I thought on this the Lord whispered...

As it is in the natural, so is it in the spiritual...

In the same way that our carelessness (or even the carelessness of others) can lead to physical injuries, so too can our spiritual carelessness be detrimental to our soul. Rather than a burn or scar on our body, our sins will afflict our mind and spirit. But it is wonderful to know that Jesus came to heal all of our afflictions. He bore them on the cross and because of Him we receive physical and spiritual healing. Isaiah tells of Jesus' purpose for coming to earth. Isaiah 53:5 says, "But he was wounded for our transgressions, he was bruised for our iniquities; the chastisement of our peace was upon him; and with his stripes we are healed" (ASV). In Barne's notes on the bible, he writes, "The chastisement by which our peace is effected or secured was laid upon him; or, he took it upon himself,' and bore it, in order that we might have peace. Each word here is exceedingly important, in order to a proper estimate of the nature of the work performed by the Redeemer." Lord Jesus I am so grateful you came to earth to bear my mistakes and sins. Help me to die to my own ways so I may find life through you! In Your name I pray! AMEN!

MAY 9

On this day in 1980, my first born, beautiful daughter Melissa was born. When she entered this world, my entire life changed for the better. I looked at this tiny baby, bone of my bone, flesh of my flesh and fell in love. She has always been a tremendous part of my heart, so beautiful inside and out! No matter what has separated us in the physical realm, no matter how many days might have gone by without her being right next to me physically, she always has been and always will be a part of me! As I think about her and the joy she has brought to me, the Lord nudged me

As it is in the natural, so is it in the spiritual...

The parent child relationship can be compared to our relationship with the Lord in many ways. My children are my greatest reward. Likewise, Psalms 123:3 tells us, "Behold, children are a heritage from the Lord, the fruit of the womb a reward" (ESV). When a child is born, they become a son or a daughter; likewise, when we receive Jesus, we become sons and daughters of the Lord. John 1:12 says, "But as many as received him, to them gave he power to become the sons of God, even to them that believe on his name..." (KJV). My children became a part of my every thought and action the moment I knew they were conceived. Likewise, as we recognize his presence in us, the Lord becomes a part of our every thought and action. As a mother cares for our children, so too does the Lord care about our every single need and goes with us through each trial and each joy in this life. Lord you have taught me that just as I love and cherish my daughter no matter what, and I want to share in her joys and also her pain, (as I do all of my children and grandchildren!) so too, do you love each of us! Thank you for showing us your amazing love! Amen!

MAY 10

Driving through the mountains, we encountered blinding curves where we were not able to see what was coming. There are hills so steep that when you climb them you must shift into a lower gear in order to make it to the top, and when going down them, you have to ride your brakes in order to maintain control. There are moments that the view is so beautiful it takes your breath away, and then there are times when the fog is so thick you can't see two feet in front of you. At times, we encounter weather that frustrates us and impedes our progress. Sometimes we are so impatiently trying to get where we want to go, that we take the short cut and lose our way. Most of us would never set out on a trip without at least looking at a map to find directions that will help us reach our destination. As I thought about this, the Lord quickened to me that...

As it is in the natural, so is it in the spiritual....

Our life is like a trip through the mountains and His Holy Word is our spiritual roadmap. He has given us instruction in the way we should go; yet we still become confused or frustrated because of the curves and the hills and the weather. The really awesome thing is that God has already been there ahead of us and we need only to ask Him and He will guide us. In Psalms 32:8, "The LORD says, "I will guide you along the best pathway for your life. I will advise you and watch over you" (KJV). Lord, as I travel down life's road, help me to look to You for help in navigating the unknown path ahead of me. Help me to listen for Your voice and hear Your gentle urging so that I may know the way that I should go. I believe You know all things and have provided a way for me to know Your will in my life. I know that You are with me through the valleys, the blinding corners, the steep hills and the impeding weather. Lord Jesus, help me seek Your way in prayer and look to Your Word for guidance, for it truly is a lamp unto my feet and a light unto my path. In Jesus' name, Amen!

MAY 11

As spring marches onward, I am debating on whether or not to grow a garden this year. We are planning on being gone quite a bit this summer and it seems that unless I am daily working in my garden the thorns and weeds suddenly appear and overtake the place. The truth of the matter is that these unwanted plants start out as tiny seeds that float in, and once they are allowed to take root, they will overrun the formerly clean, good soil and ruin anything else that is planted. As I thought about this, the Lord reminded me...

As it is in the natural, so is it in the spiritual...

My heart is much like my garden. It may begin clean and beautiful after prayer and devotions, but as I go through my day, I inevitably encounter all kinds of weeds in the form of attitudes, problems, temptations and trials. These little troublesome particles float into our life continually and unless we are careful to remove them, they will take root and crowd out the good seeds that have been planted. Jesus tells about the parable of the sower who sows seeds into a variety of places but the weeds were one of the things that choked out the seeds. Indeed, we must daily go before the Master Gardener, allow him to remove the thorns and weeds that try to sprout up in us, lest they overtake our lives. David writes in Psalms 51:10, "Create in me a clean heart, O God; and renew a right spirit within me" (KJV). Lord, thank you for being the Gardener of my soul and for daily showing me what I need to do to be fruitful for Your kingdom. Amen!

MAY 12

Today is the birthday of my beautiful granddaughter, Bella. She is our only red-headed child. Her beautifully thick, silky, long hair is an indescribably beautiful, rich dark auburn. I always tell her that people would pay a lot of money to have that color hair! Her hair matches her personality...her laughter brings such beauty to any room, as does her hair, but don't mess with her cuz that old adage about a red-head's temper is true! She can fend for herself! I also tell her that I hope she never changes her hair color because she could never create anything more beautiful and I'm afraid she would regret it dearly! My grandma's heart wants nothing more than to keep her from any pain or heartache or regret, even though I know she won't always listen to my voice. As I thought on this the Lord prompted me...

As it is in the natural, so is it in the spiritual...

In the same way that I want to advise, guide and protect all of my grandchildren, so too does the Lord desire that we heed his voice in all things. He guides us with his word and his spirit, yet we often go ahead with our own whims and then end up regretting them! There are many bible verses that teach the importance of hearing God's voice. Psalms 25:4-5 is a favorite of mine: "Make me to know your ways, O Lord; teach me your paths. Lead me in your truth and teach me, for you are the God of my salvation; for you I wait all the day long" (ESV). When we are willing to listen to the ONE who only wants the very best for us, we can avoid the pain of regret. Dear Lord, we know that if we will only seek you through prayer and bible study, you will indeed speak to us, lead us and guide us! We are so thankful for this gift! In Jesus' name, Amen!

MAY 13

My husband was talking about how he was feeling bad that he had gotten angry last night when one of his track athletes left the meet early (and he still had the mile relay to run!!). Dan had really gotten after the kid on the phone when he got ahold of him. I told him that perhaps this was an opportunity for him to sit his team down and teach them a lesson on grace. The kid made a bad mistake based on the information he had at the time (one of his other relay members was injured and out of the relay so he assumed they wouldn't run it but he didn't check with my husband). As I thought on this the Lord pointed out...

As it is in the natural, so it is in the spiritual...

My husband was so disappointed and angry about the bad decision that young man made and likewise, how must God feel when we turn aside from what we know we ought to be doing and do that which is convenient or easy or desirable for our flesh? The truth is we have to live with the consequences of our actions. The kid will likely have to sit out one meet to pay the penalty for his mistake. The penalty for our sins has been paid with the precious blood of Christ. Now when we make mistakes, we will have pain that follows us here in this life, but we are freed from eternal damnation when we ask the Lord for forgiveness. I John 1:9 reminds us…" 9 If we confess our sins, he is faithful and just to forgive us our sins, and to cleanse us from all unrighteousness" (KJV). We know not how many times God's mercy and grace have covered our mistakes! Thank you Lord for your grace, mercy and forgiveness. Amen!

MAY 14

This morning I took the swifter upstairs to do a bit of cleaning. The sun was shining and making it very clear that my house had not been dusted in recent days. Due to my schedule, I have been leaving at dark and returning home just before dark so the dust was not noticeable until light shined into my home. It is my desire that my home is beautiful and clean so if we have guests, I will not be ashamed of the dirt and dust. As I dusted, the Lord revealed to me that…

As it is in the natural, so is it in the spiritual…

Just as sunshine reveals the dusty corners of our home that have been neglected, so too does the LIGHT of this WORLD, JESUS Christ reveal the dusty corners of our hearts that have been neglected. In John 8:12, "Again Jesus spoke to them, saying, I am the light of the world. Whoever follows me will not walk in darkness, but will have the light of life" (ESV). When Jesus' light shines into our hearts, we can see how badly we need to be changed and cleansed from our sinful ways. Lord, help me to allow your light to shine in my heart. I want to get the cobwebs and dust out so that it will be a beautiful, clean place of for You to reside! In Jesus' name, Amen!

MAY 15

This morning's sky was a brilliant splash of orange and pink painted across the eastern horizon. As I looked at it, I remember the old adage: "Red sky in the morning, sailors take warning!" I wondered whether my travel plans would be impeded by bad weather that day. Soon, the brilliant orange and pinks faded to gray and with it, the warning for caution also faded. The Lord impressed upon me this truth…

As it is in the natural, so is it in the spiritual…

We are given signs and warnings from the Lord to beware and be cautious in our daily journeys. Often, however, we do not pay attention to the vivid warning and as we do so, the sign becomes faded. If we ignore his warnings long enough, they will disappear from our horizon altogether and we will no longer be able to detect when things might be hazardous. We will no longer recognize the spiritual implications of signals being sent our way. Hebrews 12:25-26 warns, "25 See that ye refuse not him that speaketh. For if they escaped not who refused him that spake on earth, much more shall not we escape, if we turn away from him that speaketh from heaven: 26 Whose voice then shook the earth: but now he hath promised, saying, Yet once more I shake not the earth only, but also heaven" (KJV). Dear Lord, please awaken my soul once again to your voice that I may heed your warnings and that still small voice that lingers in my soul. Please do not let me ignore things you send my way! In Jesus' name, Amen!

MAY 16

This week will be a full moon, and with that comes all kinds of lore surrounding the full moon. It is said that more babies are born on a full moon than any other day of the month. It is also said that the hospitals and mental health clinics are busier on the day before and after a full moon. The moon has a magnetic pull strong enough to affect the tides in our oceans so it makes sense that it can have a strong effect on our body.

As it is in the natural, so is it in the spiritual…

We are not just physical beings but spiritual as well; and therefore, things not only pull and tug at our physical body, but also there are invisible, powerful forces that are trying to pull us in a certain direction. Ephesians 6:12 says "We wrestle not against flesh and blood, bud against principalities, against powers, against the rulers of the darkness of this world, against spiritual wickedness in high places." The better we grasp this truth, the more equipped we will be to fend off the forces that would seek to pull us in the wrong direction. Lord open my eyes to the forces that are trying to pull me and help me to gravitate toward you in every moment!

MAY 17

Exercise and muscle fitness is something I concern myself with occasionally. I go in spurts, feeling motivated to work out faithfully for weeks at a time and then I will lapse into a state of laziness where I do nothing at all for weeks at a time. I know this inconsistency is NOT ideal and that I am losing all that I had previously gained during my dedicated weeks, but I cannot figure out how to stay motivated! UGH. If I want to be in shape, I must get on that bike whether I feel like it or not. I must eat healthier meals whether I feel like it or not! As I was pondering this during my morning devotions, the Lord quickened something to me…

As it is in the natural, so is it in the spiritual….

We heard a wonderful message where the minister talked about obedience being a vital key in our ability to enter into the presence and ultimately the will of God. In the same way that we must do certain things in order to be healthier, so too must we do certain things to be more holy! We must get on our knees and pray, we must take time to study the bible, we must fast, we must obey what we know God is asking us to do, whether we feel like it or not or we will NEVER build ourselves up in our faith. Just as the excelling athlete must establish a dedicated routine in order to accomplish their goals, so must the Christian establish a dedicated routine in order to accomplish what God has in store for us. Lord, please put within my heart the dedication and commitment and obedience to do that which you call me to do, no matter how I might feel, and help me to become stronger each day so that I may accomplish your will and purpose in my life. Jesus, himself told us…in Luke 11:28, "Blessed rather are those who hear the word of God and obey it" (NIV). Lord, thank you for your promises! By the simple act of obedience, I can have your blessings and enter into your presence. Help me to daily set out to obey and listen for your voice. In Jesus' name, Amen!

MAY 18

Today is our regional track and field meet. It will be a day full of the thrill of victory and the agony of defeat. These athletes have spent many hours honing their skill, running, jumping, throwing, and overcoming obstacles that would bring them to this decisive day. The question of the day: "Will I make it to STATES?" "Have I done enough?" As I thought about this, the Lord nudged me and whispered…

As it is in the natural, so is it in the spiritual...

Just as many athletes today will be anxious about their future, fearful they won't make it to that next level…the highest level of competition at the State Track and Field Meet, so too, many believers are continually battling with the fear that perhaps they won't make it to that next level, the highest level of life, through the gates of Heaven. They are anxious about whether they have done enough to earn their way, despite their daily routine of prayer, church, giving, serving. There are many beliefs that exist regarding this age-old question. Will I make it to Heaven? Jesus told Nicodemus in John 4, "Very truly I tell you, no one can enter the kingdom of God unless they are born of water and the Spirit. 6 Flesh gives birth to flesh, but the Spirit gives birth to spirit. 7 You should not be surprised at my saying, 'You must be born again' (NIV). He also said, 21 "Not everyone who says to Me, 'Lord, Lord,' will enter the kingdom of heaven, but he who does the will of My Father who is in heaven will enter. 22 Many will say to Me on that day, 'Lord, Lord, did we not prophesy in Your name, and in Your name cast out demons, and in Your name perform many miracles?' 23 And then I will declare to them, 'I never knew you; depart from Me, you who practice lawlessness.' Ephesians 2:8-9 says, "For by grace you have been saved through faith, and this is not your own doing; it is the gift of God; not a result of works, so that no one may boast (ESV). Not all Christians believe the race is won in the same way. Bottom line: we must tune into the voice of our Lord. We must "Work out [your] own salvation with fear and trembling" (Phil. 2:12). Friends, I encourage you to search the word, and fight the good fight of faith so we can win OUR race. Lord, for each one who reads these words, help them look to you, not tradition or someone else to tell them how to enter the race which leads to the kingdom of heaven. We must run the race YOU have set before us. In Jesus' name, Amen!

MAY 19

Today while walking on the beach I noticed that the footprints of a lady ahead of me were visible 10 yards or so ahead of me, but by the time I got there, they were all but vanished from the waves. As I thought about this, the Lord let me see...

As it is in the natural, so is it in the spiritual...

In the same way that those footprints were washed away by the waves of the ocean, so too are our sins washed away in baptism. In the bible, people were baptized immediately after they believed in Jesus. Acts 2:38 was the first account, "Repent, and let every one of you be baptized in the name of Jesus Christ for the remission of sins; and you shall receive the gift of the Holy Spirit" (KJV). Other accounts were found in Acts 8:36-38 and Acts 10:48 where Peter actually commanded that they be baptized in the name of the Lord Jesus after they had received the gift of the Holy Spirit. Acts 19 gives the account of disciples who were baptized by John being baptized again in the name of Jesus after Paul gave them a bible study. Acts 22:16 says, "And now why tarriest thou? arise, and be baptized, and wash away thy sins, calling on his name" (ASV). Lord, thank you for providing a way for us to have every sin washed away forever. Help us to spread this good news to all who will listen! In Jesus' name, Amen!

MAY 20

One day, I was talking to an acquaintance I hadn't seen for a long time. I listened as she laid out her list of complaints about her life and as she went on about the situations that were going on in the lives of her family. When I tried to get a word of advice in, she suddenly had to get going, and I was left with the impression that she really did not want solutions to her problems, she just wanted to complain. As I pondered this, the Lord spoke to me...

As it is in the natural, so is it in the spiritual...

While the Lord desires for us to make the effort to communicate with him, he doesn't want a one-way dialogue of requests and complaints. An important part of communication is LISTENING. He is our heavenly Father and He wants relationship with us at the highest level possible, which means we not only speak to Him, we must also listen. John 10:27 says, "My sheep hear my voice, and I know them, and they follow me. I give them eternal life, and they will never perish, and no one will snatch them out of my hand" (ESV). Please help me Lord as I communicate with you, to be sure to listen closely for your voice so that I may hear You and follow in your way! In Jesus' name, Amen!

MAY 21

It is mid Spring and the sun is shining brightly. After a long, snowy, cold winter, I am excited to step out into the warm sunshine. Finally! As I open my door, the cold north wind catches me full in the face, taking my breath away and sending shivers to the bone. I quickly retreat and put on my warm coat. As I was slipping my arms into the down filled sleeves, the Lord quickened to me that:

As it is in the natural, so is it in the spiritual...

Just as we need protection from unexpected, bitter cold weather, so too do we need to wrap ourselves in Christ to protect our heart, mind and soul from the unexpected, adversities that fall daily into our lives. Things can look bright and warm in our life, but suddenly we are hit in the face by a bitter storm that takes our breath away. God's word tells us that as many of us who are baptized into Christ, have put on Christ (Galatians 3:27 emphasis mine); we are clothed with salvation (Psalms 132:16; Isaiah 61:10) and we are to clothe ourselves in humility toward one another; God opposes the proud but gives grace to the humble (I Peter 5:5); put on the full armor of God (Ephesians 6:11-17); to put on Christ and make no provision for the flesh (Romans 13:14); and to put on, as the elect of God, holy and beloved, bowels of mercies, kindness, humbleness of mind, meekness, longsuffering; forebearing one another, and forgiving one another...(Colossians 3:12-13). Lord, we thank you for your promises, our salvation, and for all of the many benefits that come to us when we PUT ON Christ Jesus. In Jesus' name, AMEN.

MAY 22

We have all had great service in a restaurant and we've all had not so great service! A good waitress knows how to take care of their customers. They keep the coffee cup full, they make sure the food is delivered hot, they bring all the necessities and condiments needed or requested and most of all, they do so cheerfully and without hesitation. They give their service generously. As I thought on this, I realized that…

As it is in the natural, so is it in the spiritual...

Each moment of every day, we have opportunities to serve God and others through our actions and our attitudes. Jesus Himself came to earth and showed us how to serve selflessly and graciously without any attitude. But how often do we grumble as we are serving? Proverbs 11:25 tells us, "A generous person will prosper; whoever refreshes others will be refreshed" (NIV). Lord, help me to serve with a cheerful heart full of desire to please YOU first, and others as well.

MAY 23

Seasons come and go. This point was addressed by my pastor on Sunday and he reminded us that seasons allow a window of opportunity in which we must accomplish certain things, lest the window closes and the opportunity is missed. When it is spring, we must plant the seeds in the ground or if we wait too long to plant, the season will go by and the crop will not grow during the growing season and will not be ripe for harvest during harvest season. He pointed out that…

As it is in the natural, so is it in the spiritual…

Just as we must take advantage of the seasons of sowing and reaping in the natural, so too we must take advantage of those seasons in the spiritual. If we do not sow seeds in our spiritual life, we will never reap a crop. II Corinthians 9:6 says, "6 But this I say, He which soweth sparingly shall reap also sparingly; and he which soweth bountifully shall reap also bountifully" (KJV). If we want to reap, we must sow. We must spread the message of God's love to a lost world if we want to see changes. Help us Lord, to boldly sow the precious seeds of your gospel so that You may reap a harvest of souls. In Jesus' name, Amen!

MAY 24

My husband and I were up early one Saturday morning and just meditating on the Lord when he had a thought. He said that when we are trying to use words to describe something to a small child (such as hot or cold, or perhaps the way some new food tastes) we fall short on words. They cannot fully comprehend and understand what we are trying to explain because they have not yet experienced it. As we talked the Lord revealed to us both...

As it is in the natural, so is it in the spiritual...

Just as words fail us when explaining those tangible experiences with our five senses, the same is even more true when it comes to explaining the intangible experience of the Lord's presence. A person who has not entered into the presence of God cannot fully comprehend things in the spiritual realm. I Cor. 2:14 says "Then natural man does not receive the things of the Spirit of God for they are folly to him; and he cannot know them because they are spiritually discerned (KJV). Once a person has experienced the unspeakable indwelling Spirit of God, they are partakers of His supernatural power and their understanding is opened. Lord, as we seek you, let us not stop short of what you have purposed for each of us. Through your name I pray! Amen!

MAY 25

When reading poetry, we must be able to make a connection to what was written or else the meaning escapes us. With no connection, it fails to affect us or inspire us. It truly helps us to study the author so that we might get a glimpse into their background, experiences and mindset before we approach their work. Then we can more fully appreciate the words they have written. As I thought on this it occurred to me that...

As it is in the natural, so is it in the spiritual...

If we have not made an attempt to know the Lord, or if we have not felt His love, goodness, mercy and grace, it may be difficult to pick up His word and make a connection. Sadly, the truths of the Word of God may fail to affect us. Hebrews 4:12 declares, "For the word of God is quick, and powerful, and sharper than any two-edged sword, piercing even to the dividing asunder of soul and spirit, and of the joints and marrow, and is a discerner of the thoughts and intents of the heart" (KJV). When we seek to KNOW the Lord through meditation in prayer and through the study of his Word, then that precious Word will astound us, change us, influence us and inspire us.

Romans 11:33 declares, "O the depth of the riches both of the wisdom and knowledge of God! How unsearchable are his judgments, and his ways past finding out!" (KJV). Let us strive to know you Lord and let your Word penetrate our human minds and elevate us to a spiritual realm where we can more fully appreciate you.

MAY 26

Recently I was at a playground watching kids who were squealing with delight as they rode up and down on a teeter totter. It occurred to me that in order to be lifted up on the teeter totter, you must exert some energy. To get the best lift, you must have your feet firmly planted on the ground and push off of it. You go up and then gravity causes you to come back down. Once your feet hit the ground again, you must then use the strength you have to push yourself back up. When the teeter totter is on sand, you don't have as much velocity as you do when it is built on asphalt or other hard surfaces and you have to work much harder to be lifted up. As I thought on this, the Lord nudged me and revealed…

As it is in the natural, so is it in the spiritual…

As I seek to rise up to new heights in my walk with the Lord, I must have my feet planted on the solid rock of Jesus Christ. II Timothy 2:19 says, "Nevertheless, the firm foundation of God stands, having this seal, "The Lord knows those who are His," and, "Everyone who names the name of the Lord is to abstain from wickedness" (NAS). I want to have my feet planted on this firm foundation built by the Lord. I want him to know that I am his! Jesus Christ is the rock of my salvation! Upon Him, I stand. Thank you Lord, for you never move nor change! You are my solid rock! Amen!

MAY 27

As mentioned yesterday, riding on a teeter totter as a young child can be very exhilarating! However, as I found out recently, as we mature, it can be repetitive and uncomfortable to the point that we simply want our feet on the ground! As I thought about this, the Lord pointed out…

As it is in the natural, so is it in the spiritual…

My spiritual journey can be much like a teeter totter. At times I exert much time and energy into prayer and bible study and spiritual things in an attempt to lift myself up higher. It seems, though, that inevitably I find out that while those heights are exhilarating, I ultimately just want my feet on solid ground. It is here where I can find that firm foundation that exists only in my faith in what Jesus Christ has accomplished for ME. I Corinthians 3:11 says, "For no one can lay a foundation other than the one already laid, which is Jesus Christ. Lord" (BSB). Dear Lord, I thank you for showing me that I do not need the drastic ups and downs of teeter totter Christianity, but rather, the firm foundation of Jesus Christ upon which I can stand! Amen!

MAY 28

Walking through the playground I passed by the roundabout carousal. There were children hanging on for dear life squealing with delight as they crawled their way toward the center to gain better stability and avoid being thrown off. As I thought about this, the Lord illuminated to me…

As it is in the natural, so is it in the spiritual...

I believe God has a desire for us to live not far from him, out on the edge, clinging desperately so we don't fall off, but rather, his desire is that we draw closer to him, where we can feel safe and find rest. Psalms 73:28 says, "But it is good for me to draw near to God: I have put my trust in the Lord GOD, that I may declare all thy works" (KJV). Dear Lord we recognize that as we move closer to you, we reduce the risk of falling away from you! We also see that our power is generated from You so we must remain close so we will not fall! Thank you for your love, your power and your refuge. In Jesus' name, Amen!

MAY 29

Water is vitally necessary for life. Without water, a person would die. Our bodies are made up of 75% water and it requires water to be healthy. I have noticed also that the more water I drink on a regular basis, the more I crave it if I am not taking in enough. As I thought on this the Lord nudged me...

As it is in the natural, so is it in the spiritual...

He reminded me that in the same way I need water to be alive, and now even crave it when I don't get enough, I also need Jesus - the living water - in order to be alive spiritually. Without him in my life, my spirit would wither up and die. I need daily time in prayer and study of God's word to water my spirit and soul. As Jesus promised in John 4:14, "But whosoever drinketh of the water that I shall give him shall never thirst; but the water that I shall give him shall be in him a well of water springing up into everlasting life" (KJV).

MAY 30

I was listening to someone talk about getting strong. She talked about how a body builder starts with small weights to strengthen his muscles. He doesn't jump right in and lift 100-pound barbell. As he gains strength, he adds weight to his bar and is able to slowly gain more and more confidence in his physical ability. As I listened, the Lord was showing me that...

As it is in the natural, so is it in the spiritual...

Just as physical strength must be built slowly, so too must we build up our spiritual being in small increments. We must start small and build our faith by trusting God for those daily things...those small, seemingly insignificant things that we typically rely on ourselves for...plans for the day, where to shop, a good parking space, a lunch choice, which route to take, and simple things like that. If we train ourselves to listen in the small things, we can learn to hear his voice and obey him. Then when the heavy things of life come, we will be prepared to listen for God, and trust and follow Him. Isaiah 30:21 promises, "And thine ears shall hear a word behind thee, saying, This is the way, walk ye in it, when ye turn to the right hand, and when ye turn to the left" (KJV) Indeed, I have experienced the voice of God leading me in such a way. Lord, it truly amazes me how incredibly concerned you are over every small thing we do. Help me to build myself spiritually each day by trusting you more with each thought and decision I make! In Jesus' name, Amen.

MAY 31

As I contemplate how to go about getting back in shape physically, I realize that I must endure some pain in order to achieve my goals. If I want to have strong legs, arms and healthy heart, I must treat my body well and put it through some rigorous activity. I can't sit on the couch and expect to grow stronger! I must get up and DO something and it may bring a bit of discomfort in the process. The key is to be consistent because if I stop for a few days or a week or a month, I will be right back where I began. As I thought about this, the Lord reminded me that...

As it is in the natural, so is it in the spiritual…

Just as my body must endure some pain in order to be more fit, so too must my spirit endure some pain in order to be fit for the Work of God's Kingdom. I must exercise self-restraint, and I must bring my desires and my will and my spirit into subjection so that I can be ready and able to do the work God is preparing me for. If I slack off for a day or two or a week or a month, I will find myself right back where I started in the same condition that I was in when I began the quest for strength. I love Paul's prayer in Ephesians 3:16 "That he would grant you, according to the riches of his glory, to be strengthened with might by his Spirit in the inner man; 17 That Christ may dwell in your hearts by faith; that ye, being rooted and grounded in love, 18 May be able to comprehend with all saints what is the breadth, and length, and depth and height;19 And to know the love of Christ, which passeth knowledge, that ye might be filled with all the fulness of God" (KJV). Oh Lord, please help me to daily build my spiritual self so that I might be strengthened by your Spirit for all good works for Your Kingdom. In Jesus' name. Amen.

JUNE 1

I was on my hands and knees in my garden, covering seeds with dirt, chastising myself and wishing I had taken more time and care to prepare the soil with compost and fertilizer. I whispered a little prayer, "Lord, even though I have not made better preparations, please let these seeds grow and be fruitful." Suddenly, the Lord dropped a series of thoughts and scriptures into my heart...

As it is in the natural, so is it in the spiritual…

In an instant, all of the biblical references about planting and reaping what we sow came to me in a flash of realization that if I treated my heart and mind the same way I treat my garden, then what kind of spiritual fruits would I expect to grow? It was a kind and gentle reminder from the Lord that we must invest time and effort into his kingdom if we want to reap anything. If we are not producing fruit then we must look at our preparation efforts. Galatians 6:7 reminds us, "Do not deceive yourselves. God is not to be scoffed at. For whatever a man sows, that he will also reap" (WNT). Lord, help me to sow my time and energy into the spiritual, so that I may reap spiritual goodness in due season. Dear Lord, thank you for showing me this truth! I want to cultivate the soil of my heart so that the seed of your word will take root and grow and bring fruit into my life and the lives of those I love. Amen!

JUNE 2

Continuing from yesterday, I will share more of what the Lord revealed as I planted my garden. As I patted the warm earth over the seeds, I continued to receive tidbits from the Lord. The soil we choose to plant seeds must be good soil. We must not scatter it on the hardened path where it will not sink in. We must not plant in dry, rocky soil or thorny ground. Sometimes additional preparation is required to prepare our soil so the seeds can receive nutrients from the soil in which they are planted. The Lord whispered...

As it is in the natural, so is it in the spiritual...

As the sower must have good soil to plant his seed, so too must I have my heart ready to actually receive the seed of God's word. I must properly prepare myself through repentance and prayer and even tears to water my hardened heart. Otherwise, the seeds will not take root, but just lay there and die. In Luke 8, Jesus teaches, "5 A farmer went out to sow his seed. As he was scattering the seed, some fell along the path; it was trampled on, and the birds ate it up. 6 Some fell on rocky ground, and when it came up, the plants withered because they had no moisture. 7 Other seed fell among thorns, which grew up with it and choked the plants. 8 Still other seed fell on good soil. It came up and yielded a crop, a hundred times more than was sown."

When he said this, he called out, "Whoever has ears to hear, let them hear" (NIV). Lord help me to hear your words and prepare my heart to receive the good seed of your word today! In Jesus' name, Amen!

JUNE 3

One thing a gardener knows, After the seeds are planted, they not only need continued fertilization at regular intervals, but they also require an ample amount of water. Without moisture, plants soon wither and die. As I thought about this and whispered a prayer for rain, the Lord opened my mind to understand...

As it is in the natural, so is it in the spiritual...

In the same was those tiny seeds need rain after being planted, so too do I need the seeds of God's word which are sown into my mind and heart to be watered. Just as rain in the natural brings growth, refreshment and fruitfulness, so also do showers from Heaven bring goodness for my soul. Psalms 126:5 tells us, "They that sow in tears, shall reap in joy." Tears that flow as we are receiving that precious seed from heaven will be more securely planted in our hearts. Dear Lord, help me to embrace your precious word as the ground embraces the farmer's seed. Help me cover the word with tears of joy and thankfulness, that they may produce fruit in due season. In Jesus' name, Amen!

JUNE 4

As I wait and watch for my garden to sprout this week I am praying for good growing weather! The seeds desperately need warmth and light of the sun to spur the tiny seed onward to growth. A hard frost or temperatures that are close to freezing will not help these tiny seeds sprout and grow! Longer days of sunlight are what is needed! As I thought on this the Lord reminded me...

As it is in the natural, so is it in the spiritual...

In the same regard, so too does my heart desperately need the warmth and light of the SON of God to spur me on and help me to grow! John 1 emphasizes this about the Lord Jesus, "3 Through him all things were made; without him nothing was made that has been made. 4 In him was life, and that life was the light of all mankind. 5 The light shines in the darkness, and the darkness has not overcome it" (NIV). Thank you Jesus, for you indeed are the light of this world, and in you there is no darkness at all! I can be sure that if I remain IN YOU, I will grow and produce fruit for Your kingdom. Amen!

JUNE 5

After a seed pokes through the ground they are still at risk for things like insects, disease and varmints who would like to snack on the tender roots just sprouting. We go to great lengths to protect our gardens from these harms. We spray, sprinkle and put powder on leaves. We put electric fences and borders around the garden. We set up scarecrows and check them frequently for signs of an invasion. Again, the Lord revealed to me this truth...

As it is in the natural, so is it in the spiritual...

In the same way that our garden is vulnerable to the attacks of an invader, so too are those precious seeds which have been sown into our hearts. We hear a wonderful word from our pastor on Sunday and make a commitment to go deeper with the Lord, but even before our tires hit the road, we are questioning it. Where does this doubt or fear come from? Well of course it isn't the Lord! It is the enemy of our soul who seeks to kill, steal and destroy anything good that the Lord has planted. The parable of the sower tells us in Mark 4:15, "Some people are like seed along the path, where the word is sown. As soon as they hear it, Satan comes and takes away the word that was sown in them" (NIV). Guard your heart people! Proverbs 4:23 tells us, "Guard your heart above all else, for it is the source of life" (CSB). Dear Lord, help me this day to understand how vital it is that I be on the look-out for the thief, the enemy of my soul, to come and try to steal away your precious seed from my heart. Please alert me and help me set my fences high! In Jesus' name, Amen!

JUNE 6

We must continually fight the weeds that spring up (and seem to grow even more quickly than the seed that was planted!) Careful removal of the weed is necessary. If you simply cut it off with the edge of a hoe, it will grow back because the root has not been destroyed. It will come back crooked and mangled but stronger than ever. No, you must remove the entire weed, and shake all of the dirt off to allow the root to dry and die in order to kill it. If the root has even a little bit of soil left clinging to it, it will remain alive and will find a way to take root again. The Lord illuminated to me...

As it is in the natural, so is it in the spiritual...

Likewise, in the spiritual, if I remove something from my life but yet continue to tamper with it, I essentially am replanting the root of that evil weed into my heart and it will grow back, mangled and angry and even more difficult to pull out and destroy. Colossians 3:5 tells us, "For if you live according to the flesh, you will die; but if by the Spirit you put to death the deeds of the body, you will live" (BSB). We do this through dying daily to the desires of our flesh and turning our life over for the work of God's kingdom. Lord, I thank you for this wonderful truth and for teaching me how to remove sin and death from my life that I might grow healthy and vital for your kingdom. In Jesus' name, Amen!

JUNE 7

True north. I watched a show about people who were lost in the wilderness and the main reason was they had lost their sense of direction. When one cannot tell where they are or where they are headed, confusion sets in, followed by frustration and desperation. If they would only have learned where true north lies by reading the signs given by God (sunrise, and sunset) they could have found their way back home. As I thought of this, the Lord pointed out that...

As it is in the natural, so is it in the spiritual...

Just as we become lost when we do not align ourselves with true North in the physical world, so too can we become lost when we fail to align ourselves with the true North of our Spiritual world. The Lord has established a path for each one of His children and we must daily go to Him to ask for direction, especially when we have perhaps stepped off of the path we once followed so closely. If we can simply locate our True North in Christ Jesus and His calling for our life, we will soon be out of the wilderness and back on track. Psalms 107:4-6 "They wandered in the wilderness in a desolate way; they found no city to dwell in. Hungry and thirsty their soul fainted in them. Then they cried out to the Lord in their trouble, and He delivered them out of their distresses" (NKJV). Thank you Lord for giving us your word and your spirit to guide us and give us direction in this wilderness we call life! Amen!

JUNE 8

A chameleon is a very interesting creature. I first encountered one when I was a child on vacation in Florida visiting our aunt and uncle. This curious little creature was on a green plant when my uncle pointed him out. "Watch this!" He whispered as he slid a stick under the tiny green reptile. In a matter of a minute or less, right before my eyes, the chameleon had turned the exact shade of color as the grayish brown stick. "WHOA!" I exclaimed! "That is so COOL!" Little did I know how that little lizard lesson would be used of the Lord to show me...

As it is in the natural, so is it in the spiritual...

In the same way that a chameleon can change its color to blend into their immediate environment, so too do I have the tendency to change depending on who I am with. The impact of this wavering behavior was made crystal clear to me one day when a fellow "believer" became totally different when the "cool kids" showed up. Needless to say, the Lord used that to show me how detrimental it is when I change my colors around certain people rather than sticking with my beliefs. Ephesians 4 explains how God gave apostles, prophets, evangelists, pastors and teachers to build up the body of Christ and reach unity in our faith and knowledge of Jesus so we can mature to the full stature of Jesus Christ. Wow. That's a tall order! But the promise that follows is pretty huge: "14 Then we will no longer be infants, tossed about by the waves and carried around by every wind of teaching and by the clever cunning of men in their deceitful scheming. 15 Instead, speaking the truth in love, we will in all things grow up into Christ Himself, who is the head" (BSB). Lord, thank you for those you placed in ministry to build up your church. Help me to follow Godly instruction and stay true to my beliefs, no matter who I am around. In Jesus' name, Amen!

JUNE 9

While rushing to work this week one day, I nosed my vehicle out to pass and glancing in the rear-view mirror, I noticed a bubble top two cars behind me. I immediately eased back into my lane and assessed the situation for a short distance. It was soon apparent this car was a State Police Trooper. I decided to set my cruise at 55 mph and be a few minutes later than I had wanted to be. He turned at the corner five miles from my workplace, so I relaxed and I soon again had an opportunity to pass a slower vehicle. As I nosed out, I again glanced back and again noticed a bubble two cars behind me! I was flabbergasted! But again, I slowed my pace and resigned to driving the speed limit. As I did so, the Lord quickened to me that…

As it is in the natural, so is it in the spiritual...

As I slowed my vehicle the second time, I noticed the bubble top on the police car, the Lord whispered… "If my children would live their lives with the knowledge that I am always there, watching them, I wonder how they would act?" This illumination startled me into the realization that I ought to live each moment of my life in a way that is pleasing to my Lord. Proverbs 15:3 tells us "The eyes of the Lord are in every place, beholding the evil and the good" (KJV). I ought to always be mindful that He IS there, watching and waiting for me to be and do what he created me to be and do. Lord, please help me remember that you are ever present.

JUNE 10

Any farmer knows that when a grain of wheat falls into the ground, it must first die before it can sprout into a plant. Without death, life cannot come forth. Until that seed sheds it's former shell - it's hard exterior - and allows the nutrients of the soil to absorb into it, it cannot become what it was intended to be. It will never produce anything unless it is broken down and changed into a soft sprout that can grow into a productive stem. As I pondered this, the Lord reminded me that…

As it is in the natural, so is it in the spiritual…

If I am like the grain of wheat, I must be planted and die (to self-will) before I can ever become what God intends me to be. I must allow God to remove the hardness of my heart so that he can change me and make me soft and willing to grow in Him. Only then can I produce what I was created to produce. John 12:23 says, "But Jesus answered them, saying, The hour has come that the Son of Man should be glorified. 24 Most assuredly, I say to you, unless a grain of wheat falls into the ground and dies, it remains alone; but if it dies, it produces much grain. 25 He who loves his life will lose it, and he who hates his life in this world will keep it for eternal life. 26 If anyone serves Me, let him follow Me; and where I am, there My servant will be also. If anyone serves Me, him My Father will honor" (NKJV). Dear Lord, my purpose will never be revealed until I am willing to die to my will and live for your purpose! Amen!

JUNE 11

There are no guarantees with farming. There is only trust and faith. A farmer has faith to put a seed in the ground, add a little fertilizer and then let God do the rest. God provides the sunlight and the rain which are key in the survival of that tiny seed. The farmer can do little or nothing besides plant and pray. As I thought about this, the Lord reminded me that…

As it is in the natural, so is it in the spiritual…

In the same way a farmer must have faith to plant seeds and fertilize them, so too, we must have faith that when we plant seeds into the hearts of others, and fertilize the seed with prayer, it is GOD who sends light and showers upon that heart to grow that seed. Without these two elements, the seed with soon perish. Matthew 5:13 reminds us, "Ye are the light of the world…" and goes on to exhort us to "Let your light so shine before men that they may see your good works and glorify your Father which is in heaven" (KJV). We must remember that God draws people to him but he sends us to shine HIS light into their lives. Lord, help me to remember that it is only my job to plant the seed and fertilize it with prayer. Then I must trust that you will bring forth the harvest of those souls. Thank you for showing me this simple truth! Amen!

JUNE 12

As a child grows, he becomes independent in certain tasks. When he begins feeding himself, for example, he may develop a taste for certain foods and a dislike for others. However, just because a child likes certain foods does not mean the food is necessarily 'good' for him. This realization of what is healthy and unhealthy comes from maturation and experience. As I was pondering this, the Lord quickened to me that...

As it is in the natural, so is it in the spiritual...

As we grow up spiritually, we must learn what things sustain us toward greater spiritual growth. Likewise, we must also learn which things can be a detriment to us and hinder our growth. If we consume too much worldly 'junk' we lose our hunger for the things of God. We must carefully choose what we put on our 'plate': what we watch, listen to, read and how we spend our time. As we turn away from unhealthy choices and activities and turn toward God, our hunger for Him increases. In John 6:27, Jesus tells us, "Labour not for the meat which perisheth, but for that meat which endureth unto everlasting life, which the Son of man shall give unto you: for him hath God the Father sealed" (KJV).
Lord, please stir up that hunger for You and help me to be wise in my daily choices. AMEN!

JUNE 13

I listened to a wonderful message again this week by one of our Pentecostal preachers. He talked about the church and how it was 'beautiful for situation.' Mount Zion, the church in Jerusalem, was not built down on level ground, but rather, it was elevated and not necessarily easily accessible. Those making the trek to Zion knew it was a tough journey, full of hills and valleys and it would take commitment and effort to make the climb, but once there, they found it to be a place of refuge and rest and spiritual renewal. Zion was beautiful because in comparison to its surroundings, it was high and lifted up. As he spoke, he reminded us that…

As it is in the natural, so is it in the spiritual…

Just as the Jerusalem church required a journey and great effort to access, likewise, in order to gain access to the spiritual riches, we have to make sacrifices. We cannot expect to remain on the same level spiritually if we want to be an effective witness to the life-changing power of Jesus Christ. Psalms 48:1 says: "Great is the LORD, and greatly to be praised in the city of our God, in the mountain of his holiness. 2. Beautiful for situation, the joy of the whole earth, is mount Zion, on the sides of the north, the city of the great King. 3. God is known in her palaces for a refuge of the world" (KJV). Dear Lord, people truly do want and need a refuge; let us make that trek to your true church found only in Jesus Christ, high and lifted up. Amen!

JUNE 14

This morning, as I was reading my bible and listening to the rain, I suddenly detected the sound of a single bird, chirping out a joyful song. I smiled at my husband and said there's a bird out there singing, even in the rain. As I said this aloud, the Lord whispered…

As it is in the natural, so is it in the spiritual…

I want to be like that bird, when the stormy, rainy days come into my life, I want to be so full of joy that instead of a complaint, a song of praise bursts out of my mouth. The bible exhorts us in Psalms 96:1 to "O sing unto the LORD a new song: sing unto the LORD, all the earth" and in Psalms 30:5 it says that "weeping may endure for a night, but joy cometh in the morning" (KJV). Thank you for the song of that bird this morning and the joyful noise which turned my heart towards you this morning! Amen!

JUNE 15

Today is my grandson Baylor's birthday. He is my daughter Kristin's middle boy and is such a joy to my heart. Baylor is the type of kid that is rather fickle and a bit reserved in giving out affection. He is true to his feelings with his personal boundaries and that is not a bad thing! If he doesn't really want a hug, no amount of coaxing or pleading will make him give one. He doesn't succumb to direct pressure from mom and dad either! "NO" is his final decision. Baylor responds better to the indirect path of play to get him to warm up to you. My husband will just lay down on the floor and pretty soon, here comes Bay (and the other two!) rolling around and laughing and tackling Grandpa. As I think about this, the Lord quickens to me that...

As it is in the natural, so is it in the spiritual...

In the same way that my dear grandson sets boundaries and fiercely sticks to them, so too can we learn from him in the spiritual realm. Many times, we fall into the trap of feeling pressured to conform to the changing world around us and do that which is expected of us by our society. We are expected to politely follow the expectations of others even though we know that is not what we want to do or what the Lord would have us do. We succumb to peer pressure, in our conversation, in leisure activities, in political and social viewpoints, just so we don't offend anyone. But the Lord has called us to stand firm in our faith! Ephesians 6:13 tells us, "Therefore, take up the full armor of God, so that you will be able to resist in the evil day, and having done everything, to stand firm" (NAS). Thank you for your word Lord. Help us to daily draw from it to help us be firm in our convictions and beliefs in a world where there is so much pressure to conform. In Jesus' name, Amen!

JUNE 16

As morning dawns on this rainy day, I relish in the sounds that envelope me. Water drops hitting the window pane, the wind raking through the still empty branches on our walnut trees and howling around the corners of our snug, warm house, birds chirping even despite the not-so-nice weather. As it draws closer to daylight, I can see this is going to be a cloudy dreary morning, but somehow, my heart is light and unaffected. As I think about this, God whispers to me...

As it is in the natural, so is it in the spiritual...

When dreary situations and circumstances surround us, we must remember that our joy does not come from this world around us, but rather it only comes from the Lord. We must not derive our mood from the weather or the situation we are facing, but rather, we must intentionally keep a joyful heart and give praise and glory to our Father in Heaven because of who He is, even despite our current dreary forecast. Philippians 4 reminds us to "Rejoice in the Lord always, and again I say Rejoice!" (KJV). Lord, thank you for showing me that even when the cloudy, rainy days come, we must rejoice! Amen!

JUNE 17

Our power went out last night just after dark. I was astonished at how pitch black our home is without any of the clocks that usually illuminate the kitchen. I turned on my I-phone flashlight and located our two lanterns. As I lit them, I was astonished at how much light such a tiny flame gave off in a room that had been in complete darkness. A moment later I also found out how much heat such a tiny flame gives off when I touched the glass chimney to adjust it! Yeowch! As I pondered this thought, the Lord illuminated my heart...

As it is in the natural, so is it in the spiritual...

In the same way that a tiny flame of fire lights up an entire room and provides much warmth, so too does a tiny flicker of God's love. We Christians carry this flame inside our hearts the minute God ignites us with his Holy Spirit. In II Corinthians 4:6, Paul writes, "For God, who said, "Let light shine out of darkness," made His light shine in our hearts to give us the light of the knowledge of the glory of God in the face of Jesus Christ (BSB). Dear Lord, I praise you for your light which burns brightly in the hearts of those who believe. I ask that you would allow the light of your Holy Spirit to glow from our hearts and penetrate the darkness to bring illumination and warmth to others in need of your love. In Jesus' name, Amen!

JUNE 18

As I sit here this morning, I glance out the window and notice the eastern sky gradually transforming from darkness. The change begins at the horizon with just a tiny sliver of light but, surprisingly and amazingly before I know it, the entire sky has changed from darkness to a soft blue/gray of early morning. The apparent source of light is golden orange still rising out of the East and the transformation is far from complete in these early moments of daylight, but the beauty of this sunrise has impacted me…for the Lord has whispered in my heart…

As it is in the natural, so too is it in the spiritual…

Just as the sunrise transforms the darkness in such a splendid beautiful way, so too does the Light of this World transform the darkness of a human heart. When we allow Jesus to shine his light into our lives, we are transformed. I Peter 2:9 says that we should "show forth the praises of Him who has called us out of darkness into His marvelous light" (KJV). Sin in one's life creates darkness, but God has called us to step into the light. Help me bask in the light you have given me today Lord so that I may never be overcome by darkness. Amen.

JUNE 19

Father's Day is a special time when we celebrate our dads. We give honor to the man who gave us life, who we hopefully admire, the man who we look to for provisions such as food and clothing; the one who gave us shelter. As children we looked to our fathers for guidance in the way we should go and forgiveness when we messed up. We wanted to please our father above all else! We look to our father for protection from the evils of this world and we cherish this relationship more than anything! As I think about this, the Lord quickens to me…

As it is in the natural, so is it in the spiritual…

The relationship between a child and their father is much like that between our heavenly Father and us. This is made clear throughout scripture. My favorite example is found in The Lord's Prayer. We begin by addressing God as, "Our Father, which art in Heaven;" we give honor to His Holiness, "Hallowed be thy name;" we reveal our desire for HIS righteousness, peace and joy by requesting "thy kingdom come;" we heed His authority, "thy will be done on earth as it is in Heaven;" We acknowledge his continual provision, "Give us this day our daily bread;" we bow to his eminence in our lives when we ask him to "forgive us our trespasses as we forgive those who trespass against us;" we understand His power when we ask, "and lead us not into temptation but deliver us from evil;" and finally, we acknowledge his divine authority, "for thine is the kingdom, the power, and the glory forever and ever, Amen" (KJV). Thank you, Heavenly Father for giving us NEW life through your spirit. Thank you for your provision, your protection, your forgiveness, your guidance and most of all your great love for each of your children! Amen!

JUNE 20

The story of Samson and Delilah is very interesting. Samson was a man of unbelievable strength with a mission from God. He was a judge over Israel and an enemy of the Philistines. He fell in love with Delilah, who plotted with the Philistine leaders to discover his source of strength and destroy him. She was Samson's weakness. Despite her repeated schemes to get him to tell her his source of power Judges 16:16 tells us, "She tormented him with her nagging day after day until he was sick to death of it" (NLT). Finally, he gave in and revealed to her all of his heart. Samson's flesh was weak and he allowed this woman, whom he though he loved, to torment him and now she would destroy him. She got him drunk and cut off his hair, the source of his power. He was captured and tortured by his enemies. In one final act, Samson went on a suicidal vengeance mission to destroy the Philistines but his gift from God had been squandered. As I thought about this story, the Lord brought an interesting parallel to mind...

As it is in the natural, so is it in the spiritual...

Just like Samson, we have been called with a purpose to serve in God's kingdom. We each have a ministry laid before us and have been given a source of strength through the Holy Ghost to perform it. However, like Samson, there is a deceiver lying in wait to steal, kill, and destroy us. This enemy will find any method he can to wear us down, torment us, nag us and then strip the source of power from us and remove us from our mission. He will entice us and lull us to him in any area he sees a weakness, be it lust of the flesh (addictions, sexual sins), lust of the eyes (greed, envy) or pride of life (vanity, selfishness) and the list goes on. Like Samson, when we let our guard down, the enemy will try to cut off our source of our spiritual power – which is strengthened through prayer, fasting, bible study and worship - because his mission is to destroy our ministry and ultimately, our life. In II Corinthians 2:11 Paul emphasizes the importance of daily renewal of our attitudes and our hearts before Christ Jesus, "So that we should not be outwitted by Satan; for we are not ignorant of his schemes" (BSB). Dear Lord, please show me my heart this day. If I have any temptation, unforgiveness, anger, lust, or other sins that are ensnaring me, please eradicate them this moment so that I can protect the power I have received from your Holy Spirit. In Jesus' name, Amen!

JUNE 21

"Don't know which way we're headed"- I was texting someone about having lunch and trying to set up plans, but when I wrote that I wasn't sure yet which way we were headed – we weren't sure where we wanted to spend the day, but we would keep them posted. As I said to my husband "it's hard to make plans when we don't know our final destination," he looked at me as the Lord nudged both of us…

As it is in the natural, so is it in the spiritual…

Many of us are still unsure of where our final destination will be. Because of this lack of decisiveness, we will spend much of our lifetime wandering and wasting our days with frivolous activities and meanderings. Until we decide where we truly want to end up, we cannot travel a productive road spiritually. Paul tells Timothy, "I have fought a good fight, I have finished my course, I have kept the faith: Henceforth there is laid up for me a crown of righteousness, which the Lord, the righteous judge, shall give me at that day: and not to me only, but unto all them also that love his appearing" (II Timothy 4:7-8) The course he speaks of is a pathway that has been clearly laid out in God's word so that each of us could be 'followers' of Jesus Christ. Note that Paul begins by saying, "I fought a good fight." This signifies that it will not be easy. We are in a battle which begins with making up our minds once and for all where we want to end up! Then we must stay on course and stick to our path no matter where others may be heading and no matter how enticing the other route might seem. Once this decision is settled, it becomes much easier to make plans for our day! Lord, help me keep in mind that my destination is heaven and my course is to follow you each day. Help me not to stray from the course you have set for me! Help me to run this race as you would have me to do each step of the way! In Jesus' name, Amen.

JUNE 22

The Emerald Ash Borer is an insect that came to the US from Asia in the early years of this century. Within a decade, it has invaded our woodlands here in Michigan and is killing millions of ash trees. In fact, it is now considered to be the most destructive forest pest ever known in North America (Emerald Ash Borer Information Network. (n.d.) Retrieved from www.emeraldashborer.info). Upon investigation, I learned that the bug itself is not the problem as much as the larvae. The bug lays the eggs and then those larvae burrow into the bark and deep into the tree and destroy the tissues that allow the tree to absorb water and nutrients. The first thing to die is the canopy and within a year of infestation 1/3 of the branches will die. The process continues until the tree is completely drained of life. As I thought about this devastating problem, the Lord quickened to me that ...

As it is in the natural, so is it in the spiritual...

Just as a tiny insect can bore its way into a strong and healthy tree and eventually kill it, so too can tiny intruders bore their way into a believer's heart. If not eradicated, they will destroy our mind, prevent us from absorbing the truth of God's word and assuredly kill, steal and destroy our once strong and thriving soul. Jesus said in John 10:10, "The thief cometh not, but for to steal, and to kill, and to destroy: I am come that they might have life, and that they might have it more abundantly" (KJV). Lord, help me to recognize when intruding pests attempt to attach themselves to my heart and prevent me from hearing what you have for me each day! Let your word be the insecticide that removes them that I may be healthy and strong in You! Amen!

JUNE 23

This morning we were packing up the truck to head to Iowa to visit our kids and grandkids. Our little dog, Jewel, keenly aware that we were getting ready to leave, was a bit distressed. She was glued to the door and at the first opportunity, she bolted fromo the house and leapt into the truck to occupy her position. It was if she was saying, "No way am I getting left behind! Above all else, I need to be with you." My heart was touched by Jewel and her swift, decisive action this morning; running from what she must have viewed as her prison, to what she viewed as freedom inside the truck where she would be with the ones she loved. As I was chuckling about this, the Lord pointed out that...

As it is in the natural, so is it in the spiritual...

Just as my heart was touched by Jewel's passionate desire to be with us, so too must the Lord's heart be touched when his children run to be with him. Yes, we must fight through the obstacles of life in order to be in his presence, but there is nothing like it once we are safely there. In Psalm 16:11 David writes, "Thou wilt shew me the path of life; In thy presence is fullness of joy; in your right had there are pleasures for evermore" (KJV). In the presence of the Lord is where our hearts are made content. The troubles of life fade away when we are with our loving Father. My sweet little dog has once again been a reminder of the kind of love we ought to display towards the Lord.

JUNE 24

Just examine your hand for a moment. Think about what tasks your hands have completed within the past hour; the past day; the past week and so on. Think for one moment about the intricate design of the human body and how each part serves a very important purpose. Without our various parts, we would be incomplete and the other parts of the body would be forced to compensate in order to fulfill the tasks we humans must complete. As I thought on this, the Lord revealed to me that…

As it is in the natural, so is it in the spiritual…

Just as our human body functions more effectively when all of its parts are present and working, so too does the body of Christ function more effectively when all of its members are present and working. Our church is the body of Christ. We are each members in particular and we each have a calling to fulfill in order for the entire body to accomplish what God has set before us. I Corinthians 12 explains in detail that we are all given different gifts and all have our own functions to perform. Verse 18 says, "But in fact, God has arranged the members of the body, every one of them, according to His design" (BSB). He goes on to encourage the body to recognize that just as our eye needs our hand and our head needs our feet, so too do we need each other and ought to have mutual concern and care for one another. Dear Lord, help us to look at our brethren as you have taught us; that we are all placed there for a purpose and that we all ought to love one another as if each member was vital to our own survival. Amen!

JUNE 25

When we are traveling, I sometimes become keenly aware of the vastness of this world in which we live and of the innumerable number of people who cross my path. It occurs to me that each of these humans has their own story to tell, their own life filled with joys and pains, blessings and sorrows, dreams and hopes. Some do not have anyone to talk to. Many seek help to sort out their thoughts and feelings through counselors or professionals who are trained to listen and offer support. As I thought about this, the Lord whispered…

As it is in the natural, so is it in the spiritual…

We may encounter a thousand people in our daily journeys, with a thousand different stories, but our heavenly father knows each and every detail of each and every one of his children's lives. Luke 12:7 says, "And even the very hairs of your head are all numbered. So, do not be afraid; you are worth more than many sparrows" (BSB). Indeed! Our Heavenly Father knows the number of hairs on my head! He is fully aware of every single joy or sorrow in our life and when we feel like no one is listening to our story or hearing our cry in our times of distress, or joy, or grief, we can rest assured that the Lord is listening and waiting with open arms to embrace us. He truly is my confidant and my counselor, who is there to listen to my every thought, my every joy, my every concern. He already knows each of the moments of life and he has the answers I need. He is the one I can run to and the sustainer of my sanity. Thank you for your unmatchable love Lord! Amen!

JUNE 26

Visiting my daughter and her family at their lake home, I noticed that as the sun was setting in the sky, the water was smoothing out like silk. It seemed to remain in this glasslike state until after sunrise the next morning. When daylight fully arrives, the water is no longer still. The glassy surface has been disturbed by the wind that accompanies the sunlight. As I thought about this phenomenon, the Lord whispered to me…

As it is in the natural, so is it in the spiritual…

Sometimes we become complacent in our lives. We are satisfied with peace and quiet. Many exist in utter darkness regarding the truth of the Gospel, and seem to live life with no conflicts, no problems, and smooth waters. The Lord wants us to remember today that Jesus said he did not come to bring peace but a sword or conflict (Matthew 10:34 - Gods Word). Throughout the bible the Holy Spirit is represented by wind and the Lord Jesus is called the light of the world. In the spiritual realm, Jesus' light and spirit disrupt our former way of life and create waves where things were once seemingly smooth. When we make up our mind to follow Jesus, we will have to be prepared to trust Him to guide and direct us when the water becomes rough. Lord, I know that sailing for your kingdom does not mean I will have smooth waters every day, but that inevitably, in this world, I will have tribulation. Help me to trust in you to get me through the rough days I will face. I know you are in control! In Jesus' name, Amen!

JUNE 27

Here in Iowa with my daughter and her family, we have been on the boat most evenings as the sun goes down. As I mentioned yesterday, right at dark, the waters become often become smooth like glass and there is barely a ripple to disturb the mirrored reflection. When water is this still it is very easy to detect even the slightest disturbance on the surface. As thought about this, the Lord illuminated to me...

As it is in the natural, so is it in the spiritual...

When darkness falls into our lives, whether it be illness, injury or anguish, we tend to become still, we tend to become reflective and we tend to become more sensitive to the slightest disturbances. This stillness, this reflectiveness, this sensitivity, is necessary for us to hear the voice of our Father, who is daily waiting for us to draw near and be in his presence. It is in His presence where we can make sense of things, where we can find peace, joy and tranquility in this life which can quickly create ripples and waves in our life. Psalms 23 reminds us that "He leadeth me beside the still waters" and then after that, "He restoreth my soul, He leadeth me in the paths of righteousness for His name's sake..." (KJV). Take time each morning to find that place of still waters where the Lord can calm the ripples and waves in your life, restore your soul, and lead you in His paths.

JUNE 28

Each time I find myself on a lake, I proclaim that I have found "My Happy Place." I have always loved the water, whether it is a lake, an ocean, or a river, there is just something calming and quite therapeutic to my soul when I am there. Doctors of long ago used to prescribe seaside visits to those suffering from mental health issues. Apparently, there truly are calming effects to the mind and soul when we are near the water. As I thought about this, the Lord nudged me...

As it is in the natural, so is it in the spiritual...

Just as many people seek out physical bodies of water for physical refreshment and fulfillment, so too must I seek out that living water than never runs dry to fulfill me and sustain my spiritual being. Jesus said, "He who believes in me as the scripture hath said, "From his innermost being will flow rivers of living water" (NAS). Jesus was speaking about His Spirit, which dwells within us when we are born again. Lord, when we need true peace and freedom from the stresses of this life, we must seek out that life giving water that only comes from YOU! Amen!

JUNE 29

Sitting on the deck overlooking the lake on this cloudy Sunday, I relish in the quiet, absorbing the beauty around me. Soon, I hear the gentle rumble of thunder in the distance. The approaching storm is announcing itself long before it actually arrives. As it grows closer, the thunder becomes more demanding. As I thought about this, the Lord whispered...

As it is in the natural, so is it in the spiritual...

Just as the approaching storm sends warning signals, so too the Holy Spirit sends rumblings into our spirit when impending storms are headed our way. In order to benefit from this warning system however, we must tune our spiritual ears to hear what the Lord is saying to us. Proverbs 3:6 says, "Seek his will in all you do and he will show you which path to take" (NLT). Thank you Lord for allowing me to find that quiet time each day to allow you to speak into my life and direct my footsteps. Amen!

JUNE 30

Technology affords us a continual connection to information, entertainment, interactions right at our fingertips. We only need reach in our pocket to "connect." In any given restaurant you will see families all sitting at the table engaged in their own private mode of entertainment on their own personal device. Likewise, today, the Lord whispered to me...

As it is in the natural, so is it in the spiritual...

Just as these external connections can cause us to slip away from human conversations and interactions, so too can other interferences create spiritual disconnect from the Lord. Thoughts from the enemy, our busy schedule, our to-do list, all of these can cause us to cut our time short or eliminate it all together. Soon we find ourselves without that much needed time with the Lord. The Lord urges us to 'be still and know that I am God' (Psalms 46:10, KJV). We need a break from the continual external inputs that surround us. We must intentionally set aside some quiet time in order to gain rest. We must first unplug, disconnect and find a place of peace and tranquility so that we can leave room for the voice that matters most in our lives. That still small voice of the Lord Jesus. Amen!

JULY 1

We took a trip to Iowa this month to visit our kids and grandkids there. I had a few pots of plants and flowers that I had set under the shade and then a few days into my trip I remembered to ask my brother to water them a couple of times. Well, apparently, two waterings in eleven days is not enough because they were severely dried up and I lost about half of them. I turned my attention to a few of the plants that still had some green stems, though the leaves were brown and withered. To my amazement, with daily sprinkles of water and some pruning, they sprang back to life! As I was rejoicing in this revival of my plants, the Lord revealed to me that…

As it is in the natural, so is it in the spiritual…

Your faith is like these precious living plants. Without daily care you may soon find your spirit withered, unproductive, and ultimately without hope. By seeking God's voice and presence through prayer and reading his word and by pruning our lives through obedience to His commandments, you can bring restoration to your dried-up spirit and revival to your heart and soul. Soon you will be producing fruit again that is good for others! Leviticus 26:3-4 promises: "If ye walk in my statutes, and keep my commandments, and do them; 4. Then I will give you rain in due season, and the land shall yield her increase, and the trees of the field shall yield their fruit" (KJV). Lord, thank you for your promises. Thank you for your faithfulness. Help me to daily prune the dead and withered parts of my spirit and receive the spiritual rain you so graciously send to me to help me to grow and produce fruit that is good! In Jesus' name, Amen!

JULY 2

Sitting on the beach a week ago, my husband watched as the abandoned sandcastle build by a small child slowly eroded from the waves. He told me that it was interesting because he thought it would have washed away from the top down, but this was not the case; instead, the structure was sinking because the sandy foundation upon which it was built was shifting each time a wave came in. Eventually the castle toppled and sunk into the beach. As we talked, the Lord illuminated that…

As it is in the natural, so is it in the spiritual…

Just as Jesus said in Matthew 7:24 "Anyone who listens to my teaching and follows it is wise, like a person who builds a house on solid rock. 25 Though the rain comes in torrents and the floodwaters rise and the winds beat against that house, it won't collapse because it is built on bedrock. 26 But anyone who hears my teaching and doesn't obey it is foolish, like a person who builds a house on sand. 27 When the rains and floods come and the winds beat against that house, it will collapse with a mighty crash." We can choose to heed the teachings of Jesus or go our own way and attempt to build our lives upon worthless things which have no stability or security. Lord help me to not only hear your words, but to obey them so that my foundation is built upon you, my rock and my salvation! In Jesus' name!

JULY 3

While reading Exodus this morning, I was once again amazed over what a detailed and intricate God we serve. This is where God gave instructions to Moses for the tabernacle; that place where the Lord manifested his presence to the Israelites. He specified every single detail including the size of the finished tabernacle; the specific kind of material and exact measurement for each part of the tabernacle; the colors of each different fabric for each particular use in the tabernacle; the exact position where each and every item that would be used in the tabernacle; the number of boards; the ounces of gold, silver and brass right down to the sockets that would be cast. Along with the construction of the tabernacle and the altar and each part of it, he also gave very specific instructions on how the people were to approach the Lord with their sacrifices. He provides every tiny detail for the garments that the priests must wear while ministering in the tabernacle, even down to the undergarments; the steps that needed to be taken for the consecration of the priests; how to prepare the unleavened bread and cakes; instructions on which animal was to be sacrificed and when; each step in the taking of that life and offering that sacrifice including what to do with the blood, the fat, the hide and the entrails of the animals. God gave instruction on exactly how the altar was to be constructed and how the offerings were to be performed and which portion of the animal was to be used on which day of the year for the various offerings (sin offering, burnt offering, wave offering and heave offering). The division of the areas of the tabernacle were also of extreme importance, from the outer court to the brazen laver, from the altar, to the holy of holies which contained the Golden Lampstand, Table of Shewbread and the Ark of the Covenant where the manifest presence of God resided. Only the high priest was allowed to enter into this most holy place after he had undergone the proper steps of making a blood sacrifice and washing with water for purification. He always entered with a rope around his ankle just in case the offering was unacceptable and the Lord smote him. Indeed, our God is a God of order and intricate detail. He left nothing for the priests to wonder about regarding how they were to approach him. He set forth a pattern requiring death and then cleansing before one had access to His presence within the holy of holies. As I thought about this, it occurred to me that...

As it is in the natural, so is it in the spiritual...

The tabernacle of Moses is a type and shadow of what was to come. For sins to be forgiven, an innocent life must be taken; blood must be shed; then a cleansing must occur by washing with water and finally an entrance into the Holy of Holies where the presence of God dwelled. But God had a better plan. Jeremiah 31:33 says, "But this [shall be] the covenant that I will make with the house of Israel; After those days, saith the LORD, I will put my law in their inward parts, and write it in their hearts; and will be their God, and they shall be my people" (KJV). Let us take a few days to consider this marvelous new plan of God, and how he brought an end to the old and ushered in a new and better way for man to approach the God of this Universe, the King of Kings and Lord of Lords. As we approach Independence Day, let us also take time to examine and celebrate the amazing freedoms we have been given because of the death, burial and resurrection of Jesus Christ, who is The Lamb of God, God Incarnate, Redeemer and Mighty Savior. Thank you Lord, for as Paul writes, "Therefore, there is now no condemnation for those who are in Christ Jesus. 2 For in Christ Jesus the law of the Spirit of life has set you free from the law of sin and death" (Romans 8:2-3, BSB) In Jesus' name, Amen!

JULY 4

Today is Independence Day. A day when Americans celebrate our freedom from the tyranny of the British Crown. Our Declaration of Independence contains a list of nearly thirty evidences of the many oppressions imposed upon the colonists by the far-reaching King of Britain. Reading the Declaration of Independence, the reason that compelled those freedom seekers to lay down their lives is made clear. This monumental day gives us cause to reflect upon our freedoms which I, for one, take for granted. We live in a country with so many freedoms, it takes an awakening of sorts for us to understand just how fortunate and blessed we are as a nation. As I ponder this great day, which celebrates America's independence, the Lord whispers a reminder...

As it is in the natural, so is it in the spiritual...

The freedoms we celebrate from the repressive rule of a distant ruler can be readily compared to the greatest example of freedom this world has ever known: freedom from slavery to our sinful nature; freedom from guilt and shame; freedom from condemnation and death - which is eternal separation from God. In the natural, the Declaration of Independence is a legal document created by man and is applicable to all who will follow the laws of this land. In the spiritual, the New Covenant is a lawful promise created by the God of this Universe and is available to all who believe. The new testament is rich with scriptures showing how the law of Moses was a pattern for the New Covenant. Acts 13:39 says, "Through Him, everyone who believes is set free from every sin, a justification you were not able to obtain under the law of Moses" (NIV). Paul compares how much greater the new covenant is since through repentance and turning to the lord we are able to receive forgiveness and freedom! II Corinthians 3:17 says, "Now the Lord is that Spirit, and where the Spirit of the Lord is, there is liberty" (KJV). Anyone who has experienced God's Spirit will testify that this is truly a removal of chains; a transformation of the heart where the glory of the Lord overwhelms your heart and soul and delivers you from bondage to this world so you can become a child of God; a citizen of the heavenly realms. It is this new birth which transforms us from hopelessness to hope; from fear to faith; from death to life. Thank you Lord, for sending your Holy Spirit to indwell believers that we might obtain freedom, and power over sin in this world through You! Amen!

JULY 5

The first piece one encountered as they entered the tabernacle of Moses was the brazen altar, where the blood from the sacrificial animals was sprinkled to atone for the sins of the people. The need for death to occur to cover sins goes back to the fall of mankind. God told Adam in Genesis 2:17, "But of the tree of the knowledge of good and evil, thou shalt not eat of it: for in the day that thou eatest thereof thou shalt surely die" (KJV). We know this was a spiritual death because they did not drop dead. They hid from God and tried to cover their nakedness with fig leaves. However, the Lord provided animal skins as an appropriate covering. This first shedding of blood and covering by God demonstrates that our attempts to cover our sins are not adequate, but rather we must look to the Lord to find His way in all things! The first step God ordained for the priests in the tabernacle is also the death of an innocent and the shedding of blood. As I think about this, I realize that God wants each of us to see...

As it is in the natural, so is it in the spiritual...

The brazen altar points back to the Garden of Eden and forward to the cross of Jesus. Hebrews 9:22 tells us, "Indeed, under the law almost everything is purified with blood, and without the shedding of blood there is no forgiveness of sins" (ESV). God established in Genesis that sin requires death when an innocent animal's life was taken to cover Adam and Eve's sin. The sacrificial death of Jesus Christ was THE final act of redemption with blood. No more lambs were to be sacrificed on the altar of the tabernacle to atone for the sins of man. God Almighty robed Himself in flesh and entered this world at Bethlehem with a plan of salvation for all who would believe. Roman's 6:23, says, "For the wages of sin is death; but the gift of God is eternal life through Jesus Christ our Lord" (KJV). Jesus ministered on the earth for 33 years, fully knowing that He would be THE perfect sacrificial lamb of God and the final High Priest. Hebrew's 10 explains, "11 Under the old covenant, the priest stands and ministers before the altar day after day, offering the same sacrifices again and again, which can never take away sins. 12 But our High Priest offered himself to God as a single sacrifice for sins, good for all time. Then he sat down in the place of honor at God's right hand" (NLT). It's almost too much to comprehend! This connection between the old and new testament is astounding. We will continue to explore the tabernacle and its connection to the new testament message over the next two days. Dear Lord, we cannot fathom the truth of your word in our human minds. Please send your Holy Spirit to bring revelation to us and help us recognize our desperate need for redemption, and help us see the amazing grace, mercy and love you have for us. You cherish us so much you have made a way that we can live eternally in your presence. Thank you Lord! Amen!

JULY 6

The next station within the tabernacle was the brazen laver where the priest had to cleanse himself by washing his hands and feet. In Exodus 30:17-20, The Lord told Moses and Aaron to make the bronze laver and place it between the tabernacle of meeting and the altar of incense; and when Aaron and his sons enter the tent of meeting, "They shall wash with water, so that they will not die; or when they approach the altar to minister, by offering up in smoke a fire sacrifice to the LORD. So, they shall wash their hands and their feet, so that they will not die." Needless to say, cleansing in water was a highly important step in the redemption of their sins and absolutely necessary if they wanted to stay alive as they entered the presence of God! The Lord wants us to see…

As it is in the natural, so is it in the spiritual…

Just as the priest had to obey this step of washing in the brazen laver before ministering before the Lord, so too are we to be cleansed. Jesus instructed Peter and the disciples to go and preach to all nations, commanding them to be baptized in His name (Matthew 28:19, Mark 16:17, Luke 24:47). In Act's 2:38 on the day of Pentecost, Peter gave the very first New Testament sermon, telling all who had witnessed the ushering in of a new and marvelous covenant, "Repent, and be baptized in Jesus' name every one of you for the remission of sins, and you shall receive the gift of the Holy Ghost. 39 For the promise is unto you, and to your children, and to all that are afar off, even as many as the Lord our God shall call" (KJV). The Brazen laver in the old testament tabernacle was indeed a foreshadowing of the New Testament act of baptism. Believers today enter the waters of baptism to identify with Jesus in his death, burial and resurrection. Romans 6 tells us: When we are buried with him in baptism, we are united with Jesus Christ in his death and our former nature- or "old man" is passed away and all things become new." Our old way of thinking and behaving dies as we put on Christ (Galatians 3:27). Lord, you have made the gospel message very clear in your word. Let us exercise faith and obedience that we may be able to enter your holy Kingdom. Thank you for your Word. Your word is truth. In Jesus' name, Amen!

JULY 7

The final destination for the high priest in the tabernacle was his entrance into the Holy of Holies. The Holy of Holies was concealed by a thick curtain, or veil, and only the high priest could enter therein, and his life literally depended on whether the sacrifices he presented on behalf of the people were acceptable to God. This entrance into God's presence was the pinnacle of the High Priest's year and all of the people waited outside to see if their sins would be atoned for one more year. After Jesus' death, Matthew 25:50-52 tells us, "When Jesus had cried out again in a loud voice, He yielded up His spirit. At that moment the veil of the temple was torn in two from top to bottom. The earth quaked and the rocks were split. The tombs broke open, and the bodies of many saints who had fallen asleep were raised" (BSB). As I read this, the Lord revealed that...

As it is in the natural, so is it in the spiritual...

The renting of the veil in the temple was a monumental occurrence. No human could have torn the thirty-foot high curtain! The power of God rent the veil in half, which symbolizes to all believers that our access to the presence of God is now completely open. Three days later, that same power of God resurrected Jesus Christ from the grave. How does a believer follow Christ in this important step? Jesus instructed his disciples in Acts 1:4-5, "Wait for the promise of the Father, which, saith he, ye have heard of me. 5 For John truly baptized with water; but ye shall be baptized with the Holy Ghost not many days hence" (KJV). They obeyed and waited, fasting and praying until the day of Pentecost. When the mighty rushing sound from Heaven came and the Holy Ghost was poured out upon those believers, bystanders were amazed for they heard them speaking with other tongues. They thought they were intoxicated, but Peter explained this was the fulfillment of Joel's prophecy and Jesus' promise, which is the Holy Ghost indwelling believers to give them power! The bible says "Now when they heard this they were pricked in their heart and asked Peter and the rest of the apostles, "What shall we do?" Peter presented the new testament gospel message given to him by Jesus. Acts 2:38 says, "Repent, and be baptized in Jesus' name every one of you for the remission of sins, and you shall receive the gift of the Holy Ghost. 39 For the promise is unto you, and to your children, and to all that are afar off, even as many as the Lord our God shall call" (KJV). From that monumental day, a new covenant was firmly put in place by our Heavenly Father. The altar where innocent animals died was replaced with repentance, or death to self-will as we sacrifice our life to him with a sincere heart (Paul wrote that we must "die daily" through repentance). The washing of the priest's hands in the brazen laver where blood was cleansed from his hands is replaced with water baptism in Jesus' name to wash away our sins. The Holy of Holies where God's presence resided exclusively for the high priest is now replaced by believers receiving the Holy Spirit of Christ. This beautiful Gospel is the message of hope we must take to a lost and confused world. So many are desperately seeking answers to life's problems and we have it! So many are not living in the FREEDOM so easily accessible through faith in Jesus Christ and what he did on the cross to purchase our freedom! Let us be bold in this day to share the Word of God with any who should inquire as to the hope that lives in us! In Jesus' name, Amen!

JULY 8

Driving down the winding hilly roads in the Rocky Mountains can be treacherous. One has to be focused on the road right ahead, lest they find themselves in the ravine. So many things can distract us; cell phones, the radio, wildlife in the field, the scenic view, and a million other things. As I thought about this, the Lord shined his light…

As it is in the natural, so is it in the spiritual…

When we get our eyes off of the path the Lord has set us on and start rubber-necking off to the left or right, we can find ourselves in a spiritual ravine. Perhaps it's that new boat, or that lake home we dream about, or that Netflix series everyone is talking about, or sports, or your golf game, or hunting, or even church events and activities, or a million other things. These things in and of themselves are not evil, but they can become perilous when we allow them to distract us from the path the Lord has directed us on. Paul exhorts us: "Therefore, holy brothers and sisters, who share in the heavenly calling, fix your thoughts on Jesus, whom we acknowledge as our apostle and high priest" (NIV). Lord, may you help me fix my eyes on Jesus, and keep me on the right road and out of the ravines that would otherwise bring disaster into my life. In Jesus' Name, Amen!

JULY 9

It is finally summer here in Michigan…the trees are filling up with nuts and fruit, the neighbor's gardens are overflowing with vegetation, but regretfully, not mine…I didn't plant one because we were supposed to be taking a long trip for a good portion of the summer. But now, plans have changed, and because I did not sow seed, I will not see any fruit from a garden this summer. As I was pondering all of this, the Lord reminded me that…

As it is in the natural, so is it in the spiritual…

In the same way that a garden will not produce vegetation or fruit if seeds are not sown, so too, unless you sow a spiritual seed into the hearts of those people the Lord puts in your life, nothing will come forth to harvest. We are given new opportunities each day to sow into the lives of others, be it a word aptly spoken to someone searching for answers or just the simple daily faithfulness to the Lord as an example to others. Yet sometimes we do not grasp the opportunity. Perhaps we have no confidence the seeds will take root, or perhaps we think we will be too busy to tend to the tender new lives that might result. Maybe our own human imperfections keep us from sharing the gospel message of hope to others. Whatever the reason, when we do not step out in faith and plant a seed, we are voiding any possibility of that seed taking root and springing up into a fruitful life for the kingdom of God. Galatians 6 makes this truth clear: "...7 Do not be deceived: God is not to be mocked. Whatever a man sows, he will reap in return. 8 The one who sows to please his flesh, from the flesh will reap destruction; but the one who sows to please the Spirit, from the Spirit will reap eternal life. 9 Let us not grow weary in well-doing, for in due time we will reap a harvest, if we do not give up" (BSB). Dear Lord, help me to remember the principle of sowing and reaping as I encounter others in my daily goings. Lord help me to have faith to sow seeds for your kingdom today and every day. In doing so, I trust that you are the Lord over the harvest for your kingdom. In Jesus' amazing name. Amen.

JULY 10

My husband and I have talked about planting a few fruit trees for many years. However, we have not done it thus far because we are either too busy in the spring or don't have the money to spare on the trees. It occurs to me that we could now be enjoying peaches, cherries, apples and pears if we had only made the sacrifice of time and cost and planted some trees! As I pondered this the Lord reminded me...

As it is in the natural, so is it in the spiritual...

The fruit harvested from trees is edible and good for the body, but the fruit of the spirit is even more vital for this life. Galatians 5:22-

23 lists these fruits: Love, Joy, Peace, Patience, Kindness, Goodness, Faithfulness, Gentleness and Self-Control. Fruit is harvested from nine different 'seedlings' we must plant into our spirit and soul and then we must water and fertilize them with the word of God and with prayer. They do not grow or reproduce on their own, and if we are not careful to protect them, disease and insects can kill and destroy them. Lord help me to continually nurture the fruit of YOUR Holy Spirit so that which comes forth from my life may be pleasing to you.

JULY 11

As we were driving home last night, we noticed the cloudless sky and we also noticed the sunset was not as colorful and expansive as it can be in Michigan during the summer. I remember reading how the clouds actually help create beautiful sunsets due to the reflecting of the sun's rays. As I thought about this the Lord quickened to me…

As it is in the natural, so is it in the spiritual…

Just as cloudy days can create awesome, beautiful sunsets, so too the clouds of our troubles and trials can create in us a desire to look to the Lord and to realize that even though we struggle, our faith in Christ Jesus is a glorious thing. I Peter 1:6-7 "In this you greatly rejoice, though now for a little while you may have had to suffer grief in various trials 7 so that the proven character of your faith - more precious than gold, which perishes even though refined by fire - may result in praise, glory, and honor at the revelation of Jesus Christ" (BSB). Lord, I am so thankful that when we encounter dark and cloudy times in this life, You make all things beautiful and hopeful and full of glory. Hallelujah! Amen!

JULY 12

Yesterday, we pulled into a campground on the Rifle River. It is our first time here so we had not yet explored the place. We were given a map and my first question was: "Which sites are full hook-up?" For you non-RV folks, full hookup means you can have unlimited use of your own camper's facilities because you have hook up directly to the drainage system. We were only staying a few days, so the full hook up is not usually a necessity, but when the lady said she thought only one of these sites was still available, that made me want to race to that spot and claim it as if it were the most coveted campsite on the grounds! So, we did. We pulled in and we noted the lack of room and lack of shade on our site, the campfire ring that was in an awkward place right near the neighboring families and the road, and we realized we would really have no peace here, but we set up anyway. Afterwards, we took a bike ride around and much to my dismay, we found many other sites that were large, shaded, private and much more desirable even without "Full" hook ups! Hmmm. Now, I wanted to move but it would take a great deal of labor and work to accomplish that task. Oh, the misery of regret for making a rash decision without having all of the information! As I pondered this dilemma, the Lord whispered...

As it is in the natural, so is it in the spiritual...

When we fail to seek the Lord's counsel in our spiritual life, we often rush in and make decisions that end up in regret. Proverbs 28:26 says, "26 He who trusts in himself is a fool, but one who walks in wisdom will be safe" (BSB). By failing to wait on the Lord, we can create a great deal of stress, regret and unnecessary labor to get us back to that place where we find peace, serenity and joy. By considering our choices prayerfully before we jump in, we will have peace in knowing we are living in His will and it will be well worth it! Dear Lord, help me to learn this lesson of life, that seeking your will in prayer is always the most rewarding plan. AMEN!

JULY 13

I absolutely LOVE summer. I typically love being in the sun, especially when I am anywhere near water either swimming, fishing or just relaxing. However, I have experienced many a day where I failed to protect myself from the sun, and I ended up miserably burned and then itching for days due to over exposure. Now, I apply at least 30 SPF sunscreen before I go out to prevent sunburn and the annoying rash, and I try to make sure I cover my children and grandchildren to protect them. I am so much happier since I have been consistent with this regimen. As I thought about this, the Lord shined a light on this truth to me...

As it is in the natural, so is it in the spiritual...

Just as we must protect our skin from the harmful effects of the sun, so too must we put on the protection our Heavenly Father provides for us. Prayer is the premium form of spiritual protection and we have immediate access to it continuously. Yet how many of us go about our day, forgetting to cover ourselves and our loved ones with this most vital application? Without prayer, we are more at risk for external elements to have their negative effect on us. Without prayer, we are more susceptible to being 'burned' by the daily stresses and temptations of this world. Our heavenly father provided us with the precious ointment of prayer so we can cover ourselves and our loved ones with His divine protection. Psalms 121 reminds us: 5. "The Lord watches over you! The Lord stands beside you as your protective shade. 6. The sun will not harm you by day nor the moon by night. 7.The LORD keeps you from all harm and watches over your life. 8. The LORD keeps watch over you as you come and go, both now and forever" (NLT). Lord help me to daily apply prayer to my life and the life of my loved ones. Thank you for being my covering and for giving me peace as I find refuge in your protective hand. In Jesus' name, Amen.

JULY 14

Last night, I turned on the porch light to let our dog out and within seconds, I noticed a swarm of bugs near the open door. I quickly closed the slider and watched as more and more bugs were drawn to the light. As I thought about that the Lord quickened to me that...

As it is in the natural, so is it in the spiritual...

Just as those bugs were drawn to the light from the bulb in our porch fixture, so too are others drawn to the light of the world as it shines from within us believers! Jesus reminded us in Matthew 5:14. "Ye are the light of this world. A city that is set on a hill cannot be hid. 15. Neither do men light a candle, and put it under a bushel, but on a candlestick; and it giveth light unto all that are in the house. 16. Let your light so shine before men, that they may see your good works, and glorify your Father which is in heaven" (KJV). Lord, help me remember that I have your light within me and my purpose is to illuminate YOU to the world around me. May your light shine in each word and action that proceeds from me, so that those who are in darkness may be drawn to YOU. In Jesus' Name, Amen!

JULY 15

Yesterday we were blessed to spend time at beautiful Higgin's Lake with my family on my sister's boat. It was a perfect day and Higgin's lake is so beautiful with turquoise and midnight blue segregating shallow waters from deep. There are many areas where you can walk knee deep, then waist deep and then...well that next step - is a drop off of perhaps forty, eighty or even one hundred feet deep! Not surprising, these areas are where you will see boats congregating together, anchoring near the drop offs to enjoy the thrill of taking that deep step...or dive from sand to the depths of the lake! As I thought about the alluring beauty of these drop offs the Lord whispered...

As it is in the natural, so is it in the spiritual...

Just as the beauty of these natural drop offs lure us to explore, so too can the lure of certain lifestyles draw us to walk towards unknown, dangerous waters. The world promises beauty and excitement while the truth is that the next step could find us way over our heads. David so eloquently reminds us; "For you have delivered me from death and my feet from stumbling, that I may walk before God in the light of life" (Psalms 56:13). When we walk in God's light, we won't sink under sinful choices. Lord, help me to walk daily in your light. Illuminate my path so that I do not step into the deep and dangerous waters of sin. In Jesus' name, Amen!

JULY 16

I'm not sure what it is about a rainy day that I love. Maybe it's the simple fact that no outdoors work need be done. Perhaps it's the knowledge that our land needs a good soaker every now and then to green things up. Maybe it's the sound of the rain drops on the windows and roof that lull me into a quiet meditative mood. Whatever the reason, I eagerly await today as the forecast is showing a very good chance for a lengthy rain. As I though on this, the Lord whispered to me…

As it is in the natural, so is it in the spiritual…

In the same way I look forward to the cleansing rain from the sky, so too do I look forward and eagerly crave that cleansing spiritual rain from heaven. I yearn for those days when I can spend time reading and writing and pondering the things of the Lord. Those days spent in solitude where I can receive that much needed spiritual rain to nourish my dry and thirsty soul and to help grow my faith. Psalms 143:6 recounts: "I lift my hands to you in prayer; I thirst for you as a parched land thirsts for rain" (NLT). Dear Lord Jesus…thank you for pouring out your spirit upon us like rain and your showers of blessings to quench our daily thirst. Help us to remember that we need only ask in order to receive your miraculous, thirst quenching water from heaven. In Jesus' name, Amen!

JULY 17

The Bible story of David and Goliath has a tremendous message for us today. David, a young shepherd boy, was sent by his father to check on his older brothers, who were with Saul's army preparing to battle the Philistines. When David arrived, he witnessed the giant's daily taunt to the Israelites, defying the armies of Israel and challenging them to send out a man to fight him. David asked some men nearby what prize would be given the man who kills Goliath. He couldn't believe this uncircumcised Philistine should defy the armies of the living God. Despite his older brothers' rebukes, David volunteered for the showdown. Saul saw David's determination and offered his own armor, but David rejected the king's armor, because he had not proved it. Instead he wore his own coat, picked up his own shepherd's staff and sling and chose five smooth stones from a brook. He bravely faced Goliath saying, "You come against me with sword and spear and javelin, but I come against you in the name of the Lord Almighty, the God of the armies of Israel, whom you have defied. 46 This day the Lord will deliver you into my hands, and I'll strike you down and cut off your head. This very day I will give the carcasses of the Philistine army to the birds and the wild animals, and the whole world will know that there is a God in Israel. 47 All those gathered here will know that it is not by sword or spear that the Lord saves; for the battle is the Lord's, and he will give all of you into our hands" (NIV). The young shepherd stood on the Lord's promise and killed that giant. As I think about this story, the Lord is showing me…

As it is in the natural, so is it in the spiritual…

We all face battles in this life. Many of these battles are seemingly impossible to win. However, we must realize that although we are just mere shepherds with a few small stones to cast at our giants, we are not alone. When we face impossible situations, when we struggle with that goliath that taunts us, and defies the One who leads us, and comes against us with deadly weapons, we must stand firm and call on the name of the LORD. Paul wrote in 2 Corinthians 10:3, "For though we live in the flesh, we do not wage war according to the flesh. 4. The weapons of our warfare are not the weapons of the world. Instead, they have divine power to demolish strongholds. 5. We tear down arguments, and every presumption set up against the knowledge of God; and we take captive every thought to make it obedient to Christ..." (BSB). Lord, help me to pick up your spiritual weapons when I am facing my giants. My own human intellect and reasoning are fleshly weapons, but your Holy Word and your Holy Spirit are powerful and mighty, and through Your name I find victory! In Jesus' name, Amen!

JULY 18

Visiting my daughter at their lake home this summer, we would often go out on their pontoon and head to a swimming hole to cool off. We had rafts and floating seats so we could just anchor the boat, jump in and then stay right in the water floating around and relaxing. It was soon apparent and necessary however, that we tie ourselves to the anchored boat, or we would soon find ourselves drifting far away from it. As I think about this, the Lord illuminates to me that...

As it is in the natural, so is it in the spiritual...

We Christians can sometimes find ourselves drifting away from the Lord spiritually if we are not careful to anchor ourselves to Him. When we become busy with the daily activities of life, or when we face discouragement or difficulties, we can quickly drift away from God in a very short amount of time. Soon we may find ourselves distressed and crying for help. Hebrews 2:1 tells us, "So we must listen very carefully to the truth we have heard, or we may drift away from it" (NLT). The passage goes on to remind us that our very salvation is at stake. When we choose to turn away from God, we lose out on His amazing promises. Heavenly Father, thank you for your Word. Thank you for continuing to bring truth to us and for reaching for us when we drift. Help me to stay close to my anchor, the Lord Jesus! Amen!

JULY 19

Hiking in the Rocky Mountain National Park above the tree line, we were entering what is called the alpine zone. The altitude is above 12,000 feet and therefore no trees can grow but only a few hardy plants and animals live here. Amazingly we saw some of the most beautiful flowers which only bloom for a short season after the long winter snow melts. As I thought about how these most beautiful things can grow out of the harshest conditions, but only after the sunlight is warm enough to melt the snow, the Lord reminded me...

As it is in the natural, so is it in the spiritual...

In the same way that the flora of alpine regions is both hardy and beautiful, so too can a person who has endured tough times and harsh conditions in life become something amazingly beautiful when God's light hits them. They spring forth as a tender blossom and reveal the beauty of God's love despite what they must have endured. Only the light and only the love of God can do this! We can't produce this kind of beauty in and of ourselves. Jesus talked about living in the light of his presence throughout the new testament. In John 12:46 He said "I have come into the world as a light, so that no one who believes in Me should remain in darkness" (BSB). Thank you for your light, which brings all good things into bloom! Amen!

JULY 20

This morning was exceptionally foggy. I could not see my neighbor's farm which is only a few hundred yards away. As the sun began to brighten, the fog was dispelled by the light. Soon, it was clear and bright and no fog could be seen. As I thought about this, the Lord pointed out that ...

As it is in the natural, so is it in the spiritual...

Just as the light of the sun chases away fog from my morning, so too does the LIGHT of the SON dispel fog from my life! When I am in a fog, I cannot see which way to go and I am blindly traveling down a road that may lead me somewhere I do not wish to go. When the LIGHT of Jesus Christ shines into my heart, that fog is lifted and I can see clearly the direction he has asked me to go. At times, the fog is lifted only far enough for me to take a few steps in faith, but he gives me clarity to follow him when I allow his light to shine forth into my spirit. John 8:12 is a powerful verse: "Again Jesus spoke to them, saying, "I am the light of the world. Whoever follows me will not walk in darkness, but will have the light of life" (ESV). Lord, please help me to always follow you so that I may have the light of life to guide my every step. In Jesus' name, Amen!

JULY 21

Occasionally, in the middle of summer, I find myself craving winter months and darkness. That season seems to give me permission to be a bit lazy while confined to my comfortable home. When the sun is shining and it's warm outside, I am compelled (I think it is the voice of my earthly father, who was a bit on the workaholic side) to get up and do something 'productive'. Perhaps that is why a part of me loves dark, rainy days and/or dark winter months where I don't feel obligated to be continually busy doing something. As I thought on this, the Lord showed me...

As it is in the natural, so is it in the spiritual...

Just as my flesh craves physical idleness at times, so too does my spirit crave idleness. Some of the dark days we experience cause us to withdraw from productivity within our spirit! I John 1:7 reminds us: "But if we walk in the light, as he is in the light, we have fellowship one with another, and the blood of Jesus Christ his Son cleanseth us from all sin" (KJV). Just as I need sunshine to motivate me to get up and get something accomplished in my day, so too, I need to do my part and get up and walk in the light of the Lord so that I might have fellowship with others and in doing so I can do a work for HIS glory, and HIS kingdom!

JULY 22

Sitting in the boat on the lake fishing one hot day, I was literally praying for clouds to block the beating sun and protect us from its scorching heat. Each time a cloud covered the sun, I whispered a prayer of thanks! Each time it left, I yearned and prayed for more to return. As I was thinking about this, the Lord quickened to me that…

As it is in the natural, so is it in the spiritual...

The presence of God manifested to the children of Israel as a cloud by day (and a pillar of fire by night) (Exodus 13). This cloud was their great source of protection from the unknowns of the wilderness! Indeed, when am in the presence of God, I feel sheltered and protected. Psalms 18:2 reminds me, "The LORD is my protector; he is my strong fortress. My God is my protection, and with him I am safe. He protects me like a shield; he defends me and keeps me safe" (GNT). Out of his presence it can feel like I am in that boat with scorching heat draining me of my ability to carry on! Dear Lord, I need the cloud of Your presence to bring peace in knowing you are my guide and my shelter and my protector!

JULY 23

Today is my son in law, Steve's birthday. He began dating our daughter when they were both in high school, and they now live in

Iowa with our two teenage grandkids. Steve's love for hunting, fishing, and the great outdoors led him to start filming his hunts. What began as a dream, eventually led to the creation of a television show, which has been airing for more than five years. He focuses a great deal of time, effort and energy into the development and production of the show, and it is awesome to watch my daughter and grandchildren become actively involved in this amazing life experience. As I think about this, the Lord reveals to me...

As it is in the natural, so is it in the spiritual...

In the same way that my son in law's love and dedication for hunting and fishing has been the catalyst for a life of amazing outdoor adventures for himself and his family, so too ought our passion and love for the Lord be the driving force in our life, propelling us to live in a way that glorifies Him and draws others into our adventure. Proverbs 16:3 promises, "Commit to the Lord whatever you do, and he will establish your plans" (NIV). I'm thankful that Steve leads my daughter and grandchildren to follow him into the great outdoors as well as walking this life with a strong faith in the Lord. Thank-you God, for all that you have done to establish our plans as we commit our ways to you! Amen!

JULY 24

Sitting at a ball game in 100-degree weather, we were praying for some clouds and a cool breeze. I love nice warm weather, but let me tell you, we were yearning for a little relief that day. I was trying to imagine how anyone got anything accomplished in this kind of heat! It is a mere struggle to even survive in such heat! As we were praying for a break from the stifling heat, the Lord revealed to me...

As it is in the natural, so is it in the spiritual...

When we humans are uncomfortable, we seek refuge from whatever it is that is causing the discomfort. Likewise, our spiritual weather can bring excessive heat into our lives. We can experience days of perfectly delightful weather when all is well in our soul, but there will inevitably be days where you must seek shelter from the harsh elements that stifle us and hinder our ability to do just about anything. As believers, we are able to turn to the Lord for relief when we encounter these difficult times. Isaiah 49:10 reminds us, "They shall not hunger nor thirst; neither shall the heat nor sun smite them: for he that hath mercy on them shall lead them, even by the springs of water shall he guide them" (KJV). His love is an everlasting river of living water that we have continual access to through His Holy Spirit. He brings a refreshing that is incomparable to even the sweetest breeze and shady spot out of the sun. Lord, Thank you for your Spiritual refreshing. I could not survive this world without YOU! Amen!

JULY 25

The morning sky is indescribable today with shades of gray, blue and pink streaking across the sky and drops of moisture hanging in the air in the form of a light fog reflecting the light as the sun rises. As I walk out onto my patio to drink in this calming scene, it occurs to me how much we miss when we rush through life without taking time to bask in a moment. How often do we ignore the beauty around us because we are so busy and so distracted by 'life' and our own agenda? As I thought on this, the Lord whispered to me…

As it is in the natural, so is it in the spiritual…

Busyness can not only impede our ability to truly see the physical world around us, but it can also totally block our ability to 'see' the spiritual world around us as well. When we do not take time to bask in God's presence through reading his word and prayer, we rob ourselves out of the most amazing part of this earthly life-the indescribably joy that comes from our connection to our Creator. Psalms 16:11, "Thy wilt shew me in the path of life; in thy presence is fullness of joy; at thy right hand there are pleasures for evermore" (KJV). Lord, thank you for your abiding presence. Help me to seek your peace and your presence even in the midst of my busy life. Amen.

JULY 26

The air feels heavy with moisture as the sun rises this morning. The clouds have won, and yet behind them, the sun is still there, attempting to shine through at any given opportunity. The resulting scene is breathtakingly beautiful with the sunlight reflecting off of the clouds. The very obstacles that are trying to block the sun are actually creating beauty. As I thought on this, the Lord nudged me...

As it is in the natural, so is it in the spiritual...

Life has troubles, every day. It is how we view them that makes the difference. Just as the clouds provide the substance that allows the sun to reflect and create beauty, so too can we look at life's troubles as an opportunity for God to shine his beauty onto our situation. In Isaiah 61, the prophet was anointed to preach the Gospel of good tidings to the meek and to bind up the broken-hearted and proclaim liberty to the captives and those who are bound by life's difficulties. Verse 3 says, "To appoint unto them...beauty for ashes, the oil of joy for mourning; the garment of praise for the spirit of heaviness that they might be called trees of righteousness, the planning of the Lord that he might be glorified." Thank you Lord for helping us to see that cloudy days and troubles of life are an opportunity for your glory to shine forth into our lives. May we recognize and grasp this, and give all the honor and glory to you. In Jesus' majestic name. Amen.

JULY 27

Water always flows into the path of least resistance. As long as there is a source that continues to supply water to even the smallest stream, it will continue to grow. Even if it dries up occasionally, that groove that was originally formed remains and it makes it that much easier for water to flow the next time there is rain. With continued precipitation, the stream is deepened and widened into a creek, and eventually it will become a mighty river; essentially unstoppable. As I thought on this, the Lord opened my awareness and pointed out that...

As it is in the natural, so is it in the spiritual...

The Lord showed me in a flash that just as water finds the path of least resistance, so too will our flesh. When we go with the flow and allow our flesh to direct us, we find ourselves creating habitual flow in a certain direction. Soon our habit has carved out a larger creek and before we realize what is happening, it has grown into a deep and treacherous river. Even if we stop up the flow and change the course of our spiritual river for a season or two, that original ditch still remains. If we are not careful, we may dip our toe into our former streams and find ourselves being carried away by dangerous waters once again. Isaiah 43:18 tells us, "18 Remember ye not the former things, neither consider the things of old. 19 Behold, I will do a new thing; now it shall spring forth; shall ye not know it? I will even make a way in the wilderness, and rivers in the desert" (KJV). Thank you Lord. As I allow You to forge new waterways that will replenish my soul with spiritual blessings and keep me from my old pathways. Amen!

JULY 28

Pulling weeds in late July was no fun task as a farmer's daughter. The lamb's quarters were just that...about as big around as a hind quarter of a lamb! They were extremely tough and nearly impossible to pull out of the dry ground, so my dad usually waited until after a nice long rain and then sent us kids out on the errand to pull these monster weeds. As I thought about this, the Lord made it clear...

As it is in the natural, so is it in the spiritual...

In the same way a tough old weed is easier to remove after a rain, so too are tough old sins much easier to remove after we have experienced that much needed spiritual shower from the Lord. Shedding tears is an emotional experience. Doing so in God's presence it can very essential to our spiritual growth. This may happen in many ways from a quiet but sincere time of prayer, to a joyful time of worship, or a powerful word from your pastor. It can come from the beauty of God's creation or the sorrows this life can bring. We humans have been uniquely made to shed tears for many causes but the truth is, it is during these most vulnerable times, we can make the biggest changes in our lives. If we allow the Holy Spirit to do a work in us when we are tearfully tender, He can remove those stubborn weeds so we will have a successful harvest from what God has planted within us. Psalms 126:6 encourages us, "He who goes out weeping, bearing the seed for sowing, shall come home with shouts of joy, bringing his sheaves with him" (ESV). Thank you Lord, for my tears. I pray they soften my heart that I may remove the stubborn weeds trying to take root, so I might bring in a harvest for your kingdom! Amen!

JULY 29

Today is my mama's birthday. It is hard to put into words the impact that my mom has had on me. She is the one I call every day to check up on and fill her in on the details of my life whether it's good or bad. She always listens to me and is interested in what is happening. No matter what I have gone through in this bumpy ride we call 'life' my mom has been my hero, my cheerleader, my refuge, my friend, my confidant, my voice of reason. As I think on this, the Lord illuminates to me that...

As it is in the natural, so is it in the spiritual...

Just as I look to my mom each day to share my life with, so too the

Lord wants us to look to him for our spiritual needs. Exodus 20:12 says "You must honor and respect your father and your mother. Do this so that you will have a full life in the land that the Lord your God gives you" (ERV). This commandment comes with a promise that if we honor our parents, we will be taken care of spiritually and God will give us a full life. Lord, we know that when we honor our parents, it produces good spiritual blessings. I thank you that you gave me a mom worthy of praise and easy to love! Amen!

JULY 30

A friend of ours from church said he had taken a slow drive around the county recently on his way home. He was saddened by the stunted growth of the cornfields due to the lack of rain this summer. He noticed, however, that even though those stalks of corn were small and the field was very dry, they did not fail to reach toward the sky, with seemingly all of their strength, awaiting a shower from heaven. He continued to point out that…

As it is in the natural, so is it in the spiritual…

Just as those stalks of corn indeed do reach upward when they are thirsty and in need of water, likewise should we also be stretching forth our arms toward heaven to receive what the Lord is just waiting to pour out on us. When we are thirsty for whatever the Lord has, we can simply reach out in earnest expectation to receive. Psalms 143:6 I stretch forth my hands unto thee: my soul thirsteth after thee as a thirsty land (KJV). Lord do not let me hesitate to turn my face up and lift my hands to you when in need of any small or great thing, for it is you who sends rain to water the thirsty ground and my thirsty soul. In Jesus' name, Amen!

JULY 31

The morning mist was hovering over the sugar beet field this morning at when the Lord called me out of my sleepy bed to come and commune with him. What a beautiful sight for my eyes to behold! As the mist lingered and the thirsty leaves of the beets drank in the precious dew, the Lord spoke to me:

As it is in the natural, so is it in the spiritual...

The Lord reminded me that just as this precious mist from heaven waters the thirsty crops, His spirit hovers over us, drenching us with his presence and providing us with life sustaining dew to quench our dry and thirsty soul. In Genesis 27:28, Isaac blessed his son Jacob with these words, "May God give to you the dew of heaven and the richness of the earth—an abundance of grain and new wine" (BSB). Oh Lord, may your presence ever hover over each of us, and may we always thirst after the water only you can provide that we may live in the richness and abundance of your love. Amen!

AUGUST 1

Kayaking down a swift river like the Au Sable is a one directional sport. You will quickly find that if you try to paddle against the current you will be working very hard and it will seem as if you are not going anywhere. In fact, even trying to stand still in this river can be a challenge due to the strong pull of the water. As I thought about this the Lord was showing me that...

As it is in the natural, so is it in the spiritual...

Some days, when we are attempting to do what is right and follow Jesus, we feel as if we are swimming against a strong current of the world, pulling us in a different direction. It can literally feel as if we are drowning and helpless. But when we find ourselves in these situations, we can remember the promises found in Isaiah 43:2: "When you pass through the waters, I will be with you; and through the rivers, they will not overwhelm you..."(ESV). He promises that no matter where we go, he will carry us through. Thank you, Lord Jesus, for your promises are true. I know that wherever I go, you will carry me through my troubles. Amen!

AUGUST 2

Yesterday we shared the day with some friends who we don't see very often. We used to go to church with them and were pretty close until we moved back home and since then we only see each other maybe once a year for dinner. We made plans for them to come for a visit. They were worried about bringing the kids but we welcomed all of them to come so we could get to know the kids and spend some time with our friends. After they arrived, we packed up and drove the short trip to the lake, where there was a nice sandy beach. The kids LOVED it. They romped and collected shells and played for several hours. We sat and visited and reminisced. After the beach, we went for supper and then came back to our house and built a bonfire, made S'mores, and played corn bag toss (corn hole). They left satisfied and happy and as we bid them goodbye, we were so glad we made the effort to rekindle that friendship. As I sit here this morning, thinking on that, the Lord whispered a truth to me...

As it is in the natural, so is it in the spiritual…

It became clear to me in that moment that my relationship with the Lord will either grow or wane depending on ME. He is always there waiting for us. He is always knocking gently at our heart's door and wants us to let him in so he can commune with us. We only need to open the door and welcome him in. In Revelation 3:20, the Lord says, "Behold, I stand at the door, and knock: if any man hear my voice, and open the door, I will come in to him, and will sup with him, and he with me" (KJV). Dear Lord, please keep my heart ready and willing to invite you in at all times so that my friendship with you never grows awkward or unfamiliar. Let me always be ready and willing to open the door for you to come in and dine with me. In Jesus' precious name, Amen!

AUGUST 3

I was in the yard working recently and kept looking up toward the sky in hopes of seeing a few clouds to give us a break from the blazing sun. I recall some specific times in my life when I would pray for rain or pray that the rain would not hit us, and to my amazement, my prayer would come to be! As I looked up and whispered a prayer to God for this relief, he quickened to me...

As it is in the natural, so is it in the spiritual...

God protected the children of Israel in a supernatural way, with a cloud by day and a pillar of fire by night: Exodus 14: 19-20 says, "Then the Angel of God, who had gone before the camp of Israel, withdrew and went behind them. The pillar of cloud also moved from before them and stood behind them, 20 so that it came between the camps of Egypt and Israel. The cloud was there in the darkness, but it lit up the night. So, all night long neither camp went near the other" (BSB). Wesley's notes clarified what I thought to be true. He writes: "The angel of God - Whose ministry was made use of in the pillar of cloud and fire, went from before the camp of Israel, where they did not now need a guide; there was no danger of missing their way through the sea, and came behind them, where now they needed a guard, the Egyptians being just ready to seize the hindmost of them. There it was of use to the Israelites, not only to protect them, but to light them through the sea; and at the same time, it confounded the Egyptians, so that they lost sight of their prey, just when they were ready to lay hands on it. The word and providence of God have a black and dark side towards sin and sinners, but a bright and pleasant side towards those that are Israelites indeed" (Wesley's notes. (n.d.). Retrieved from https://biblehub.com/commentaries/wes/exodus/14.htm). Lord how can we doubt your love for your children? Thank you for being the light which guides and the cloud that protects me. Help me to follow your light which leads me out of my own personal Egypt. In Jesus' name! Amen!

AUGUST 4

This morning there are many clouds in the sky. The clouds cover the sun, which we know is there, but it is temporarily concealed. The wind must blow those clouds away for the sun to be revealed once again where we can feel its warmth upon our face. The Lord took this opportunity to point out to me...

As it is in the natural, so it is in the spiritual...

Just as a cloudy day can hide the sun, so too do the spiritual clouds in our life sometimes conceal the Son of God from shining his light into our lives. The cares of this world, doubts, worries, distractions, sin, and disobedience can cover the glory of God and prevent others from seeing Him in us. The blessing of God's light shining in our life requires time in God's presence; a strong refreshing wind of the Holy Spirit to blow those clouds away so that we can once again bask in the glory and warmth of HIS presence. Job 37 recounts the sovereignty and complete omnipotence of God. Verse 15 asks, "Do you know how God dispatches the clouds or makes the lightning flash?" (BSB). May we always remember that no matter how many clouds try to block the light, HE is ever present, waiting for us to call on the power of the Holy Ghost to blow those dark, gray obstacles away. It is through His might and His power that we can overcome our cloudy days that his light may shine through! Thank you Lord for this reminder! Amen!

AUGUST 5

A windstorm recently passed through our area and after it was over there were many tree branches strewn about on the ground. It is apparent that only the well attached, stronger branches were able to withstand the storm that had come upon them. As I was contemplating this natural truth, the Lord spoke to me...

As it is in the natural, so is it in the spiritual...

When battering winds and stormy days come into our lives, some will fall away, break their connection with their life source and be left scattered and broken. It is the branch that is firmly attached to its source that will be able to survive the winds of this life. Jesus said in John 15:5, "I am the vine, ye are the branches: He that abideth in me, and I in him, the same beareth much fruit: for apart from me ye can do nothing. 6 If a man abide not in me, he is cast forth as a branch, and is withered; and they gather them, and cast them into the fire, and they are burned. 7 If ye abide in me, and my words abide in you, ask whatsoever ye will, and it shall be done unto you." This is powerful! Dear Jesus, I am so thankful to know that as I cling to my You, I am able to bear good fruit! Help me remember this as I enter each day! In Your name! Amen!

AUGUST 6

I plucked a few flowers from my garden the other day and now they have lost their beauty. They are nothing but shriveled petals drifting onto my countertop. The harsh reality is that once you cut a flower from its life source, it is dead, and the effects will soon be seen. As I thought about this the Lord whispered…

As it is in the natural, so is it in the spiritual….

The Lord reminded me that when you cut a living thing from its life source, it will surely die. He reminded me how Adam and Eve were disconnected after they chose to disobey Him. Their monumental sin caused death to enter into this world which is essentially separation from God-our life source. The effects were felt from that moment on by their children and all of those who came into this world. 1 Peter 1:24 reminds us… "People are like grass; their beauty is like a flower in the field. The grass withers and the flower fades. 25 But the word of the Lord remains forever" (NTL). As we walk through this life, we can choose to either turn away from our life source - Jesus Christ - or we can attach ourselves to him and receive eternal life through being born again of His Spirit, which never dies. Dear Lord, help each of us become alive evermore by staying connected to our life source - YOU! In Jesus' name, Amen!

AUGUST 7

This weekend as we drove to our daughter's home in Bay City, my husband asked which way I wanted to go. I began to think about the ways this seemingly small decision could affect our lives. In fact, every time we drive somewhere, we must decide which route to take. Often, it depends on our mood and whether there may be construction along one path, but those who have encountered tragedies while driving can tell you: that seemingly small decision was costly. As I thought about this, the Lord whispered to me...

As it is in the natural, so is it in the spiritual...

Our libraries are filled with metaphors, poems, fables, idioms and books on forks in the road, the road less traveled, taking the high road and so on. These writings are all talking about choices. Just as we have to make seemingly small choices regarding our travels (and countless other things each day), so also, we are making choices each day regarding where we are heading spiritually. Rejecting the path which the Lord has clearly presented to us through His word can lead us down some bumpy, painful paths in this life. Oh, yes, there may be laughs and good times along that road, but the destination is not one of inner peace and eternal joy. Psalms 25:12 promises: "Those who have reverence for the LORD will learn from him the path they should follow" (GNT). Proverbs 12:28 is a bit more blunt: "There is life in the path of righteousness, but another path leads to death" (BSB). Lord we acknowledge that when we choose to follow YOU, we are promised eternal life as our destination, and despite the bumps and curves and detours, we are granted peace, joy and assurance in our final destination. Amen!

AUGUST 8

Today is my hubby's birthday. I can't really express how much I love this man. I always try to figure out what to get him, but he is a tough one to buy for, because he is a little on the particular side. So, I am always a bit frustrated if I can't figure something out. One year I got him a giant flat screen television as a surprise. It was especially fulfilling to give him a gift that was a bit on the extravagant side. It was amazing to see the joy upon his face when I actually pulled off (or so I thought) the surprise and got him something he really wanted. As I thought on this, the Lord nudged me...

As it is in the natural, so is it in the spiritual...

The Lord wanted me to see that he is the master and creator of extravagant gift giving! First and foremost, he has given us a tremendous gift of salvation. Ephesians 2:8 says, "For it is by grace you have been saved through faith, and this not from yourselves; it is the gift of God, 9 not by works, so that no one can boast" (BSB). When God's gift of the Holy Spirit was first poured out, Peter, on the Day of Pentecost, exhorted those who had witnessed the Holy Spirit baptizing those in the upper room; "38 Peter replied, Repent and be baptized, every one of you, in the name of Jesus Christ for the forgiveness of your sins, and you will receive the gift of the Holy Spirit. 39 This promise belongs to you and to your children and to all who are far off, to all whom the Lord our God will call to Himself..." (BSB). The gift of the Holy Spirit of is God's most extravagant gift to humanity, for it came with a cost of the precious Blood of his only son, Jesus Christ. Thank you Lord for the precious gift of your Spirit, who fills us with your power to overcome the sin of this world. Help me to daily receive the Holy Spirit power that I may do all that pleases you! In Jesus' name, Amen!

AUGUST 9

Rain is either a friend or foe depending on your perspective. For the farmer who is in need of a growing shower, it is a blessing while for another who wants to get the hay or wheat off it is a curse! For those not in the business of reaping and sowing, it is difficult to understand why some rejoice in the rain…to them it is simply a nuisance and an irritation. Thinking about this paradigm, the Lord revealed to me…

As it is in the natural, so is it in the spiritual…

For those who are trying to grow in the Lord, spiritual rain is welcomed for it brings us in right standing with Him. The Lord speaking through Isaiah says in 45:8, "You heavens above, rain down my righteousness; let the clouds shower it down. Let the earth open wide, let salvation spring up, let righteousness flourish with it; I, the LORD, have created it" (NIV). Those precious drops from heaven when we are in His presence sustain us during the dry moments. Lord I thank you for your showers from heaven. I ask that you bless those who are standing with open arms to receive it from you and I ask that you create a thirst in those who do not yet understand. In Jesus' name, Amen!

AUGUST 10

Driving along the road the other evening, we noticed some beautiful ponds. We were talking about how nice it would be to have a place with a large pond so we could kayak and fish and just enjoy nature. We then drove past a pond that was anything but beautiful. It was stagnant and rotten and nothing good could possibly come out of that body of water. We began to talk about ponds and how in order for them to be clean and healthy, they must be spring fed. We agreed that there must be a continual source of fresh living water flowing into it in order for it to be clean, healthy and productive. The Lord quickened to me…

As it is in the natural, so is it in the spiritual…

If we do not intentionally gain access to Jesus, who is the source for a continual spring of fresh living water flowing into our spirit, we too will become stagnant. We won't grow spiritually and nothing good will come from us. Jesus explained this in John 7:37: In the last day, that great day of the feast, Jesus stood and cried, saying, If any man thirst, let him come unto me, and drink. 38 He that believeth on me, as the scripture hath said, out of his belly shall flow rivers of living water. 39 (But this spake he of the Spirit, which they that believe on him should receive: for the Holy Ghost was not yet given; because that Jesus was not yet glorified.)" (KJV). Lord Jesus, thank you for your spirit which gives me fresh and new "living" water each day as I spend time with you in prayer and in reading Your word. I give all praise for all good and fresh things to YOU! Amen!

AUGUST 11

Yesterday, my granddaughter ran to me at her ball game and snuggled up close to me. When I am busy and unable to see my kids and grandkids, my heart aches for those moments of cuddle time when I can pour out my love on them. My husband shared with me that the Lord showed him this morning...

As it is in the natural, so is it in the spiritual...

God is our creator and our Heavenly Father, and just as we ache for the love of our children and grandchildren, so too, he aches for us to come near him and snuggle up and soak up his love. Just as I pour out love and kisses onto my grandchildren, so, too, he wants to pour out his love upon us. Romans 5: 5 says, "And hope does not put us to shame, because God's love has been poured out into our hearts through the Holy Spirit, who has been given to us" (NIV). Let us allow God to pour his love into our hearts by spending precious time in his presence, so that we may have love to pour into others. In Jesus' name!

AUGUST 12

Yesterday I was admiring the flowers pots in my yard. It's amazing what a splash of color can do to improve one's mood! This morning as I was reading my bible, the eastern sky was streaked with shades of pinks and gold as the sun began its ascent into the sky. I once again pondered how it is amazing what a splash of color can do to improve one's mood! As I thought on this, the Lord whispered to me...

As it is in the natural, so is it in the spiritual...

Just as darkness, bleakness, gray, and black are all words and 'colors' associated with depression, so, too, light, bright, colorful and white are all words and 'colors' associated with joy. It occurred to me that each of us has an opportunity every single day to embrace depressing thoughts, words and actions, or to embrace joyful thoughts, words and actions. Proverbs 23:7 says "As a man thinketh in his heart, so is he" (KJV). This means that the moods and attitudes and thoughts we choose to embrace and act on actually ARE who we are. The attitude we carry into our day will be what others notice and identify us as. If we want to bring light, color and joy into other's lives, we must be in contact with the SOURCE of light, color and joy! JESUS. Lord we know that in and of ourselves, we become too entangled with the cares of life. We need time with YOU to drive the dark, gray, dreary thoughts from our hearts and replace them with light, colorful, joy. It's amazing what a splash of color can do for one's mood! AMEN!

AUGUST 13

Today we were talking about driving and getting lost and I said "Yep, it only takes one wrong turn and you end up somewhere you never wanted to go." Suddenly, the Lord whispered...

As it is in the natural, so is it in the spiritual...

There are countless people sitting in jails and prisons who will tell you that one mistake led them down the wrong path. We need to be in continual contact with God for guidance of each of our spiritual journey because it will be him who will speak wisdom to us through the Holy Ghost. John 14:26 says "But the Comforter, which is the Holy Ghost, whom the father will send in my name, he shall teach you all things, and bring all things to your remembrance, whatsoever I have said unto you" (KJV). Psalms 32:8 says, "I will instruct thee and teach thee in the way which thou shalt go: I will guide thee with mine eye" (KJV). Dear Lord, many of your Holy Scriptures teach us that you are the one whom we should seek for guidance, direction and wisdom. Thank you that Thy word is a lamp unto my feet and a light unto my path! Amen!

AUGUST 14

I saw my former pastor's wife at family camp this week and she immediately asked me "How are you doing?" with a knowing look. She always gets right to the heart of the matter with me whenever we see each other. She is one of several people I consider as a counselor and mentor to me. I have called on her for Godly wisdom at various times in my life when I needed it. As I thought of this encounter, it reminded me that…

As it is in the natural, so is it in the spiritual…

When we come into contact with God's spirit, he gets right to the heart of the matter and if we are open to his influence, he immediately becomes our counselor and mentor and can show us all truth about our situation. Romans 8 tells us that those who live in accordance with the Holy Spirit, have their minds set on what the Spirit desires and his mind is then life and peace. Jesus said in John 14:16, "And I will ask the Father, and He will give you another Comforter (Counselor, Helper, Intercessor, Advocate, Strengthener, and Standby), that He may remain with you forever --" (Amp). Dear Lord, -Indeed, you have sent your Spirit to indwell us and bring us comfort, counsel, intercession and strength; to be our forever mentor and lead us into all truth. Thank you for this amazing gift! Amen!

AUGUST 15

I love playgrounds, but I am not a fan of the merry-go-round. The circular motion of that ride always gets me feeling disoriented and weak. Any time I have ever ridden on a round and round ride, I have felt this way and I just want it to stop so I can exit as quickly as possible! I have found that by sitting very close to the center mechanism, I can ward off the dizziness a bit but as soon as I get out away from the center, things get pretty crazy! As I think about this, the Lord quickened to me that…

As it is in the natural, so is it in the spiritual…

At times throughout my spiritual life, I have felt like I am riding on a Merry-go-round! In prayer, God helped me see that rather than stay out on the edge where things spin wildly and the ride is dizzying and disorienting, I needed to gravitate toward the center of it all which is Christ Jesus. If I stay close where HE lives and moves and breathes, and where we can access his POWER. James 4:8 directs us, "Draw near to God, and he will draw near to you…" (ESV). Dear Lord, give me clarity of mind and a resolve to live for you. AMEN!

AUGUST 16

We woke up this morning to a humming sound in our chimney and quickly became suspicious that we had a bee infestation. Lo and behold, my husband investigated and found that indeed we had just that- a honey bee infestation. In reading on this topic, I discovered a few interesting facts. One fact is that honey bees reproduce and grown in numbers within their hive and then need to split up, so the queen sends scouts to find a new residence. Once it is located, the queen takes half of the bees to the new location en mass (all at once). This is why all of a sudden, we ended up with these pesky visitors in our chimney! After a frantic run to town for bee spray, my husband was advised by his honey-bee farmer friend to light a small smoky fire in the chimney trap door and maybe they would leave. I prayed as he lit the fire and after a scare with a flame shooting up the chimney (dear Lord please not a chimney fire too!!) the bee humming subsided with the exception of a few stragglers in our kitchen flue, the hive must have left! Hallelujah! As I rejoiced, the Lord revealed to me…

As it is in the natural, so is it in the spiritual…

The Lord illuminated to me that just as quickly as this hive of bees found a new home in our chimney literally overnight, so too can a spiritual infestation occur in our heart and mind if we do not carefully and prayerfully allow God to inspect and protect on a daily basis! We must exterminate the enemy immediately at the first sign of infestation before it gets a stronghold within our spiritual being and wreaks havoc upon our lives. Psalms 44:5 says, "Through You we repel our foes; through Your name we trample our enemies" (BSB). Dear Lord, when we rely on our own strength, we are helpless against our enemy attacks, but when we trust in You, we are able to eradicate the enemy from our situation! Thank you for your presence, which penetrates our life like smoke to that bee swarm! In Jesus' name, Amen!

AUGUST 17

We went canoeing with our friends on the Au Sable river recently. One of our buddies rented a kayak. He was playing around and testing out the maneuverability of the vessel when suddenly he was upside down in the river! Fortunately, he was in shallow water and able to stand up and grab his hat, but the river quickly swept his sunglasses away before he could retrieve them. We all laughed about this blunder for days after the trip and I still chuckle when I recall the incident, but God has also shown me that...

As it is in the natural, so is it in the spiritual...

When we venture into unfamiliar territory, we are susceptible to perils unbeknownst to us. Our lack of experience can create potentially dangerous circumstances if we don't know how to react to unexpected events. Likewise, when we walk into deeper waters spiritually, we must be on alert for a myriad of potentially perilous situations. I John 4:1 warns us: "Beloved, believe not every spirit, but try the spirits whether they are of God: because many false prophets are gone out into the world" (BSB). Lord you have shown us that by prayerfully considering our movements and allow You to lead, guide and direct us, we can be secure in YOUR protection. It is when we venture into unfamiliar waters on our own strength and wit that we can get into trouble. Thank you for this truth. AMEN!

AUGUST 18

As I begin to think of starting school again, I am excited to know that my job is more than just that of a teacher of Special Education students. I know that I am a called out one, chosen for a special purpose to love, encourage and inspire those little hearts and minds so that they might reach higher, embrace their gifts and their purpose and strive to become the best they can be! As I think on this, I realized that...

As it is in the natural, so is it in the spiritual...

Just as it is my desire to see these children overcome obstacles and begin to understand their worth and their capabilities, so too it is the Lord's desire to see HIS children overcome obstacles and begin to understand OUR worth and OUR capabilities! Ephesians 2:4 says, "But God is so rich in mercy, and he loved us so much, 5 that even though we were dead because of our sins, he gave us life when he raised Christ from the dead. (It is only by God's grace that you have been saved!)"

(NLT). You see, each of us is of great value to the LORD! If only we can recognize that it is each of US that he desires. He wants our hearts! Jesus told us that when one sinner repents, there is rejoicing in the presence of the angels of God (Luke 15:10). As I begin this school year, I pray for the children. I pray they might understand not only their academic potential, but also that God loves them and desires for them to find their true potential in HIM. AMEN.

AUGUST 19

When I think of a King, and his kingdom, I envision an elderly, bearded man sitting on a giant throne while those around him seek after his approval and his blessings. If you want the good life, you must obey him and bow to his wishes, and if he is a good king, he has mercy and compassion on his subjects. As I was thinking on this, the Lord suddenly illuminated to me that...

As it is in the natural, so is it in the spiritual...

It only follows that we might view God's kingdom in a similar fashion. We all want to live the good life in the physical realm. Perhaps we look to him for those things we perceive as blessings: a comfortable home, a nice vehicle, a good job, good friends and so on. But these things are only temporal. The bible tells us, "The Kingdom of God is NOT meat and drink (physical things that WE consider to be blessings) but righteousness, peace and joy in the Holy Ghost" (Romans 14:17). The Lord Jesus stepped away from his heavenly throne and royal attire and robed himself in flesh and came to this earth to seek and save the lost! Like the good earthly king, Jesus wants us to fellowship with him and embrace life in HIS kingdom. This invisible kingdom is filled to overflowing, but not with physical blessings. If you've ever stepped out of the realm of this physical world to seek a relationship with the King of Kings, you understand that His blessings go far beyond the physical things we seek. We have access to His Righteousness, His Peace and the Joy that only comes from the Holy Ghost. AMEN!

AUGUST 20

I awaken to the sound of raindrops on the window and am immediately sedated. What is it within my soul that loves rain? I ponder. As a farmer's kid, when it rained, we had a day of relative rest. No picking stones or pulling weeds! YAY! Perhaps this is it but it seems to hold a deeper connotation. As I whispered a prayer of thanks for the gently drops from heaven, the Lord quickened a truth to me...

As it is in the natural, so is it in the spiritual...

In the bible, rain is often a parallel for blessings from God. We all know in some deep place in our hearts that God truly is in control of the weather. Jeremiah 5:22 asks, "Are there any among the false gods of the nations that can bring rain? Or can the heavens give showers? Are you not he, O LORD our God? We set our hope on you, for you do all these things (ESV). We all go through dry spells in our spiritual walk, but ohh the refreshing that a rain from heaven can bring to that thirsty soul. Lord, help me to look up expectantly when my soul is feeling dry and void of your touch. Help me to remember that all of my blessings come from you so that I will always look up and wait on the rain from heaven to water my soul.

AUGUST 21

Light illuminates. As the dawn of this quiet morning illuminates the entire sky, I notice that things that were unseen just a moment ago, are now visible. Where there were shadows a moment ago, now I see the outline of the trees. Then where the outline was only visible, another moment passes and I can see the branches of the tree. Finally, as the light becomes greater, the color of the trees develops and the beauty of God's creation is revealed fully. As I thought on this, the Lord reminded me...

As it is in the natural, so is it in the spiritual...

Just as the morning light illuminates the world around us, so too does the Light of this World illuminate what is in our hearts. As we allow Him in, His light illuminate the darkest corners of our heart and mind so that we may see clearly. Ephesians 5:13 tells us that "Everything exposed by the light becomes visible and everything that is illuminated becomes a light" (NIV). God's Word translation says, "Light exposes the true character of everything." When we allow Christ to enter our hearts, he sheds light on those things we need to address and remove. Once they are made apparent to us, it is much easier to deal with. Dear Lord, thank you for shining the light of your Holy Spirit into my heart that I may see clearly into even the darkest corners. Help me to clean out each corner that I may have nothing lurking in the shadows of my soul. In Jesus' name, Amen!

AUGUST 22

Light reveals. Continuing on the thoughts of yesterday...One day, I was cleaning the back room closet and ran across a headlamp. I put it on and checked the light to see how well it worked. As I wandered around the house, I noticed that I could see dust bunnies where I previously had not noticed! WOW. This was a revelatory thing for my house cleaning days! Obviously, we need light in order to see so we can clean the clutter, sweep out the dirt and cobwebs and ensure there are no unwanted residents living in our homes. But that focused beam on my head allowed me to see so much more it was astounding! As I thought on this, the Lord revealed to me that...

As it is in the natural, so is it in the spiritual...

Just as we need light to clean our homes well and to rid ourselves of unwanted items, so too must we have the Light of Christ shining in our hearts so that we can "See" the dust, clutter and unwanted residents living in our heart. I John 1:9 says "If we confess our sins, he is faithful to forgive us of our sins and cleanse us from all unrighteousness." Before we can even confess, we must first let His Light shine into those dark corners so He can show us the clutter, dirt, cobwebs and even unwanted residents that have taken up their home there! Lord thank you for your light! Thank you for helping me clean my heart that it would be a dwelling place for YOU! Amen!

AUGUST 23

Light comforts. Most of us have been afraid of the dark at one time or another. My grandchildren all want night lights when they go to bed. I like one too so getting up in the night isn't too treacherous! I remember as a child times when I allowed my imaginations to transform harmless objects into dreadful terrors. I saw things that were not really there because of my limited vision, and I allowed my mind to create monsters where there really were none to be seen. As I thought on this…the Lord whispered to me…

As it is in the natural, so is it in the spiritual…

In the same way that turning on a light switch can chase away unwarranted fears and shed light to reveal that there is nothing to fear, so too can this be in our spiritual life when we allow God's light to shine into those dark and fearful areas of our life so that we can see that there is nothing to fear when we allow God reside within us. David writes in Psalms 27:1, "The LORD is my light and my salvation; whom shall I fear? the LORD is the strength of my life; of whom shall I be afraid?" (KJV). Lord thank you for your light, which comforts us when we are fearful. Let us always turn to you for that illumination when we cannot see in the dark! In Jesus' name, Amen!

AUGUST 24

In 1991, my husband and I took a leap of faith and began our new life together as husband and wife. We met in March and were married five months later. I am sure there were many who said it couldn't last, but we proved them wrong. One thing that we have learned (and this is what I tell newlyweds) is that love is a decision. It's a commitment, not a romantic feeling. The feelings you have must be there, granted, but those will not survive the storms of life without a firm foundation built upon the decisive resolve that you will work together and stick together and stay in the marriage no matter what. You must put on the blinders and look only to your spouse for comfort and love. A wandering eye will destroy a marriage. As I think on this, the Lord pointed out...

As it is in the natural, so is it in the spiritual...

The bible is full of warnings about spiritual adultery. The children of Israel continually suffered consequences of turning to idolatry and putting their faith in false gods rather the being faithful to the living God. In today's world we are drawn away from God by all of the enticements this world offers. We forget to put God first and look to him for our needs. James 4:4 puts it bluntly: "You adulterers and adulteresses! Do you not know that friendship with the world is enmity with God? Therefore, whoever wishes to be a friend of the world makes himself an enemy of God" (KJV). Essentially, he is talking about our heart. When we desire the things of this world more than we desire God we are committing spiritual adultery. We must commit our hearts to God and Him alone. Dear Lord, help me to keep my heart pure unto You. Help me to put on my blinders and resist anything that may attempt to capture my heart and draw me away from You! In Jesus' name!

AUGUST 25

As summer draws near its bittersweet end and I begin counting the hours until I must get to my classroom to prepare for our school open house, I reflect over the weeks of freedom my husband and I have enjoyed. Our oldest daughter and her family moved to Iowa this summer and we were able to help them pack and prepare for the move. We enjoyed a couple of camping trips with our middle daughter and her family as well as taking a day to help them with a small facelift in their living room. We were able to help our son and his family with their home remodeling project and we have had the ability to spend time with all of our grandkids and some close friends and family throughout this summer. Without this precious time on our hands, we would never have created these memories. As I ponder this, the Lord reminds me…

As it is in the natural, so is it in the spiritual…

Just as we try to make the most of our time off, also too must we as believers redeem the time we have in the spiritual realm. In his letter the Ephesians, Paul exhorts believers "14 Wherefore he saith, Awake thou that sleepest, and arise from the dead, and Christ shall give thee light. 15 See then that ye walk circumspectly, not as fools, but as wise,16 Redeeming the time, because the days are evil.17 Wherefore be ye not unwise, but understanding what the will of the Lord is" (KJV). In other words, we, who are the children of God must make the most of the opportunities given us to bless others, lead and guide them by our example, and love them as Jesus first loved us. Lord thank you for each moment you graciously give to me. Help me to look to you each day and ask for guidance and direction that I might bless others. In Jesus' name, Amen!

AUGUST 26

Watching my grandchildren grow and learn is one of life's most rewarding and amazing things. The love that exists between myself and them is so great, but it is not comparable to that of their parents. When one of my grandbabies is hurting or upset, and their parents are near, they will most often cry out for "Mama" or "Daddy." This seems logical since these are the people who have poured their love and adoration upon the infant throughout their first months of life. As I pondered this, the Lord quickened to me that…

As it is in the natural, so is it in the spiritual…

Just as a baby calls out to their earthly parents when in need, so too will a child of God instinctively call out to their heavenly father when in need. In Romans, chapter 8, Paul writes to believers about our spiritual adoption by God through Christ Jesus. He reminds us that we who are led by the Spirit of God are the sons of God. Our relationship with our heavenly Father is apparent because we have been partakers of His Spirit. Paul writes, "…ye have received the Spirit of adoption whereby we cry, Abba, Father." He goes on to say that "16 the Spirit itself beareth witness with our spirit, what we are the children of God" (KJV). Lord, thank you for making me your child and being right there each time I whisper or cry your name! Thank you, Heavenly Father for all of your wonderful blessings! Amen!

AUGUST 27

My pickle plants actually grew very nicely this year for a change. Typically, they don't grow bushy or lush and therefore, they produce very little. A few days ago, I noticed that my lovely bushy pickle plants were turning yellowish despite the fact that they were just beginning to produce cucumbers. They appeared to be at the end of their season rather than in production mode. I was trying to figure this out when I mentioned it to my husband and he reminded me that the pickle farmer who just bought our car last week had said something about a disease the pickles were susceptible to this year where they simply up and die. He said that is probably what happened to our pickles since we didn't spray or sprinkle them. I felt like someone had snuck in and robbed me of the reward of my labors! Apparently, careful guarding of our garden is necessary to protect and keep diseases, bugs and weeds from killing our fruit before we get a chance to harvest it. As I thought on this the Lord pointed out…

As it is in the natural, so is it in the spiritual…

Many have invested years of their life serving God, but if we are not careful, the enemy can sneak in and ruin everything that we've so diligently worked to establish. John 10:10-11 reminds us that "The thief comes only to steal, kill and destroy. I came that they might have life and have it abundantly" (NLT). Careful guarding of our heart can be likened to the careful tending of our vegetable gardens. Dear Lord, please help me to be watchful as the enemy tries to sneak in and plant seeds of destruction into the garden of my heart. In Jesus' name, Amen!

AUGUST 28

Something happened while praying recently; I asked the Lord why it seems I am always in a battle with my flesh and my will, while some people seem to have no problem living a life devoid of God. He quickly planted an image in my mind of two boxers in a ring and whispered: "If you aren't in a fight, you aren't fighting the GOOD fight!" I immediately said a prayer of thanks as he illuminated that…

As it is in the natural, so is it in the spiritual…

We may wonder why others around us seem to live their lives so easily without Jesus. They seem to live happily without pesky spiritual struggles tugging them to change their habits or lifestyle. I have tried life without a relationship with Jesus, and I can live only short periods of time free and clear from the convictions that erode my 'fun' times. It's like the Lord is continually pulling me and calling me to rise up and leave behind the things that once nearly destroyed me. He reminded me as I Peter 2:9-11 says: "But ye are a chosen generation, a royal priesthood, an holy nation, a peculiar people; that ye should shew forth the praises of him who hath called you out of darkness into his marvelous light; 10 Which in time past were not a people, but are now the people of God: which had not obtained mercy, but now have obtained mercy.11 Dearly beloved, I beseech you as strangers and pilgrims, abstain from fleshly lusts, which war against the soul…" (KJV). Lord, help me to recognize that when I am facing struggles and battles, it is YOU who is calling me to fight this war against my soul. Let me be thankful there is still a battle and that I am still in it! AMEN.

AUGUST 29

I love watching the sunrise when it begins as a sliver of orange and gradually spreads upward across the eastern horizon, warming the grayish blue sky with its bold color. There is just something so amazing about each of these glorious beginnings of a new day. It signals to me that I this is a brand-new day and anything is possible! As I sit here this morning, the Lord helps me see…

As it is in the natural, so is it in the spiritual…

Malachi 4:2 promises: "So shall the sun of righteousness arise to you who revere my Name, with healing in his wings, - and ye shall come forth and leap for joy like calves let loose from the stall" (TEB). Each morning brings a new opportunity for spiritual healing as we take our hearts before the Lord and usher in a new day. We ought to rise up from that morning prayer feeling the joy of freedom from any captivity that once held us! I praise you Lord Jesus for this new day! Thank you for putting joy in my morning and hope in my every breath! In Jesus' name, Amen!!

AUGUST 30

This summer we have been particularly dry in our immediate area. Our lawn is brown and the crops are suffering. As a farmer's daughter, I know the necessity of rain for our crops. I know the torment that resides in the minds of those who put the seed in the ground and then pray for just enough rain. Rain is most definitely a necessity for survival. As I thought on this, the Lord spoke to me…

As it is in the natural, so is it in the spiritual…

Isaiah 45:8 illustrates the metaphor of rain in a spiritual sense: "You heavens above, rain down my righteousness; let the clouds shower it down. Let the earth open wide, let salvation spring up, let righteousness flourish with it; I, the LORD, have created it" (NIV). It is obvious that rainy weather is a necessary element in our lives for survival. Likewise, the rain of righteousness from the Lord is also a vital element for our spiritual survival. Since no man is able to attain righteousness, Jesus Christ came to earth in our place, bringing an abundance of blessings; grace, peace, pardon, salvation and eternal life, and the Holy Ghost was poured out (as rain) to indwell believers so that we can be partakers of all of the blessings and righteousness of God. Hallelujah! Thank you Lord for sending your Spirit of righteousness!

AUGUST 31

As I mentioned yesterday, we have experienced somewhat of a drought where I live. I believe we have gotten a little over an inch of rain in the past seven weeks. Each time rain is forecasted, we get our hopes up. We hear the rumbling of thunder and see lightening but then watch in dismay as the storm sweeps around us and we are left wanting for rain. Someone commented that there seems to be a vacuum or a dome of sorts hovering over us. A study done by the University of Nebraska states that "Common to all types of drought is the fact that they originate from a deficiency of precipitation that results in water shortage for some activity (e.g., plant growth) or for some group (e.g., farmer)." (Types of Drought. Retrieved from https://drought.unl.edu/Education/DroughtIn-depth/TypesofDrought.aspx) It seems that once a pattern (or some would say a vicious cycle) of dryness sets into an area it's hard to break. As I was thinking on this, the Lord interjected...

As it is in the natural, so is it in the spiritual...

Just as patterns of drought can inhabit a region, so too can spiritual drought become a pattern with believers. Perhaps our daily patterns and habits have led us away from consecration and prayer time which draw us into the presence of God. A busy calendar or preoccupation with other things can keep us from the spiritual rainfall we so desperately need. We must intentionally change our daily habits in order to break that pattern and have the Holy Spirit rain upon our hearts. Hosea 10:12 exhorts God's people to "Sow to yourselves in righteousness, reap in mercy, break up your fallow ground; for it is time to seek the Lord, till he come and rain righteousness upon you" (KJV). Lord help me to seek you daily in prayer and turn over my heart as a plow turns the earth. Help me to await your presence which brings sweet rain into my dry and thirsty soul. I give you praise for your faithfulness. In Jesus' name, AMEN!

SEPTEMBER 1

Today is my daughter-in-law, Danielle's birthday. She is a wonderful mama and the perfect wife for my son. I believe that it is no accident when children are interested in learning. My 'daughter' is a lover of reading, and she is instilling this amazing passion into her children. She is also very passionate about inspiring her children to explore the world around them through science kits and investigating nature. This year, she picked a milkweed that was housing two monarch larvae and brought it indoors where she could teach the kids about the life cycle or this amazing creature. They watched it grow into a caterpillar and then become a pupa (chrysalis). They witnessed the caterpillar's metamorphosis into the amazing Monarch Butterfly and then they released it into nature! What an experience these kiddos had all because their mama is very intentional on teaching them through experiences. As I thought about this, the Lord quickened to me…

As it is in the natural, so is it in the spiritual…

In the same way that Dani is intentional in creating opportunities to instill a love for reading and learning about nature in her children, so too was the Lord intentional in creating a world where His power and glory cannot be denied. It was no accident that this world came into being for the Lord God Almighty provided countless evidences that He is the author and creator of this amazing world in which we live. Genesis 1:1 tells us plainly, "In the beginning God created the heavens and the earth;" Psalms 19:1 exclaims, "The heavens declare the glory of God; the skies proclaim the work of His hands;" Isaiah 45:18 declares, "For thus says the LORD— He who created the heavens; He is God; He formed the earth and fashioned it; He established it; He did not create it to be empty, but formed it to be inhabited— "I am the LORD, and there is no other;" Romans 1:20 reasons with us, "For since the creation of the world God's invisible qualities, His eternal power and divine nature, have been clearly seen, being understood from His workmanship, so that men are without excuse" (BSB). Lord I praise you for your awesome and intentional creation of every natural thing we know here on this Earth. Through this, we have the opportunity to learn and be inspired to give you glory for the beauty we enjoy each day. In Jesus' name, Amen!

SEPTEMBER 2

In our prayer room before service last Sunday, the Lord suddenly revealed to me a picture of myself, standing in a field with my hands outstretched and open (not closed). He impressed upon me that people cannot receive something that is being handed to them if they do not open their hands. He spoke into my spirit a message of truth:

As it is in the natural, so is it in the spiritual…

"You need to live your life in the spiritual posture of having open hands outstretched so that you can not only give to others but also can receive of me." As I was grasping this moment, he further instructed me to understand that when I live with closed hands (or a closed heart) I can't give, nor can I receive!! In Luke 6:38 during the sermon on the mount, Jesus instructed us, "Give, and it shall be given unto you; good measure, pressed down, and shaken together, and running over, shall men give into your bosom. For with the same measure that ye mete withal it shall be measured to you again" (KJV). Lord help me to be generous with all of the possessions you have given me. Help me to also be ready to receive from others and from you! Amen.

SEPTEMBER 3

This time of year proves to be very trying in many ways. Fall means back to school for my husband and I. It also brings fall allergies which have been very troublesome for my husband in the past. He struggles with this ailment each year and although he hates to go to the doctor, he often will do just that. While trying to find the perfect balance between modern medicine and God's ability to heal, my husband grapples with the great questions of life. Where is God when I am in despair and I can't breathe? Why won't he heal me? What am I doing to deserve this? These are some of the questions that all of mankind have pondered throughout the centuries. As I think on this, the Lord reminds me...

As it is in the natural, so is it in the spiritual...

In the same way that physical ailments cause us to suffer and seek relief, so too ought we recognize when our spirit is afflicted. Many of us continually struggling with the same spiritual ailment. We are in need of the touch of the Great Physician and yet, we try to deal with our sins and our problems on our own. Sometimes, we wonder where God is when we are in despair and can't seem to lift ourselves out. We question whether God is there at all and why we must go through these struggles! The Lord wants us to know that His word has answers for every spiritual affliction mankind has ever struggled with! Simply stated we must first recognize that we have a sin problem! I know it's not a popular statement in today's self-absorbed, self-ruled, if I think it's ok it's ok - culture to admit that we have NO hope unless we obey God's word and seek to fix our brokenness through Jesus. I John chapter 1 has our answer: "4 And these things write we unto you, that your joy may be full. 5 This then is the message which we have heard of him, and declare unto you, that God is light, and in him is no darkness at all. 6 If we say that we have fellowship with him, and walk in darkness, we lie, and do not the truth: 7 But if we walk in the light, as he is in the light, we have fellowship one with another, and the blood of Jesus Christ his Son cleanseth us from all sin. 8 If we say that we have no sin, we deceive ourselves, and the truth is not in us. 9 If we confess our sins, he is faithful and just to forgive us our sins, and to cleanse us from all unrighteousness. 10 If we say that we have not sinned, we make him a liar, and his word is not in us" (KJV, emphasis mine). Once we have come to this place, it is only then that we can be made spiritually whole...and this must be done often if not daily. Dear Lord, your word gives us vital instruction on dealing with all of our heart ailments. Help us to come to you each morning with a sincere heart seeking to be cleansed so we may embrace a healthy and fruitful spiritual life. In Jesus' name, Amen!

SEPTEMBER 4

As a teacher, I used to spend a great deal of time worrying about my teaching style, my presentation, and my pedagogical skills. My daily question was, "Am I being effective?" In recent years, the state has even developed an entire system by which teachers are evaluated based on student progress. This has caused much concern and anxiety on the part of many teachers. During my early years as a teacher, the Lord revealed to me that my students were not just brains to be filled with static information, but rather, they are individual souls to be fed with love and encouragement. They, along with my children and grandchildren, were my ministry. He reminded me that...

As it is in the natural, so is it in the spiritual...

Students are taught many things as they go through their school years. But just as academic knowledge is vital to the success of their test scores, so too, in order to survive this sometimes-brutal world, our kids need to understand that they are valuable, priceless, wondrously and marvelously created for a purpose by a loving God who has a plan for their lives. This is my mission. Above all else. Yes, I teach the material and test my students to see if they 'got it', and yes, I care that they are successful on state tests, but what matters most is that they know that I care about them and that they are precious little beings who can make a difference in this world. Psalms 32:8 says, "I will instruct you and teach you in the way you should go; I will counsel you with my loving eye on you" (NIV). Lord, help me to always remember that children, above all, need love and encouragement. Help me to teach with that knowledge etched upon my heart. In Jesus' name, Amen!

SEPTEMBER 5

My husband came in the other day after pulling weeds out back and said he had somehow gotten poison ivy or something similar on his arm. It soon became itchy as the blisters were forming. He was baffled as to how or where he came into contact with the culprit weed, since we do not have woods on our property. Nevertheless, he apparently touched some irritant and it definitely has given him an angry, blistering rash. As I thought about this, the Lord opened my eyes...

As it is in the natural, so is it in the spiritual...

Just as we can unknowingly contract poison ivy or some similar irritant, so too can we come in contact with spiritual attitudes that will undoubtedly affect our spirit. Whether it is that grouchy complainer at work, or someone sitting next to us in the pew, the attitudes of others can most definitely rub off onto us. How vital is it then that we surround ourselves with those who Love the Lord and want to submit their lives to Him and bring glory to His name? Paul discusses this in I Corinthians 15. Verse 33 reminds us, "Do not be deceived: Bad company corrupts good character" (BSB). On the other hand, as Proverbs 27:17 says, "Iron sharpeneth iron; so a man sharpeneth the countenance of his friend" (KJV). Dear Lord, help us to remember that negative attitudes, gossip and foul language can be like the poison ivy that rubs off on us even when we aren't aware of it! Give us wisdom as we strive to walk out a positive life that brings you glory! In Jesus' name, Amen!

SEPTEMBER 6

My little dog Jewel is so cute and funny. She has learned how to get my attention when she wants something. If she wants to play catch, she brings her ball to me and sets it on my lap. If she wants to go outside, she will sit across the room and "Ruff, Ruff" until I get up. She indeed has learned how to communicate her needs in a very clear way! As I thought about this, the Lord nudged me…

As it is in the natural, so is it in the spiritual…

Just as my little dog does not hesitate to bring all of her needs and wants to my attention, so we ought to bring ours to the Lord, for He is waiting for us to talk to Him! I John 5:14 reminds us, "This is the confidence which we have before Him, that, if we ask anything according to His will, He hears us. And if we know that He hears us in whatever we ask, we know that we have the requests which we have asked from Him" (NAS). Dear Lord, help me to remember that each and every need I have is of concern to you. Just as my pup trusts me Lord, help me to trust in your will and purpose for my life. In Jesus' name, Amen!

SEPTEMBER 7

The walnut tree in our back yard is quite the productive thing. It drops tons of nuts each year and, if left alone, they will quickly sprout another tree! If you aren't careful, you will soon have a forest instead of a yard! As I thought on this the Lord spoke to me...

As it is in the natural, so is it in the spiritual...

We are called to spread the good news to others who need Jesus. The word is like those walnuts, which when dropped into the right conditions, will quickly sprout a living thing that can grow and be productive and continue to spread the good news. In Mark chapter 4, Jesus explains the parable of the seed: "26 And He was saying, The kingdom of God is like a man who casts seed upon the soil; 27 and he goes to bed at night and gets up by day, and the seed sprouts and grows - how, he himself does not know. 28 The soil produces crops by itself; first the blade, then the head, then the mature grain in the head. 29 But when the crop permits, he immediately puts in the sickle, because the harvest has come" (NAS). Lord, help me to remember that each soul I encounter has potential to become like my walnut trees; that they may receive your word and produce fruit for your kingdom that your harvest might be plentiful! Help me not to be fearful to spread the word for I know you are the one who causes the seed to sprout and grow. In Jesus' name, Amen!

SEPTEMBER 8

It seems that each summer, a new weed develops in my yard. You get rid of one type of weed, but then the next year another one creeps into the yard. If you ignore them, they will not go away, but rather, they will grow larger and spread and completely take over the yard! Prevention is best, as any gardener or groundskeeper will tell you. You must prepare in advance with products formulated to keep the weeds from ever sprouting. If some are yet found, they must be eradicated completely lest they continue to spread and ruin your lawn. As I thought on this, the Lord pointed out...

As it is in the natural, so is it in the spiritual...

Just like weeds, sin is an insidious creeper, which will seemingly appear out of nowhere and attach itself into the lawn of our hearts. Prevention is the key to keeping our heart free from sin! We must learn the importance of daily prayer and meditation on God's word when we search our hearts for those tiny little weeds that would invade and take over! Then, when sin is found, it can be eradicated! You name the sin, and rest assured, it did not begin as a giant bed of weeds, but rather a small thought that was allowed to grow until it was suddenly too big to get rid of. Colossians 3:5 exhorts us: "So put to death the sinful, earthly things lurking within you. Have nothing to do with sexual immorality, impurity, lust, and evil desires. Don't be greedy, for a greedy person is an idolater, worshiping the things of this world" (NIV). Lord, I know that prayer and meditation on your word are the remedies to keeping my heart free from sin! Thank you for showing me the way to maintain a clean heart! Help me to be attentive to those tiny weeds that try to creep in and take over! In Jesus' name, Amen!

SEPTEMBER 9

The Aurora borealis, also known as Northern Lights, were said to be out last night. I got up several times and went outdoors to see if I could view them. Alas...I could not see due to the clouds, but millions upon millions of people were no doubt looking up to catch a glimpse of this phenomena. As I thought on this, the Lord whispered...

As it is in the natural, so is it in the spiritual...

In the same way that many people plan and wait and look to the north for those amazing glowing lights, so too must we plan and wait and look for God's promise of the most awesome event yet to come. In Matthew 24, Jesus describes this glorious event: "27 For as the lightning comes from the east and shines as far as the west, so will be the coming of the Son of Man" (ESV). "29 Immediately after the tribulation of those days the sun will be darkened, and the moon will not give its light, and the stars will fall from heaven, and the powers of the heavens will be shaken. 30 At that time the sign of the Son of Man will appear in heaven, and all the tribes of the earth will mourn. They will see the Son of Man coming on the clouds of heaven, with power and great glory. 31 And He will send out His angels with a loud trumpet call, and they will gather His elect from the four winds, from one end of the heavens to the other" (BSB). Indeed, millions of people eagerly await Jesus' triumphant return, that we might see Him in all of His glory, but many do not believe or are too busy and concerned with this life to care about the most glorious event yet to happen. Lord, help each of us to keep our eye on the Eastern sky and acknowledge our desperate need for Jesus Christ and the salvation that is found through His name! Amen!

SEPTEMBER 10

Today I was reading about the children of Israel and how the Lord delivered them from captivity. The odd thing was that once they were free, they began to grumble and even wished to be back in Egypt where at least they wouldn't starve. What they didn't know or believe was that just around the corner, the Lord was planning for their provision. He heard their grumbling and gave them quail and manna. Even then, they continued to be ungrateful and yearned to go back to captivity. While pondering how utterly foolish those Israelites were, the Lord opened my eyes...

As it is in the natural, so is it in the spiritual...

God has made a way for us to come out of captivity, aka, Egypt, aka our sinful life apart from HIM, and it is his desire to lead us into the Promised Land. He beckons us to leave the former sins we have entangled ourselves in and "Come unto me…all ye who are weary and heavy laden…and I will give you rest" (Matthew 11:28). When we finally "lay aside every weight and the sin which doth so easily beset us and run with patience the race that is set before us (Hebrews 12:1)" then we will truly enter into the promised land. For years, I have struggled with letting go of the things that held me captive for many years. The things of this world bring nothing good into my life, and yet, like the children of Israel, I keep looking over my shoulder as if something better is over there. I keep stepping back into Egypt, away from God's calling, to test it out one more time just in case it might bring more joy, peace or happiness to my life. Am I crazy? Of course! The bible says it is like a dog returning to its vomit when the fool returns to his folly (Proverbs 26:11; 2 Peter 2:22). Lord, please open my eyes to where I am headed… please point me toward the promised land and keep me from going back to that which once enslaved me! In Jesus' name, Amen!

SEPTEMBER 11

This day has become a memorial to millions of people all over our nation, but especially to those who lost loved ones in the attacks on New York City in 2001. Those of us who remember it can usually recall exactly where we were and what we were doing when we heard the news. The unsuspecting thousands of people who were at work in the twin towers in Manhattan that day did not know what was happening when the first plane crashed into the building. This horrifying attack on America the Beautiful was an unbelievable shock to people around the world. As I think about this and the evil minds that orchestrated such an atrocity the Lord reminds me…

As it is in the natural, so is it in the spiritual...

In the same way that the al Qaeda terrorists plotted, planned and precipitated the attacks on America on 911, so too does the enemy of our soul plot, plan and precipitate attacks on our soul. We are often unsuspecting of his wiles but we should heed the word of God: 1 Peter 5:8 tells us, "Be sober, be vigilant; because your adversary the devil, as a roaring lion, walketh about, seeking whom he may devour" (KJV). We must remember that we have a very real enemy of our soul who wants to blast our faith to smithereens. We must daily seek the Lord for His wisdom, plan and protection of this most vital element of Christianity. Without our faith, we lose hope. As Hebrew's 11:1 says, "Now faith is the substance of things hoped for, the evidence of things not seen" (KJV). Dear Lord, help us to be aware of the battle that is raging for our soul. Help us to be prepared to counter his attacks with your word, your spiritual power and my faith! In Jesus' name, Amen

SEPTEMBER 12

You are what you eat. This timeless adage simplifies the basic principle which teaches us that proper nutrition and proper exercise is necessary if we want a healthy body. When we overeat or take in too many carbs and put out too little exercise, we pay the price and gain weight, we feel sluggish, and we are lethargic and weary. As I thought about this, the Lord pointed out to me...

As it is in the natural, so is it in the spiritual...

Our spiritual self can only grow and be healthy and strong when we feed it properly. We must nurture that part of ourselves even more diligently than we do our physical body (which will eventually die anyway!). We do this by feeding on God's word (Jesus said in Matthew 4:4 "Man shall not live by bread alone, but by every word that proceedeth out of the mouth of God" (KJV); and prayer and worship and actively seeking after God. Jesus said in Matthew 5:6 "Blessed are they which do hunger and thirst after righteousness: for they shall be filled" (KJV). We must monitor what we consume in the area of music, television, radio, social media and other internet sites for they are absorbed into our spirit. If we feed upon too much junk, we will pay the price and feel spiritually sluggish, lethargic, and too weary to do that which we were called to do. We must "As newborn babes, desire the sincere milk of the word, that ye may grow thereby: if so be ye have tasted that the Lord is gracious" (1 Peter 2:2-3). Psalms 34:8 says "Oh taste and see that the Lord is good." The more we feed on the goodness of God, the less appetite we will have for 'junk' and we'll soon find that only He can satisfy our hunger. Lord turn my hunger away from the things that aren't worthwhile and toward those things that are. In Jesus' name, Amen!

SEPTEMBER 13

Today, I noticed there was dust and a few cobwebs gathering behind the little birdhouse I have beside my front door so I went and got the broom and moved the birdhouse and bench and antique ice cream pail and swept the area clean. The area was much more pleasing to the eye once it had been swept clean. I turned to continue sweeping but noticed that the rest of the porch was clean. It occurred to me that where there are objects or even clutter, dirt and debris will collect. As I noted this obvious truth, the Lord pointed out that...

As it is in the natural, so is it in the spiritual...

Just as dirt and debris collects around objects and clutter in your home, so too will dirt and debris collect around objects and clutter in your heart. We must examine our heart and give it a good sweeping out on a regular basis to ensure it is clean and pleasing for God to look upon. Through prayer, God will be faithful to show us the objects that need to be moved out and all we have to do is take hold of the broom of repentance and our hearts can be clean once again! II Corinthians 7:1 instructs us, "Because we have these promises, dear friends, let us cleanse ourselves from everything that can defile our body or spirit. And let us work toward complete holiness because we fear God" (NLT). Lord you are so full of mercy and grace. Thank you for providing a way for me to cleanse my heart and return to you daily through your mighty name and the blood of Jesus. Amen.

SEPTEMBER 14

Soup that is allowed to simmer on the stove or in a crock pot seems to be more flavorful that soup that is rushed out of the pot. Likewise, a roast that is slowly cooked is much more tender and much easier to chew than one that is undercooked. As I pondered this truth, it was quickened to me by the Lord…

As it is in the natural, so is it in the spiritual…

We are often impatient when we pray for something specific. Perhaps it is that lost loved one or healing. Perhaps we are seeking Gods will for our future in a certain area of our life. It could be some other spiritual request but, as Isaiah 40:31 promises, "But they that wait upon the Lord shall renew their strength; they shall mount up with wings as eagles; they shall run, and not be weary; and they shall walk, and not faint" (KJV). Lord, help me to remember that your timing is not necessarily my timing. Help me to learn to be patient and wait upon You at all times. In Jesus' name, Amen!

SEPTEMBER 15

When I opened my refrigerator this morning, I noticed an odor that could be described as less than pleasant. I thought to myself, "I really need to take some time and clean this out thoroughly one of these days, but I don't have time right now." As I walked away with my morning coffee, it occurred to me...

As it is in the natural, so is it in the spiritual...

When was the last time I took time for a thorough spiritual cleansing? 1 John 1: 7-10 says "7 But if we walk in the light, as he is in the light, we have fellowship one with another, and the blood of Jesus Christ his Son cleanseth us from all sin. 8 If we say that we have no sin, we deceive ourselves, and the truth is not in us. 9. If we confess our sins, he is faithful and just to forgive us our sins and cleanse us from all unrighteousness. 10. If we say we have not sinned, we make him a liar, and his word is not in us." So, three things must be done for 'cleansing' to occur: we must recognize we have sinned, we must confess those sins and ask for forgiveness and we must walk in the light, following Christ in fellowship with other believers. Just as it takes time, effort and a decision to thoroughly clean my fridge, it also requires time, effort and a decision to be clean spiritually. Lord, please help me remember to come to you regularly for spiritual cleansing so that my life is a sweet-smelling savor unto you and not an unpleasant odor. In Jesus' name, Amen!

SEPTEMBER 16

Have you ever been around someone who seems to only speak with criticism whenever they open their mouth? This type of conversation can be harmful and also contagious for it seems they are always trying to get others to agree with them. I believe this behavior comes from that person's discontentment with their own life. The old adage, "Misery loves company" is what comes to mind! As I thought about this, the Lord allowed me to see...

As it is in the natural, so is it in the spiritual...

In the natural, we hear the negativity and we see the facial expressions of these unhappy souls, but in the spiritual, we must recognize their deep and desperate need to be accepted and loved. I believe each of us have a "Jesus shaped hole" in our heart which can only be filled by Him. If we try to fill it on our own, we become disillusioned, self-centered and critical of others. There are many bible passages about gossip and the words we speak. Proverbs 6 is plain: "16 These six things doth the LORD hate: yea, seven are an abomination unto him: 17 A proud look, a lying tongue, and hands that shed innocent blood, 18 An heart that deviseth wicked imaginations, feet that be swift in running to mischief, 19 A false witness that speaketh lies, and he that soweth discord among brethren" (KJV). Lord, help me to remember each time I open my mouth to speak words, to ask of You for guidance for your words are full of wisdom and truth. In Jesus' name, Amen!

SEPTEMBER 17

I was reading in Matthew chapter 26 this morning about Judas' betrayal that led to Jesus' capture and how Peter denied Him three times in one hour, even after strongly objecting when His master foretold him of this. As I read, I thought how despicable it was that Jesus' followers would do such a terrible thing. How can we deny the One who brings us new life, hope, joy, peace, forgiveness, and purpose? As I was thinking this, the Lord revealed to me...

As it is in the natural, so is it in the spiritual...

When we are born again, we are called to a new life with a new purpose; however, when we turn back to our old habits and actions in the natural, we are, in fact, rejecting and denying the work of Christ's spirit in our lives and, in essence, we are the same as Judas and Peter. 2 Peter 2 is very strong on this: verse 20 says, "If indeed they have escaped the corruption of the world through the knowledge of our Lord and Savior Jesus Christ, only to be entangled and overcome by it again, their final condition is worse than it was at first. 21 It would have been better for them not to have known the way of righteousness than to have known it and then to turn away from the holy commandment passed on to them. 22 Of them the proverbs are true: "A dog returns to its vomit," and, "A sow that is washed goes back to her wallowing in the mud." Lord we know that our actions reveal our inward spiritual condition. When we obey and follow Your calling for our lives, we are showing faith in Your work and redemptive power; when we disobey and turn back to our old habits and ways, we are betraying YOU! The only One who can deliver us and bring the peace and joy we seek. Help us to stay true to your calling and will for our lives! In Jesus' name, Amen!

SEPTEMBER 18

Sipping my coffee, I gaze out the window as the sun peeks up over the horizon. The ripening bean field outside of my window reminds me that fall is very near. Green, lush leaves are now changing to deep golden color as they die. It is a beautiful thing when a new season is being ushered in. As I thought on this, the Lord quickened to me that…

As it is in the natural, so is it in the spiritual…

Just as nature signifies this new fall season with the dying of leaves, and the golden ripe fields, so too must we embrace a new season spiritually by allowing some things in our lives to die. We cannot move forward into newness of life until we let some things go, but many times it is difficult to do. Paul talks about this in Romans 6: 1-15 as being a form of death when he reminds us that baptism is the natural form of dying to sin. He writes that, "We are those who have died to sin" and that "We are buried with him through baptism into death so that just as Christ was raised from the dead through the glory of the Father, we too may live a new life" (NIV). He goes on to explain that sin must die in our lives in order for the spirit to rule and reign. We must daily put sin to death so that it no longer is our master by submitting to the Lord's will and not our own. Lord help me to daily commit my life to you, allowing that sinful nature to die so that I can enter this new season of life in you. In Jesus' name, Amen.

SEPTEMBER 19

Yesterday, I tore up much of my little corner garden and cleaned up the potted garden area as Autumn is coming quickly, and back-to-school busyness and cooler days are here. Gardening season was not too productive this year because we were gone away quite a bit this summer. When you aren't diligent, weeds will immediately invade the garden and they can choke out the vegetables you planted. As I thought about this, the Lord reminded me...

As it is in the natural, so is it in the spiritual...

In the same way weeds can take over a garden very quickly, so too can my thoughts take over those spiritual seeds sown into my heart. I may have heard a great sermon, been involved in an amazing time of worship and read my bible, but if I don't keep my mind on the Lord and pray continually, negative thoughts, worries and fears can quickly invade my heart and try to take control. We must take this ground back so that the Lord has control over it. The bible gives us much direction on how to do this. Paul reminds us in II Corinthians 10: 4-5 that "The weapons of our warfare are not carnal (human) but mighty through GOD to the pulling down of strongholds. Casting down imaginations and every high thing that exalteth itself against the knowledge of God" (KJV). Another translation says, "We must destroy any intellectual arrogance that oppose the knowledge of God." Romans 12:2 tells us we must not be "Conformed to this world: but be ye transformed by the renewing of your mind, that ye may prove what is that good, and acceptable, and perfect, will of God." In each of these passages we are, in essence, told that we must remove the weeds from our seedbed, our mind, so that we can renew our mind to the Glory of God. Lord, help me to cast out any thoughts that oppose you. Help me to renew my mind daily so that I can live in you will. In Jesus' name, Amen!

SEPTEMBER 20

On this day in 2013, my son and his wife welcomed their first child into this world. Brendan came to us in the midst of a flurry of concerns over his mama's prolonged labor. We were so thankful that both he and his mommy were safe and sound when he arrived. As he has grown, we can see his temperament and personality developing as my son and daughter in law guide and direct him. He is a passionate child who openly shows his emotions whether he is being sweet and loving, playful and silly, or upset and angry! I watch his mom and dad teach him how to respond to life's unpredictable moments, correcting or encouraging when needed and it always, eventually brings about resolution and peace. Oh, how I love this child! As I think about Brendan and pray for him daily, the Lord impresses upon me that...

As it is in the natural, so is it in the spiritual...

We humans were created with such a wide range of emotions and personality traits. We all have the capability to be sweet and loving, playful and silly, or upset and angry! And the truth of the matter is, the factors that determine our mood for the moment can often be out of our control! In the same way that a child responds to his environment, and must be taught by their parents how to modulate and control his reactions, so too must we listen to our heavenly Father, and learn how to navigate through this life spiritually. We should tune into the Lord's mind so that we can gain understanding about the factors that test our faith and attempt to create chaos or confusion. Isaiah 48:17 confirms, "Thus says the Lord, my Redeemer, the Holy One of Israel: "I am the Lord your God, Who teaches you to profit, Who leads you by the way you should go" (NASB). We need to obey God's voice instead of leaning on our human reasoning for He is there to guide us through this life. Like a child ought to be able to trust their parent, so too we can rest in his wisdom and have peace of mind! Amen!

SEPTEMBER 21

I went outside last night just before dark to get a little fresh air and exercise in my yard. I walked around our English walnut trees and noticed a few nuts had fallen. As I went to gather them, I noticed how small they were. I wondered for a moment why and then remembered that we had a drought for a good part of this summer. Less rain means less fruit. As I thought this the Lord nudged me...

As it is in the natural, so is it in the spiritual...

Just as the fruit from our trees will lack in production this fall due to not enough rain, so too will our spiritual fruit be lacking if we are not receiving enough precipitation from heaven. Rain is likened to the Holy Spirit throughout the bible. Hosea 6:3 promises, "Oh, that we might know the LORD! Let us press on to know him. He will respond to us as surely as the arrival of dawn or the coming of rains in early spring" (NLT). Jesus called himself the "Living Water" which John 7:37-39 explains as being the Holy Spirit. Without this living water, we would end up in spiritual drought. Our faith would dry up. If we want to be fruitful and productive and healthy spiritually, we must water our spirit and soul by allowing His presence to flood over us each day through the reading of his word and prayer. Lord, help me to remember to take time each day to allow your spirit to nourish my spirit and soul with your wondrous Living Water. In Jesus' name, Amen!

SEPTEMBER 22

My husband and I were talking about students who appear to be learning in class, but are really not getting it. They complete the work they are assigned. They use their textbook to look things up and do well on the homework. However, when it comes to the quizzes and tests, they fail miserably! They obviously did not attain this knowledge needed to pass the test! We are left wondering why they are not getting it! Is it something we are doing or not doing? Are they just going through the motions rather that truly learning the material? When reading my bible this morning the Lord revealed to me that...

As it is in the natural, so is it in the spiritual...

II Timothy 3 describes people who are always learning but never acquiring (truth or real knowledge). 7 The Amplified version says: "These weak women will listen to anybody who will teach them; they are forever inquiring and getting information, but are never able to arrive at a recognition and knowledge of the Truth" (AMP). Many who are reading this have been in church and serving the Lord for a long time. We have His spirit living in us. We read his word and even attend bible study. We agree with what it says. There is no doubt that we have been called to fight the good fight. Yet there are some areas on our personal battlefield that we have yet to conquer. We have repeatedly been lured by the enemy to step across the line. We have wavered back and forth between embracing our convictions and rejecting them. We seek counsel from those who are not kingdom minded. We seek ways to fit into this world rather than stand apart from it as light and salt. Verse 6 gives the answer saying, we are "slaves of sin and are controlled by all sorts of desires" (ISV). These passions and desires which are not from God but which we allow to invade our hearts are exactly what keeps us from truly attain the truth of God's word. Oh Lord! Help me recognize when I am following my passions and desires rather than yours! Help me to begin to truly attain the knowledge and apply what I learn so that I can pass the test each day! In Jesus' name, Amen.

SEPTEMBER 23

Have you ever tried to braid a rope or cord by just twisting two pieces? It really isn't going to hold is it? A third strand is necessary to create a strong enough braid to be of any use. As I thought and prayed on this, the Lord revealed to me that...

As it is in the natural, so is it in the spiritual...

He showed me that just as a cord can be strengthened by adding strands, so too can our marriage relationship be strengthened by making sure to 'add' the Lord and His will for our life into the cord so that we may become a three-fold cord, which is "not easily broken" (Ecclesiastes 4:12). He further opened my mind to the image of the cord unraveling if the third strand: GOD is removed. It would quickly fall apart and be rendered useless for any purpose. The awesome thing is the simple repair that occurs to the cord when that third strand is woven back together with the two. Friend, if you have come undone and feel unraveled in your life, consider the metaphor of the three-fold cord. If you are married, ask God to help create a three-fold cord between yourself, your spouse and Him. Ask the Lord to enter back into your life and/or your marriage and he will immediately bring strength to you. Heavenly Father, we thank you for the strength you bring to our marriage and our life. We desperately need you to be intertwined into all areas of our lives so that we may be strong through the trials of life. Amen!

SEPTEMBER 24

When thinking more about the three-fold cord, this morning, the Lord continued to reveal awesome insights to me. I pondered the purpose of a cord. Let us imagine that this cord was used primarily for tents. A tent is staked to the ground with cords, so obviously if any one of these cords is not strong, it jeopardizes the entire structure. As I thought of this, the Lord quickened to me...

As it is in the natural, so is it in the spiritual…

The cord represents one person. If one person within a home or within a church body comes unraveled from the purpose for which they were created, it weakens and jeopardizes everything else. The family is at a much greater risk for falling apart and the responsibilities that person held within the church may be neglected. Romans12:4 says, "A body is made up of many parts, and each of them has its own use" (CEV). We all must do our individual part by staying intertwined closely to the Lord so that we can be strong and useful for the purpose we were created to carry out. Lord, please help me to intertwine myself to you and your purpose. Help me to be useful in the area that you have designated for me. In Jesus' name, Amen.

SEPTEMBER 25

I was looking at an internet picture the other day of the Alaskan sea where it meets with the Ocean but does not mix. It created a distinct line of dark and light water that seemed to be separated by an invisible force. As I studied the picture and wondered at this amazing natural phenomenon, the Lord illuminated something to me. The two bodies of water do indeed come together and they exist side by side, but amazingly, they do not intermix and thus they retain their true color! Some say this photo is a hoax, but when I was thinking about it, the Lord turned my thoughts to this…

As it is in the natural, so is it in the spiritual…

In the same way that those two bodies of water are allegedly adjacent to one another, yet do not mix, so too are we called to go into all the world and preach the gospel, but we are not supposed to join with the world and embrace and become part of it. I John 2:1 tells us: "Love not the world, neither the things that are in the world. If any man love the world, the love of the Father is not in him" (KJV). Dear Lord, thank you for revealing these truths to me. Help us each to love others, but retain our Christian values. Protect us from the influences that come from living in this world. Help us to walk carefully as you would have us walk in every situation that we may retain our true color and fulfill our purpose as Christians and examples of you! Amen!

SEPTEMBER 26

Today, my bible reading was in Numbers 33. The reading was about the children of Israel and God's promise to them regarding the land of Canaan. He told them that they must drive out the inhabitants of that land before they possess it, or if they do not, those inhabitants will become "pricks in your eyes, thorns in your sides and shall vex you in the land wherein ye dwell" (KJV). As I read this the lord quickened to me that...

As it is in the natural, so is it in the spiritual...

God has given us a great and awesome spiritual promise through the Acts 2 experience. This new-testament covenant was issued by Peter, the Rock upon which Jesus said he would build his church. After witnessing the outpouring of the Holy Ghost, the crowd was confused. Peter gave his first new testament sermon, telling the people that they had just crucified the Messiah, and what they now see and hear was the fulfillment of Joel's prophecy (vs 16) when God promised to send the Holy Ghost. Peter then exhorted the crowd: "38 Then Peter said unto them, Repent, and be baptized every one of you in the name of Jesus Christ for the remission of sins, and ye shall receive the gift of the Holy Ghost. 39 For the promise is unto you, and to your children, and to all that are afar off, even as many as the Lord our God shall call" (KJV). Indeed, the Holy Spirit of Christ was sent here to empower us to conquer the sin which so easily besets us. Our inheritance is promised to us, but as with the children of Israel, we must not allow the enemy to reside in our life any longer, or he will surely blind us to the truth by putting 'pricks in our eyes.' He will certainly be a thorn in our side as we attempt to make progress in obedience to God's calling, and he will definitely try to vex us throughout our lifetime, even though we dwell 'in Christ.' Lord, we know that in order to live a joyful, peaceful existence as a Christian, we MUST do battle with the enemy and with your great power living in us, we can live in the promised land which you have given us! Amen!

SEPTEMBER 27

Several years ago, my sister and I went on an amazing trip to Paris. It was a surreal, once in a lifetime trip and we enjoyed all of the sights and experiences we could fit into our days! When we arrived at the airport to come home, there were armed soldiers at each entrance. Two days earlier, a diplomat had been killed by the group we now know as Isis. Seeing those soldiers in full combat gear was quite unnerving, but we went on about our business. The presence if those soldiers reminded me that we life in an unpredictable and sometimes unsafe world, but it also brought me a feeling of protection and security. As I thought on this the Lord revealed to me that…

As it is in the natural, so is it in the spiritual…

The bible repeatedly tells how God sends Angels and even armies of angels to defend, protect and deliver his saints. One example is found in Daniel chapter six when the Lord sent an angel to protect Daniel all night long in a den of hungry lions. In verse 22, Daniel told the King, "My God hath sent his angel, and hath shut the lions' mouths, that they have not hurt me…" (KJV). There are many other accounts of Angels protecting God's people. It is important to note that it is The Lord God Almighty who is in charge of the Angels and it is He who dispatches them for their various duties and responsibilities. Deuteronomy 3:22 reminds us, "22 Ye shall not fear them: for the LORD your God he shall fight for you" (KJV). Thank you Lord, for sending angels to do battle for us and guard us from harm. Hallelujah! Amen!

SEPTEMBER 28

Walking through a piece of land that had not been farmed for a number of years, I encountered thorns, small trees and thick patches of weeds and thistles growing where there was once a bountiful crop to harvest. I pondered how quickly the field was overtaken by these undesirable vegetations and how that without modern day equipment, this would be a nightmare to restore to a point where one could plant a crop that would produce well. What was once rich and productive soil is now filled with weeds, vines, brush, and thorns. Even today, when the farmer decides to go back and plant that field in an attempt to produce a good crop, he must then spend more time and effort to remove the thorns and weeds from the soil so that he can plant seed. As I thought about this, the Lord pointed out...

As it is in the natural, so is it in the spiritual...

The backslidden soul who moves aside from God is like a field that has been in 'set-aside' for a year or two. Likewise, when we turn aside from the Lord, we must deal with a lot of weed-pulling and untangling of vines, chopping down of brush and deliberate removal of thorns that have stubbornly grown up in our heart, mind and soul. Proverbs 22:5 uses this metaphor to tell us, "Thorns and snares lie on the path of the perverse; he who guards his soul stays far from them" (BSB). Lord help me to guard my heart and daily allow YOU to gently but thoroughly remove the weeds, thorns, vines and brush that can so quickly accumulate and take over. Let my heart be good soil that it might produce good things for your Kingdom. In Jesus' name, Amen!

SEPTEMBER 29

Today my husband pulled in the driveway and told me to take a look at his pick-up truck. He had taken the rear fender off the passenger side and it was quite rusted where the fender had been. A month or so ago, while cutting wood, I had accidentally backed into a tree and damaged the fender. I felt really bad because prior to that, the truck 'appeared" to be in pretty decent shape! He pointed out that the paint had just been covering up what was a truly unhealthy body. He also pointed out that there is an analogy there!

As it is in the natural, so is it in the spiritual...

It seems we focus a great deal of time and effort in our appearances in our society today. We primp and fuss over our hair or what we are wearing and all the while, the Lord is calling us to focus on renewing our MIND and our INNER MAN. By spending so much energy and time on our appearance, we neglect those things that really matter. Just as the truck's rusted body is a far greater problem than the exterior paint job, our inner problems are far more important than what we look like. Matthew 23:27 says "Woe unto you, scribes and Pharisees, hypocrites! for ye are like unto whited sepulchers, which indeed appear beautiful outward, but are within full of dead men's bones, and of all uncleanness" (KJV). Lord, please help me to focus my attention on my inner person and stop concerning myself with appearances, but rather, to be concerned with being more like YOU! In Jesus' name, Amen!

SEPTEMBER 30

We were talking to our friends about how my husband has torn apart our home so that we can add an upstairs bathroom. Our pastor's wife said "Gotta deconstruct so you can reconstruct...that'll preach!" How true it is! As she spoke, God whispered...

As it is in the natural, so is it in the spiritual...

My husband and I will have to literally deconstruct; we must tear our home apart, and the process is NOT comfortable. The entire house will be affected. We must move furniture from one place to another so we can convert a bedroom into a bathroom. We must build walls, add plumbing, electrical wiring and fixtures, and then put everything back together before we will be able to enjoy the fruits of our labors. Likewise, when we come to the Lord, we are all in need of reconstruction. In order for God to actually improve and renovate us, we must allow him to rearrange things in our lives. It's NOT comfortable! We must allow him to get involved in our life so he can re-wire, re-plumb and rebuild us wholly. Psalms 71 illuminates this truth: "19 Your righteousness reaches to the heavens, O God, You who have done great things. Who, O God, is like You? 20 Though you have shown me many troubles and misfortunes, You will revive me once again. Even from the depths of the earth You will bring me back up. 21 You will increase my honor and comfort me once again" (BSB). Lord, help me to remember that construction requires me to let go of how things are and allow changed to come. Help me to remember that this is a process and that YOU want to reconstruct me for your purposes!

OCTOBER 1

As I sit in my tree stand this crisp fall evening, a deer approaches my bait pile. The doe sniffs and looks around as she silently stepped into the range of my deadly arrow. Despite her instincts telling her something was not quite right, she proceeded toward the pile of carrots, unable to resist the temptation I had placed before her. In that moment, God quickened this truth to me...

As it is in the natural, so is it in the spiritual...

The Lord wanted me to see that our own temptations are like the bait pile. Satan uses things that are appealing, and even some things that might seem good for us to lure us out of safety and into harm's way. When we are tempted and drawn away from the Lord, things can become dangerous and even deadly. I Corinthians 10:13 says, "There hath no temptation taken you but such as is common to man: but God is faithful, who will not suffer you to be tempted above that ye are able; but will with the temptation also make a way to escape, that ye may be able to bear it" (KJV). Each of us have our own set of temptations that have proven to be a slippery slope for our spiritual well-being. These things appear to be good, but little do we know that the enemy of our soul is waiting in the shadows to bring us to an untimely death. Not just a physical death but a spiritual death that removes us from the path God had intended for us to be on. Heavenly Father, please go with me and be my protector. Let my heart know when I am stepping toward danger and give me the strength to resist temptations that are not good for me. In Jesus' name! Amen.

OCTOBER 2

This morning my sweetheart and I walked back to swap out the camera cards in our trail cameras we had hung in two different hunting spots. As we look through the pictures, it is apparent that most of the wildlife are unaware they are being photographed. Interestingly, there are a few photos of certain deer who are gaping at the camera and even stepping closer to inspect this box hanging on a tree. It is comical to see them caught in action, as if they have just realized that they are being photographed. As I think about this the Lord impressed upon me that...

As it is in the natural, so is it in the spiritual...

This "deer in the headlights" look makes me wonder how we would look in the photographs of our own lives while God is taking random snapshots of some of our moments in time. Are we always at our best? Or would some of His candid photographs reveal moments in our life we really wish we could delete? Hebrews 4:13 reminds us, "Nothing in all creation is hidden from God's sight; everything is uncovered and exposed before the eyes of Him to whom we must give account"(BSB). Indeed, God is omnipresent in all the earth and He knows our every thought and deed! Heavenly Father, help me to be mindful that you are the great photographer of each second of my life and give me wisdom to conduct myself in a way that will bring glory to you! In Jesus' name! Amen!

OCTOBER 3

The autumn season means busyness and reaping a harvest. In this season, we tend to forget about weeding the garden because we are so busy with reaping the fruits of our labors. However, those late season weeds are dangerous because they not only grow rampant once the vegetables are removed and they suddenly have more room to spread their roots, but also if they are allowed to take root, they have gained a foothold and are there to greet the gardener once the snow melts and the soil warms in the spring. We all know that weeds left unattended, choke the life out of the good things we have planted. It is vitally important then, that we do not become so busy in our seasons of life, that we forget the necessity of plucking up weeds when they first arise.

As I thought about this the Lord revealed to me...

As it is in the natural, so is it in the spiritual...

In the same way weeds must be removed from our garden if we want it to prosper, so too must we pray and fast and cleanse our heart and mind on a daily basis. We do not want to be inattentive in keeping our spirit free from thoughts that will destroy the good things God has planted. Galatians 5:19-21 lists those weeds that can quickly creep in if we aren't careful to be led by the Holy Spirit: "Now the works of the flesh are manifest, which are these, adultery, fornication, uncleanness, lasciviousness, Idolatry, witchcraft, hatred, variance, emulations, wrath, strife, seditions, heresies, envyings, murders, drunkenness, revellings, and such like: of the which I tell you before, as I have also told you in time past, that they which do such things shall not inherit the kingdom of God" (KJV). These unwanted 'weeds' must be rooted out by the work of the Holy Spirit in our lives. Lord, help me not to be so distracted with my 'to-do' list that I am not taking time for prayer and fasting to keep my spirit clean from the weeds that would try to overtake me. As I come to you today, please reveal to me those things that are attempting to invade the garden of my soul. Remove them from me and cast them out of my garden! Thank you for giving us a way to cleanse our hearts each morning. AMEN!

OCTOBER 4

Cold weather is coming quickly, and during the heating season in Michigan, we hardy folk like to burn wood. This takes a great deal of back breaking work, and although we cut during the warm weather too, we inevitably end up trudging out to the woods in the winter to cut and haul wood to get us through the long winter season. As long as we want heat, we must feed that woodstove, and it takes dedication and work to bring the wood to the source of our heat so that it can produce what we need. Thinking about this, the Lord pointed out...

As it is in the natural, so is it in the spiritual...

If we want to produce spiritual flames which warm our cold hearts and radiate that warmth to others around us, we must continually feed that Holy Spirit fire that was started in our spirit. In Matthew 3:11, John the Baptist predicts that Jesus would be the one to "baptize you with the Holy Spirit and with fire." If we stop tending any fire for even a short time, the flames will ebb and eventually go out, and if the flame goes out, it takes a great deal of effort to rekindle the fire. Dear Lord, help me keep that Holy Ghost fire burning in my heart through daily prayer and meditation on God's word and by gathering together with others who are 'on fire' for the Lord. In Jesus' name, AMEN!

OCTOBER 5

Today I was giving a test to one of my students in another classroom. After she got settled in and began the test, the lights went out. I stood up and went to the switch and flicked them off and on again and they reappeared. This continued to occur every five minutes until it dawned on me that the lights must be on a motion sensor. Finally, I located the small object on the ceiling and positioned myself directly underneath it so it would detect my movements as I graded papers while my student was testing. As I told my husband about this perplexing incident tonight, I said "There's a metaphor in there somewhere!" And sure enough the Lord whispered...

As it is in the natural, so is it in the spiritual...

In order to keep the lights on today, I had to position myself in a certain location and maintain a steady connection with the sensor. Likewise, if we want to keep the light of God shining into and through us, we must maintain a continual connection with HIM - we must position ourselves in the right place IN him so we can receive and reflect his light. 1 John 1:7 tells us "But if we walk in the light, as he is in the light, we have fellowship one with another, and the blood of Jesus Christ his Son cleanseth us from all sin" (KJV). Lord, please help me to continue moving in YOUR light so that it shines brightly in my world! In Jesus' name! Amen!

OCTOBER 6

Yesterday, while settling into our friend's guest room, my husband flipped the bed around to have the head on the opposite wall because there was a banging noise in the outside wall. In the process, he found our hostess's phone case, which she had been looking for all over the house. She was ecstatic! She had counted it as lost, so this discovery made it even more exciting to find. As I thought about this, the Lord reminded me...

As it is in the natural, so is it in the spiritual…

Most people do not move their furniture a lot, because it takes work and effort, but when they do, they not only find dust and dirt, but also coins, and sometimes even items that were lost or forgotten. Likewise, when the Lord wants to rearrange things in our life, our first reaction might be to resist the effort and work of change, and we may fear the discovery of the dust or dirt that could be revealed. However, it is also an opportunity for discovering some long-lost treasure that we have counted as lost. In Luke 15 Jesus tells the parable of the lost coin where a woman swept her entire house just to find one lost coin. He then related it, "Likewise, I say unto you, there is joy in the presence of the angels of God over one sinner that repenteth" (KJV). Lord, please help me to be willing to allow you to rearrange things in my life so that perhaps I may rediscover the hidden treasures that have been counted as lost. In Jesus' name! Amen!

OCTOBER 7

Have you ever wondered how a tiny little hangnail can create so much pain? That itty bit of tissue growing, nearly invisible, but growing in an area it isn't supposed to grow can cause quite the level of irritation and pain! It is literally so troublesome, I have a hard time focusing on anything other than finding a pair of clippers and taking care of it! As I was trying to remove one that has been bothering me the past couple of days, the Lord pointed out…

As it is in the natural, so is it in the spiritual…

Seemingly small spiritual problems can create a ton of pain in one's life. If the problem is not snipped off and removed, it can spread and cause all of your attention to be focused on it! We should not go through a day without checking ourselves for these spiritual hangnails. We can then ask God to help us remove them when they are still just a tiny little problem. Song of Solomon 2:15 warns us that the "little foxes" will "spoil the vine."

Likewise, it is the small issues that can give us big pain if we do not tend to it. Lord, help me to remove these hangnails from my life daily so they do not grow and infect my life and the life of those around me. AMEN!

OCTOBER 8

Most of us know someone who has served in the armed forces. One person I know of was home on leave after being in heavy combat for many months. He had left the battles behind and was attempting to reacclimate himself into 'normal' life. Certainly, he was relieved and eager to lay his weapons down and had hopes that he could relax and enjoy life. But as many soldiers report, a pervasive feeling invaded his ability to do so. He felt as if he had no purpose or direction in this new life of 'freedom'. As is the case with many, he felt out of place in this world. He was too keenly aware of the raging battles going on overseas and he was also cognizant of the thousands who were still engaged in the battle for their lives and the lives of others. This soldier was eager to return despite knowing full well what risks, and what fortitude and strength it would require being back in the battle again. As I thought on this, the Lord revealed to me that…

As it is in the natural, so is it in the spiritual…

When a believer turns their life over to Jesus, they are engaging in war. The bible is clear that we will battle spiritual forces when we come to Jesus. When we leave the ministry we've been called into, we are, in essence, leaving a battle field. We might temporarily merge back into 'normal' mode for a time but it is tough to fully depart in mind and spirit. I have had the experience of leaving behind my spiritual life and running full speed into the world seemingly free from the battles of the soul. I believe I felt somewhat like that soldier…relieved and somewhat eager to lay down my weapons of warfare and just rest and enjoy life! I also recall feeling that my purpose in life was being laid aside and that I was not fulfilling my calling. I recall my first time back in a worship service after having been absent altogether for a number of years. Each step I took toward the altar was a deliberate step of victory over the enemy of my soul, who has so often convinced me that this whole religion thing is just "not for me" and that "I just don't believe all of this." With each step, I felt as if I was reaching out, grasping that powerful weapon of praise to the God of this Universe, and using it to destroy the stronghold of my enemy! Hallelujah! Psalms 149:3-4 proclaims, "3 Let them praise his name with dancing and make music to him with timbrel and harp. 4 For the LORD takes delight in his people; he crowns the humble with victory" (NIV). Indeed, with God's help, we are able to proclaim that VICTORY is available to all who are hurting, all who hunger and thirst for more, all who have lost their way and all who are bound. Only through Christ, can we find freedom. In Jesus' name! Amen!

OCTOBER 9

Yesterday, my husband and I stopped to visit our nephew and niece at their new home on our way home from church. The house was nice, with new siding, windows, a fresh coat of paint and laid out quite nicely. When taking us through the home, I asked when the house was built, and to my surprise, my nephew said it was built in the late 1800's! I would have never guessed it was that old by the looks of it today! He said there is even an old burnt beam in the basement, a remnant of the home from 'Great Fire' that ravaged the Thumb of Michigan in 1881. As I thought about that this morning, it occurred to me...

As it is in the natural, so is it in the spiritual...

Some of us have been able to conceal and cover up the destruction that has ravaged our lives. Underneath our clean apparel and smiles, there lurks destructive memories and remnants of our own tragedies which could have destroyed us at one time. Many of us have been reconstructed to the point where others may never know what we have been through unless they examine the basement of our life where that "great fire" nearly destroyed us. I Peter 5:10 tells us: "In his kindness God called you to share in his eternal glory by means of Christ Jesus. So, after you have suffered a little while, he will restore, support, and strengthen you, and he will place you on a firm foundation" (NLT). Lord, thank you for reminding me that since I have rebuilt my life upon you, I am on a steady foundation where no storm or force can destroy me! Hallelujah!

OCTOBER 10

Our youngest grandson, Coby Walker Matt was born on this day in the year 2016. He is my Kristin and Nick's third child and third boy. I call him my Coby-licious because his snuggles are so delicious. With those big brown eyes and his crooked smile, he will steal your heart in an instant! He has a strong will and is such a determined child, and he strives ferociously to keep up with his older brothers! This spring as a 2 ½ year old he is riding a scooter like a little pro! Oh, how I love my Coby! We all find such delight in witnessing his fearless determination and zeal! As I think about this, the Lord opens my eyes to see...

As it is in the natural, so is it in the spiritual...

In the same way that we delight in the willpower and achievements of our children and grandchildren, so too does the Lord delight in us when we follow in his ways when we exercise our fearless determination and faith! In Romans 12, Paul is instructing Christians to be fervent in their faith. Within the list he writes, "11 Never be lacking in zeal, but keep your spiritual fervor, serving the Lord" (NIV). When we stand firm in our faith in the midst of great adversity of our day, it pleases the Lord. We must cling to what is right and abhor evil. We must do it with the zeal of a two-year old determined not to be left behind by his older brothers! Lord help us to seek your will in all of our ways and be determined and fearless in our pursuit of that path! In Jesus' precious name! Amen!

OCTOBER 11

During my morning devotions today, I read the story of Peter's denial. Jesus had told Peter that he would do exactly what he did but Peter swore an oath to stand by His Lord. When the situation developed and the naysayers pointed to Peter as an associate of Jesus, the prophecy was fulfilled. Peter denied his association with His Lord three times before the cock crowed twice and then, as if coming to his senses when he realized what had happened, he went out and wept bitterly. As I read this it occurred to me that...

As it is in the natural, so is it in the spiritual...

We may point to Peter and proclaim: I would NEVER deny Jesus... but as that thought crossed my mind the lord whispered to me....When you shrug aside the will of God in the face of peer pressure; when you fail to speak His name in faith for healing; when you do not share the wonderful gospel message of salvation with those who need it most, you too are denying Christ. The cock's crowing for us may occur as we take note of those missed opportunities we are given each day to profess our alliance to Christ Jesus. The Lord has pointed out that the main deterrent to our witnessing to others is summed up in one word: Shame. Matthew 10:33 says, "For whoever is ashamed of Me and My words in this adulterous and sinful generation, the Son of Man will also be ashamed of him when He comes in the glory of His Father with the holy angels" (NAS). We are as guilty as Peter was in denying him when we fail to utter his name to a lost and dying world who so desperately need him. Dear Lord Jesus, help me to be bold and unashamed to proclaim Your name and Your message of love and salvation in this world today. May I never be ashamed of the Gospel of Jesus Christ, which has the power to save us from our sins! In Jesus' name! Amen!

OCTOBER 12

While reading through Leviticus, I pondered how many different laws there were back in those days. I wondered how on earth anyone could possibly keep all of those statutes and laws! As I thought on this, the Lord reminded me of the freedom the children of Israel were offered, but they continued to remain in Egypt wandering for decades with little hope of ever being free. He also reminded me that...

As it is in the natural, so is it in the spiritual...

We all, like the children of Israel, have been or still are in captivity. We've been held there by our enemy and by ourselves through the lust of the flesh, the lust of the eyes, and the pride of life to entice us to remain captive to the world around us. All the while, the Lord is so close, beckoning us to step beyond the seen into the unseen, where we can taste and feel true freedom in HIM. In John 8, Jesus deals with the sin of a woman found in adultery. After forgiving her, Jesus was teaching that all mankind, even the Pharisees, were servants of sin. He says "Verily, verily, I say unto you, Whosoever committeth sin is the servant of sin" but then He goes on to proclaim that "If the Son, therefore, shall make you free, you shall be free indeed" (34, 36 KJV). Like the children of Israel, we all have been in bondage and we all need to find freedom. Through the power of the Spirit of Jesus Christ, we can do just that. Lord, please help me to daily call upon your power to set me free from the bondage of sin that so quickly encapsulates me. Help me be mindful of the snares set by the enemy to entrap me in sinful bondages. In Jesus' name, Amen.

OCTOBER 13

This week a hurricane was predicted to make landfall in the Carolinas. It was national news for several days prior to the event. People were ordered to evacuate the coastal region, and yet many chose to hunker down and stay. Sure enough, when Florence hit, lives were lost and the damage was widespread. Flooding, wind wreckage and electrical outages devastated many people and lives were lost. Why do people stay in the midst of imminent danger? Interviewers report that some people felt it was just easier to stay put and for some it was lack of preparation to leave. Some adopted the overly optimistic, "Not gonna happen to me" stance, and others held to that age old 'herd' thinking, "If the neighbor isn't going, neither am I." Still others were worried about losing their possessions. As I thought about those who choose to ignore the evacuation and stay, the Lord illuminated to me...

As it is in the natural, so is it in the spiritual...

It is a fact of life that one day we will all leave this world. At that point, we would hopefully have considered what happens next. Many people believe the bible is true and that one day, they will face heaven or hell. And yet, even many who 'believe' this have chosen to hunker down and stay put in a life without Jesus. Jesus' parables describe how the cares of life, the deceitfulness of riches, and our lust for other things come in and choke out the seeds of truth, which is the word of God, which has been spread throughout this world. Let us stop and ponder what will happen to us when that final storm of life takes us from our earthly home. Hebrews 9:27 says, "Just as man is appointed to die once, and after that to face judgment, 28 so also Christ was offered once to bear the sins of many; and He will appear a second time, not to bear sin, but to bring salvation to those who eagerly await Him...." (BSB). Safety will be found only in Christ Jesus. Lord, help me to daily consider the temporary status of my life here on earth. May I let go of the cares of this world and my concern for my earthly possessions and rather be secure and certain that you are my shelter. In Jesus' name! Amen!

OCTOBER 14

I was having a conversation yesterday with a young lady who is a senior in high school. The topic was the dress code at a Christian camp she attends. She questioned some of the requirements, which included below the knees, below the elbows and above the collarbone covering for girls and boys. Because I have studied this issue quite a bit, I shared some Bible verses with her which explain what God determines as 'nakedness' and 'immodesty.' Trust me, it is much different that most of society today! Mostly, I encouraged her to pray about it and allow the Lord to guide her choices. As the conversation ended, the Lord quickened to me that...

As it is in the natural, so is it in the spiritual...

When we come to Jesus, there are things he expects us to give over to him. We must change some things if we are truly obeying the Lord, because none of us are perfect! There is a growing process and we must be willing to allow HIM to change US; however, it occurred to me that this must be done through the gentle teaching of the ways of the Lord and not simply through a set of rules being taught. In II Corinthians 3:6, Paul explains that competence in ministry comes from God "...who hath made us able ministers of the new testament; not of the letter, but of the spirit: for the letter killeth, but the spirit giveth life" (KJV). This is an idiom of opposites showing that when one teaches the law without the understanding of the Lord's heart and purpose behind them, they can become a stumbling block rather than a steppingstone. The Lord showed me in that moment that he wants me to be a stepping stone for others to grow closer to Him, rather than a teacher of his statutes and rules. The Holy Spirit is the one who must impart conviction and direction into each of our hearts as we draw closer to the Lord and seek to please Him. Thank You Lord for this enlightening. Help me to remember that each of us is on our own path of righteousness and your Spirit is the one who gently and firmly gives us wisdom and guidance along our way! In Jesus' name! Amen!

OCTOBER 15

Walking through my brother's bean field on our way to our hunting stands, we were talking about the harvest. The conditions have to be just right to combine these fragile, yet tough plants. If it's too wet, the beans may be tough and cling to their pod and if it's too dry you will lose many due to shattering shells. The farmer must contemplate all of these factors as he enters the fields for harvest and yet harvest is what he must do. As I thought about this, the Lord pointed out...

As it is in the natural, so is it in the spiritual...

Over the years I have seen people come through our church doors in a variety of conditions. Just like the beans, some are tough and clinging to their pod of life, while others have experienced a shattered life and are trying to salvage what they can. The Lord knows the condition of each heart. We are called perform the harvest - to lovingly tell the message of salvation to all who can hear. We do not know if each soul is perfectly ripe but He does. In John 4:35, Jesus is speaking to the disciples, telling them, "Say not ye, there are yet four months, and then cometh the harvest? Behold I say unto you, Lift up your eyes and look on the fields for they are white already to harvest" (KJV). Dear Lord, help us to understand the task we have been given. We know that it is you who ripens hearts for harvest, and that our role is to assist with the harvest with loving kindness and compassion! In Jesus' name! Amen!

OCTOBER 16

The talk all week has been of the full super moon. Last night at the store, a friend said her day had been quite a full moon type of day. I was waiting to see what kind of full moon it would be. Would it be a great harvest moon? I love to see a giant orange moon! As the evening approached, however, the sky had become overcast and though I checked every so often, I never got to see the moon...not even a transparent glimpse! As I awake this morning, the moon is still nowhere to be seen. It is completely covered by clouds. If someone hadn't heard that the moon was supposed to be so special, they would have certainly never known it with the clouds like they were! As I thought on this, the Lord illuminated to me...

As it is in the natural, so is it in the spiritual...

If we have God's light shining in our hearts, others should be able to see it! In the Sermon on the Mount, Jesus taught us, "No man lights a lamp and puts a basket over it, but rather they place it on a lampstand so that it gives light to all who are in the house! In the same way we ought to let our good deeds shine out for all to see so that everyone will praise your heavenly Father" (Matthew 5:13-16). If we behave just like everyone around us, how will others see God's light in us? Dear Lord, please help me to allow your light to burn brightly in me so that your goodness can illuminate a dark world. In Jesus' name! Amen!

OCTOBER 17

The age of one to one device usage is upon us. Everywhere we go, people have their I-phone or droid in their hand or in their face accessing social media, playing games or communicating via text or chat apps. In restaurants, in lines, in outdoor parks, and yes...disturbingly, even behind the wheel of their cars! With so many people interacting through this tech world, we have become experts at ignoring what is right in front of us in order to engage with that which is simulated. The downfalls of this behavior are numerous, but the biggest problem I see is lack of connection with people sitting in the same room together! All on their phones! All ignoring each other and missing out on those precious opportunities for real interactions with those who are present in our lives! as I thought about it the Lord whispered...

As it is in the natural, so is it in the spiritual...

In the same way, how many of us frequently choose to absorb ourselves with a multitude of activities from the time we rise until we go to sleep at night and totally ignore the fact that there is ONE who is there waiting for us to talk to Him. The Lord is omnipresent and always with us, always there waiting for us to commune with him. Isaiah 30:18 tells us, "So the Lord must wait for you to come to him so he can show you his love and compassion. For the Lord is a faithful God. Blessed are those who wait for his help" (NLT). Lord, I am so thankful for your gracious patience. Thank you for always being there whenever I need you. Help me to come daily into your presence where I can find all of life's answers and the peace and joy that accompanies walking fully in your will and your ways. In Jesus' name! Amen!

OCTOBER 18

Today is my one and only son's birthday. I had two beautiful little girls, so of course I was pretty thrilled when doctor announced, "It's a big healthy boy!" This son of mine was such a darling little boy, and his sisters doted on him and spoiled him so sweetly. As he grew into a teen and a young man, this mom tended to look at her kid through rose colored lenses. Since his teenage years, this boy has always loved to try to tease and torment me, but I know he loves me. And oh, how I cherish my son and his sweet wife and their two precious children. Above all, I want my children to know that I look at them as my most treasured blessings. As I think about all of this, the Lord quickens to me a thought...

As it is in the natural, so is it in the spiritual...

In the same way that we mother's fiercely love our children, so too does the Lord love us! Psalms 123:3 tells us, "Behold, children are a heritage from the Lord, the fruit of the womb a reward" (ESV). James 1:17 says, "Every good gift and every perfect gift is from above, coming down from the Father of lights with whom there is no variation or shadow due to change" (ESV). I hope my son (and my daughters) know that they are those good and perfect gifts from God. Nothing in this world could ever change this mother's heart toward her children and so also is our Heavenly Father's love for each of His children. 1 John 3:1 exemplifies God's great love for us: "See what great love the Father has lavished on us, that we should be called children of God! And that is what we are..." (ESV). Lord your love toward us is such a perfect example of our love for our children! Help us to understand Your fathomless, unconditional love as we walk through this life, that we might pass it along for generations to come. In Jesus' name! Amen!

OCTOBER 19

Spending time with my grandchildren teaches me so much about the Love of God. I would do anything in my power to help them understand how much I love them. The joy I feel when they run to me with arms open is indescribable. It truly makes me want to spend as much time as I can with them, soaking up their love. As I thought on this the Lord pointed out...

As it is in the natural, so is it in the spiritual...

In the same way I adore and love my children and grandchildren, so too does the Lord love us and yearn for us to spend precious time with him. When we run to him with adoration and love, he welcomes us and pours his love right back into our hearts. What a wonderful relationship it is! I John 3:1 reminds us, "See what great love the Father has lavished on us, that we should be called children of God! And that is what we are!..."(NIV). Thank you Lord for your great love! Help me to daily run to you with my arms open that you may lavish your love on me and prepare me to love others. In Jesus' name! Amen!

OCTOBER 20

Most teachers will agree that one or two students can disrupt an entire class. Any teacher will tell you that the knot in their neck has a specific name. That one kid that wreaks havoc upon the entire classroom can cause the most experienced teacher to cringe and contemplate retirement. As I thought about this, the Lord nudged me and whispered…

As it is in the natural, so is it in the spiritual…

Just as one kid can usher chaos into a classroom, so too, did one man and woman usher chaos into our world in the form of sin. When Adam and Eve listened to the serpent [Satan] and disobeyed God's one commandment, [do not eat from the tree of the knowledge of good and evil] sin entered the world and along with it, death. This was not physical death, but spiritual death which meant separation from God. He cast them out of the Garden of Eden. Romans 5:12 says, "Therefore, just as sin entered the world through one man, and death through sin, death came to all people, because all sinned" (NIV). The good news is however, that Jesus Christ alone has taken away the sins of the world with the shedding of his blood. Hebrews chapter 9 explains how Christ's sacrificed his life, shed his blood, to usher in the new covenant between God and man. Without the shedding of blood there is no remission of sins, so Jesus offered himself as a living sacrifice, once and for all to bear the sins of each of us. Dear Lord Jesus, thank you for coming to earth and making a way for us to find redemption for our sins through your blood. Help us remember that each one of us can change our immediate world in a positive way this day by our words and actions. Help me to usher in peace, joy and love wherever I go. In Jesus' name! Amen.

OCTOBER 21

Germs are invisible sources of illness which one cannot see with the naked eye, and we don't really know we have ingested them until we have symptoms of that illness. We can also recognize illness in others and take precautions from those germs being transferred to us...as long as it's manifested by symptoms! When I have a student who is coughing or feverish or green around the gills, I am careful to avoid getting in their air space and I keep my sanitizing wipes close by to clean the area they were sitting once they leave. It is important to take precautions if we want to stay healthy! As I thought about this, the Lord nudged me...

As it is in the natural, so is it in the spiritual...

In the same way that we take precautions from illness, so too ought we take precautions from picking up the negative attitudes and sinful ways of others. When we are in the presence of someone who is continually gossiping about others, slandering others, always looking for something to criticize others about, we must protect our hearts from those thoughts, and guard our mouths from speaking evil. The bible calls gossip and slander sin. It is a sickness of the soul that destroys the human spirit when encountered. It turns people against each other and stirs up hatred in the heart. Jesus words are clear in Luke 6:45: "The good man out of the good treasure of his heart brings forth what is good; and the evil man out of the evil treasure brings forth what is evil; for his mouth speaks from that which fills his heart" (AMP). Lord, your word teaches us that just as we guard against sickness we must "Watch over [our] hearts with all diligence for out of it flows the springs of life" (Proverbs 4:23). Help us recognize and cleanse our hearts from the germs of sinful attitudes each day that we might spread goodness and love to others. In Jesus' name! Amen!

OCTOBER 22

I was reading a book entitled "Pulling Down Strongholds" by Derek Prince in which he discussed the dilemma of facing a physical battle against a person who is much bigger and stronger than you are. In order to defeat him, you must be able to bind his strength; tie him up and put a gag in his mouth. Then he will not be able to harm you or taunt you with ugly words that stir up fear and panic. In so many words, he went on to share the spiritual application...

As it is in the natural, so is it in the spiritual...

In order to defeat the enemy of our souls when he comes against us in spiritual battles, we must first bind him so he cannot touch us. Secondly, we must put a stop to his taunting by gagging him. How do we accomplish this seemingly impossible feat? Through the powerful weapon of prayer! In Matthew 12, Jesus teaches that we must render the enemy useless before we can defeat him! The Pharisees witnessed Jesus heal a blind and dumb man who was possessed with a devil and they accused him of being the prince of the devils. Jesus knew their thoughts and said essentially that a kingdom divided against itself would never stand. He went on to say in verse 29, "Or else how can one enter into a strong man's house, and spoil his goods, except he first bind the strong man? and then he will spoil his house" (KJV). Most of us know what our primary spiritual battle is with but do we know who it is with? There are principalities and powers and spiritual wickedness in high places that we must fight against (Ephesians 6:12) so we must repent of any sin and ask God to bind that strong man to remove its power in Jesus' name. 2 Corinthians 10:4 says: "(For the weapons of our warfare are not carnal, but mighty through God to the pulling down of strong holds;) 5 Casting down imaginations, and every high thing that exalteth itself against the knowledge of God, and bringing into captivity every thought to the obedience of Christ; 6 And having in a readiness to revenge all disobedience, when your obedience is fulfilled" (KJV emphasis mine). Thank you Lord for your word! Thank you for providing all of the power needed to life victorious lives for your kingdom by relying on YOUR power and might over every 'stronghold' by every 'strongman' that might come against us. In Jesus' name! Amen!

OCTOBER 23

A new baby is such a life changer! Parents and grandparents become consumed with every breath, blink, grunt and cry. They hover over the tiny human making sure they have a full belly, dry diaper and a warm bed. They cringe when baby cries, celebrate when baby burps, and "Oooo" and "Ahhh" when baby smiles. As baby grows into a toddler, more cringing, celebrating and "Ooooing" and "Ahhhing" continue. Indeed, we are enraptured with our little tykes. They truly bring so much joy into this life. As I thought about this, the Lord whispered to me...

As it is in the natural, so is it in the spiritual...

In the same way that we love, adore, obsess over and nurture our little loved ones, so too does the Lord look upon us with these same affections. I John 3:1 reminds us, "How great is the love the Father has lavished on us, that we should be called children of God! And that is what we are!" (NIV). Roman's 8:14 further describes this spiritual transformation. Paul writes, "14 For all who are led by the Spirit of God are children of God. 15 So you have not received a spirit that makes you fearful slaves. Instead, you received God's Spirit when he adopted you as his own children. Now we call him, "Abba, Father." 16 For his Spirit joins with our spirit to affirm that we are God's children. 17 And since we are his children, we are his heirs. In fact, together with Christ we are heirs of God's glory. But if we are to share his glory, we must also share his suffering. 18 Yet what we suffer now is nothing compared to the glory he will reveal to us later." Dear Lord, it is hard to grasp the true meaning of being a child of God. I know you have a heavenly inheritance that is mine because I am your daughter. Thank you for your unconditional love, your grace, your patience, your guidance and your gentle but firm correction. You truly are my Father and I am so grateful that you have made yourself known to us. Amen!

OCTOBER 24

Have you ever been in a new city or an unfamiliar highway and made a wrong turn? I have! And sometimes you find yourself in some nightmarish odyssey attempting to get back to the right road that you know will take you to your destination! It is truly a frustrating experience that I have had many times in this life. As I thought about this, the Lord pointed out...

As it is in the natural, so is it in the spiritual...

We all navigate through this life, striving to find our path, making mistakes and then living through that frustrating time of getting back to where we know we are supposed to be. I have been striving to grow in the Lord, and hear and follow his voice, and He is so kind and loving and gracious. Each morning as I awake, I have one of two thoughts in mind: a quiet sorrow for things I have done to displease the Lord, or a joyful peace for following His will. I am still learning how weak I am if I rely on my human nature to make directional decisions! I must whisper a prayer for strength or direction or wisdom. When I do something or say something I know will not be pleasing to the Lord, I feel regret. II Corinthians 7:10 says "Godly sorrow worketh repentance to salvation not to be repented of: but the sorrow of the world worketh death" (KJV). Thank you Lord that you are so faithful to show me your ways and that you give me that much needed direction as well as the desire to do better next time! Amen!

OCTOBER 25

We all can agree that cancer is a horrific, invasive, evil disease. It doesn't always begin with a glaring symptom, so it often goes undetected, which is why regular wellness checks are important. It usually originates in one specific area and if not eradicated, it will spread and ravage the body, and eventually it will kill you. Cancer must be dealt with through a combination of surgery where the mass is removed, chemotherapy, where chemicals flow through the body to seek and destroy any foreign, hidden cancer cells, and/or radiation treatment where intense light is used to kill the cells. As I thought about this malicious process, the Lord quickened to me that...

As it is in the natural, so is it in the spiritual...

Sin works in the same way as cancer. It is horrific, invasive and evil. It doesn't always begin with a glaring symptom, and it can go undetected and hidden for a period of time. This is why regular spiritual checkups are important. Sin often originates in one specific area of your life, and if not eradicated, it will spread and ravage the spirit, and eventually kill you. The treatment plan for sin is similar to that of cancer. We must go before the Great Physician so he can show us our sins. Then we must allow him to do a surgical work on our heart to remove the sin. We must allow the blood of Jesus Christ to cleanse us and God's spirit to flow through us to seek out any other hidden areas which need healing. Finally, we must allow his light to shine so intensely upon our hearts that He might bring us to a place of complete healing. Simply put, I John 1:7-9 gives the prescription for sin: "But if we walk in the light, as he is in the light, we have fellowship with one another, and the blood of Jesus his Son cleanses us from all sin. If we say we have no sin, we deceive ourselves, and the truth is not in us. If we confess our sins, he is faithful and just to forgive us our sins and to cleanse us from all unrighteousness" (ESV). Dear Lord I am so grateful for this remedy for the human condition of sinfulness. We all face the effects of its harm in this life and I am thankful that you have the ultimate course of treatment! Help me to daily come to you for prevention and healing! In Jesus' name! Amen!

OCTOBER 26

Some friends who visited us this week were amazed at the clear, starry sky as they went to leave. They went on and on about the difference between the sky out here in the country compared to where they live in a suburban area where the street lights dim the view of the stars. I had not thought about the way city lights might affect the crisp, bright light of the stars burning against the ebony sky. Indeed, I do relish being in such a place where the lights from 'civilization' do not dull the beauty of the night sky. As I thought on this the Lord sparked a thought in my heart...

As it is in the natural, so is it in the spiritual...

Just as light from a city impedes our vision to gaze upon the beauty of the night sky, so too can our spiritual vision be dulled and dimmed by the things of this world. If we are not careful to maintain our focus on God, life's trials, troubles and even busyness can dim or even block our view of God's purpose for us. We are called to set our sight (our minds) on things above, not on things on the earth (Col 3:2 Jubilee/KJV). Lord help me to focus on spiritual things and not be so easily distracted by life here on earth. Let me set my mind on those things which are eternal so that I can live out your purpose here today. In Jesus' name, Amen.

OCTOBER 27

We all need food to live, but sometimes we are not hungry for the right things, so we end up eating unhealthy foods. Typically, after eating something with too much sugar or too much grease, I feel the effects. I end up with an upset tummy and just do not feel right. A lifetime of this type of eating will result in an unhealthy body that can lead to a lack of productivity and many problems that are not easily eradicated. As I was thinking about this, the Lord quickened to me that...

As it is in the natural, so is it in the spiritual...

The word of God is necessary food for our soul, but many times, we crave other things to feed our human desires. We watch the wrong things and listen to the wrong things and end up with an unhealthy thought life and many problems that are not easily eradicated. We need to resist the temptation to feed these fleshly desires and discipline ourselves to feed on God's word in order to maintain a healthy mind and soul that is productive for the kingdom of God. Just as our physical bodies can remain alive only through consuming food, our spiritual selves can remain alive only through taking in and consuming the word of God and absorbing his presence. In John chapter 6, after feeding thousands with only a few loaves and fishes, the disciples asked Jesus how they could do those mighty works. Jesus told them in verse 35, "I am the bread of life: he that cometh to me shall never hunger; and he that believeth on me shall never thirst." (John 6; KJV). He goes on to prophecy about his death, burial and resurrection and provides the way to everlasting life through faith in Him. In the end some of the disciples left but some remained. Lord, help us to understand these spiritual truths: you are the Bread of Life and I must have faith to consume your Word as if my life depended upon it for survival. Thank you for showing me this amazing truth. In Jesus' name! Amen!

OCTOBER 28

This time of year, the leaves are falling, the days are getting colder and shorter, and the farmers are trying to finish up their harvest and fall plowing. As we head toward the end of this season and the beginning of the holiday season, I realize that we now need to start planning for Thanksgiving and Christmas gatherings and try to figure all of that out! From harvest to holidays we will embrace yet another new season. As I think about this, the Lord whispers...

As it is in the natural, so is it in the spiritual...

As we go through this time of harvest and transition in the natural, let us consider how we might be doing the same in our spiritual life. Have we sown seed and cared for it? Have we nurtured relationships that God has put in our lives? Have we reaped the benefits of God's amazing love? Are we prepared to plow our spiritual plot and start something new?

Hosea 10:12 encourages us, "12 Sow for yourselves righteousness and reap the fruit of loving devotion; break up your unplowed ground. For it is time to seek the LORD until He comes and sends righteousness upon you like rain" (BSB). Dear Lord, thank you for giving us the natural seasons to teach us about spiritual seasons in our life. Help us to sow and reap and seek you through it all! Amen!

OCTOBER 29

Standing in line for dinner at our Ladies Retreat, my friend Delores mentioned that she had recently cut her thumb pretty badly. She went on to say how although her left hand was not operating at full usage, her right hand was, and she was so thankful that her right hand was a part of her body so it could pick up the slack and even care for the left hand as it healed. As we talked, the light came on that...

As it is in the natural, so is it in the spiritual...

We immediately noted the spiritual application with being members of the body of Christ, and how when one of us is not at full strength and capability, another member ought to be there to care for them. In this way, the body can continue running smoothly and perform the functions it is meant to perform. Ephesians 4:16 tells us, "...The whole body, joined together by every joint with which it is equipped, when each part if working properly, makes the body grow so that it builds itself up in love." Lord, help us to remember that we, as part of the body of believers, should look to the needs of others and be ready and willing to care for those in need. In Jesus' name, Amen!

OCTOBER 30

My grandchildren always need a night light in the room at night. The illumination from that one tiny bulb shines enough light to dispel the darkness and the 'monsters' that lurk in the shadows. When it is dark, even a very small light allows them to 'see' and be comforted. How true this is! As I though on this, the Lord shined his light to show me that…

As it is in the natural, so is it in the spiritual…

Just as a light bulb helps so we can see and dispel fears, so too does God's word bring clarity to spiritual things. Psalms 119:105 reminds us that, "Thy word is a lamp unto thy feet and a light unto thy path" (KJV). When the Lord reveals the truth of his word to us, he is shining his light. We may not know what lies ahead because the shadows of tomorrow impede our sight, but if we will take up the lamp of God each day, it will guide us every step of the way. Thank you Lord, for your word is truth and light unto each step of my life. Help me to reach for it first each and every day to illuminate my way. In Jesus' name! Amen!

OCTOBER 31

Today is Halloween: aka "all hallows eve." A night that many Christians shy away from due to teachings about the origins of this spooky holiday. When researching Halloween, I discovered that this event dates back 2000 years ago to the ancient Celtic festival of Samhain. It was the celebration of their new year. This day marked the end of summer and the beginning of harvest and subsequently the cold, dark winter. Winter was associated with death, and the Celts believed that on this night the lines between life and death were blurred. They believed that the ghosts of the dead were able to return to earth and wreak havoc upon their crops, cause problems, and aid fortune tellers in seeing future events. They left treats in hopes to appease the ill-behaved spirits. As time passed, and various immigrants brought their traditions to America, the holiday has been dubbed a children's Trick or Treat day, mixed with ghosts and goblins. Many do not focus on the dark history of Halloween, but rather, they simply celebrate it as an innocent way for children to dress up and have fun trick or treating for candy! As I think about this, the Lord whispered to me…

As it is in the natural, so is it in the spiritual…

In so many areas of life, we can choose to dwell on the darkness or evils of the day, or we can choose to look at each day as an opportunity to reflect and display God's goodness. Halloween is no different. If each of us would prayerfully consider what we might do to bring Christ to the world through this day, we would be further ahead than condemning the decisions of others! God has given each of us a conscience that responds to His truth, and we all have to follow our own convictions! In Romans 14, Paul discusses not judging one another by what we eat or drink or how we regard certain days. Verse 14 says, "I am convinced and fully persuaded in the Lord Jesus that nothing is unclean in itself. But if anyone regards something as unclean, then for him it is unclean" (BSB). Paul goes on to say, "Do not allow what you consider good, then, to be spoken of as evil. 17 For the kingdom of God is not a matter of eating and drinking, but of righteousness, peace, and joy in the Holy Spirit. 18 For whoever serves Christ in this way is pleasing to God and approved by men" (BSB). Dear Lord, let us prayerfully consider how we ought to celebrate each day of the year, including Halloween, as a day that we can celebrate the unmatchable, glorious gift of salvation given to us. Let us find a way to share this beautiful gift with others to bring light and joy and peace to those who may be dwelling in darkness. In Jesus' name! Amen!

NOVEMBER 1

Walking through our woods this week, I found myself in some uncharted areas, fighting through the tangles and briers. I soon found a path apparently made by four-legged creatures and my going was much easier as long as I stuck to the previously trodden route. This wider path soon led me out into the open field. It dawned on me that this is a good spot to sit for hunting since this is obviously where the deer come in out. In this case, those unwary creatures would be better off taking the path filled with briers and thorns! As I was thinking about this the Lord revealed...

As it is in the natural, so is it in the spiritual...

In Matthew 7, Jesus tells us, "Enter ye in through the straight gate, for wide is the gate and broad is the way that leadeth to destruction, and many there be which go in thereat; because straight is the gate and narrow is the way that leads to life and few there be that find it" (KJV). If we incline ourselves to just following along a certain way of life just because everyone else is traveling that path, or just because it seems to be the easiest route, we may actually be on a road leading to destruction. It isn't easy taking the narrow, less traveled, path, but if we do, we may thankfully find safety in our Father's way. Dear Lord, thank you for calling me to walk the narrow path, though it may not be easy, and though I may feel alone at times. Your word and your promises are true. In Jesus' name, Amen.

NOVEMBER 2

As I began to write this morning, I was excited to notice that I am finally seeing the light at the end of the tunnel. I am closing in on my goal of 365 devotions! Wow! As I began to celebrate this victory, I noticed that some of my paragraphs are not aligned and some of the fonts are bold and so I began to go back and edit some of the work. This has been a process of quite a few years of writing and editing and revising and still much is yet to do! Wow...I realized right then that it takes a lot of discipline, time and patience to actually publish a book. As I thought on this the Lord whispered...

As it is in the natural, so is it in the spiritual...

The Lord gave me a glance as to how the development of a book is much the same as the development of one's spiritual self. We must work on ourselves daily. We must go back and edit (ask forgiveness and then actually change!) our mistakes. We must have patience with ourselves. We must deal with days where we have no inspiration. We must ignore those who do not support our endeavor. We must deal with our own self-doubts, procrastination, laziness and lack of passion. We must be diligent, no matter what the delay, no matter how long it takes to get it right, no matter what the obstacle because if we don't, we will not be fulfilling the gifts and calling which we know the Lord has given us. 2 Peter 1:10 says, "Therefore brothers, be all the more diligent to make your calling and election sure, for if you practice these qualities, you will never fall (ESV). Dear Lord, help me to be diligent to use the gifts and calling you have placed in me. Help me to daily walk in your will that I may never fall away from my faith in YOU. In Jesus' name! Amen!

NOVEMBER 3

The autumn weather here in Michigan undergoes drastic variances, even in the course of a day! This week on several occasions, it was in the thirties when I left for work, but warm and sunny when I headed for home. I have learned to layer up with items of clothing that can be added or removed as needed to accommodate for the changing temperatures. As I thought on this the Lord whispered to me…

As it is in the natural, so is it in the spiritual…

Just as we must consciously prepare for changing weather with our clothing, so too must we prepare for the winds of change spiritually. We may begin the week all fired up from an amazing church service, but the temperature can quickly cool if our heart is not properly clothed with Jesus Christ. Temptations, busyness, illness, stress, and even laziness are all temperature changers that we must prepare for. Romans 13:14 tells us, "But put on the Lord Jesus Christ, and don't make plans to gratify the desires of the flesh" (BSB). In other words, if we put on Jesus, we will have power over sin. We will be able to conquer those old habits and our selfish ways. Dear Lord, help me to prepare for any weather that could have an adverse effect on my relationship with you. Help me to prayerfully put on the righteousness of Christ Jesus as I begin my day. Amen!

NOVEMBER 4

My hubby started our outdoor wood burner yesterday. Temperatures are forecasted to be in the 30's each night, and we prefer waking up to a warm house. This is a job that requires constant action and tending. In order to have a warm house, you must have a fire burning. To get a fire burning, it must be ignited, and after that, you must continually feed the fire. To feed the fire, you must go cut wood. It must be dry hardwood that is ready to burn. If you put wet or rotten wood on it, the flame will be smothered. Indeed, it takes time and energy to keep the house warm. As I thought about this, the Lord pointed out…

As it is in the natural, so is it in the spiritual…

When I first surrendered my life to Christ, my heart was ignited for the things of Lord. That flame burned brightly and was tended with prayer, bible study and worship. These were the hardwoods which fed that fire and created that desire to please the Lord. Just as it is with our wood stove, it takes time and energy to keep the fire burning. The temperature of our heart is in direct relation to how often we feed it and what we feed it. If we spend our time filling our hearts with "rotten" things, our flame will eventually be smothered. Paul wrote to the Romans in Chapter 12:11, admonishing them: "Never let the fire in your heart go out. Keep it alive. Serve the Lord" (NIRV). Dear Lord, help me to tend the fires of my heart with your word and with worship and prayer. These are the best hardwoods with which to keep my heart burning for You. In Jesus' name, Amen!

NOVEMBER 5

Driving along on my way to work, I had the sudden urge to check my phone. As I reached for it the thought crossed my mind: "If you are looking at your phone, you will be taking your eyes off the road ahead of you and that can be dangerous; you'll never see that deer jump out or that vehicle come out of the blind driveway." As I thought about this, the Lord quickened to me that...

As it is in the natural, so is it in the spiritual...

The truth is, you can only be focused on one thing at a time. Many people dismiss this fact by saying they are only glancing for a second, or it's no more distracted driving than tuning the radio or adjusting the heat or AC. This may be true; however, it does not negate the fact that it is illegal, or that people cause accidents and lives are lost every day because someone was texting and driving. Likewise, how many Christians look away from the road the Lord has placed them on and become distracted from their purpose? It is dangerous to our spiritual well-being to take our eyes off of Jesus' path, because the enemy is gleefully happy to send danger and destruction into our path. Hebrews 12:2 reminds us to "Keep your eyes on Jesus, who both began and finished this race we're in. Study how he did it. Because he never lost sight of where he was headed - that exhilarating finish in and with God - he could put up with anything along the way: cross, shame, whatever. And now he's there, in the place of honor, right alongside God" (MSG). Lord help me not to lose sight of where I am headed and what you have for me! In Jesus' name! Amen!

NOVEMBER 6

Last night, I went hunting with my crossbow in the small woods behind my house. I was sitting in a tent just enjoying the serene sights and sounds of the woodland. As usual, when dusk approached, the deer came out. Right before dark, a buck stepped out about twenty-five yards away. I took aim and waited for a broadside shot. When I let my arrow fly, I was confident that it was a good shot. My hubby came back to help track the deer. We did not find him. The arrow had gone through but he believed from the evidence (or lack of blood) that the shot was too high on the body. We walked that little wooded area and searched for nearly two hours before we were satisfied. Replaying the shot in my head, I question myself: "Did I range him to determine the yardage, and did I use the correct scope line?" I could not be sure of those two things. As I sit here early this morning, the Lord whispered to me...

As it is in the natural, so is it in the spiritual...

Just like a hunter's arrow, our words can have a drastic effect on those we fling them upon. We may be in the correct place at the correct time and we may have a great opportunity to send that arrow and change a life, but if we aren't careful to measure our words, our efforts will be fruitless. Many scriptures admonish believers regarding the words we speak. Here are a few: Proverbs 18:21: "What you say can preserve life or destroy it; so, you must accept the consequences of your words" (GNT). Matthew 12:36-37, Jesus warns us, "I tell you, on the day of judgment people will give account for every careless word they speak, 37 for by your words you will be justified, and by your words you will be condemned" (ESV). Proverbs 12:18: "The words of the reckless pierce like swords, but the tongue of the wise brings healing" (NIV). Lastly, this prayer: Psalms 19:14: "May the words of my mouth and the meditation of my heart be pleasing in your sight, LORD, my rock, and my redeemer" (NIV). Help me be sure that my words are prayerfully spoken so they are life giving, not piercing to someone's soul! In Jesus' name! Amen!

NOVEMBER 7

We have two different varieties of nut trees in our yard. The Black Walnut and the English Walnut. The Black Walnuts are quite an annoying nuisance. This is mostly because we do not eat the nuts, but rather, we have to sweep them up, along with those pesky, thin twigs that fall along with the nuts. On the other hand, the English Walnut trees produce delicious nuts that only have to be picked up off the ground after the shell dries up. When thinking about these two different kinds of trees, the Lord shined a light on my understanding…

As it is in the natural, so is it in the spiritual…

We naturally prefer things that benefit us over things which are a bother to us. Sadly, this includes people. This selective attitude of human nature is unpleasing to the Lord, who taught us that even the poor, the destitute, the homeless, and yes, the annoying people in our lives deserve love, kindness and respect. The New Testament teaches about this: A rich man and a poor man who come into an assembly, and the rich is given a seat of honor while the poor is told to sit on the floor. James 2 asks, 4. "Have you not made distinctions among yourselves, and become judges with evil motives? 5. Listen, my beloved brethren: did not God choose the poor of this world to be rich in faith and heirs of the kingdom which He promised to those who love Him?" (ASV). This is a sobering glimpse into the heart of God. Lord, help me to be mindful of any tendency in my heart that would be unpleasing to you. Help me to see all people through your eyes, so I may act with compassion, love and tenderness. In Jesus' name! Amen!

NOVEMBER 8

I woke up early this morning just as it was starting to rain. There is something soothing about the sound of rain. It is something that is completely out of my realm of control. I have no say over when it starts or when it ends or how much rain will fall. I only get to listen and watch it happen. As I thought on this, the Lord whispered…

As it is in the natural, so is it in the spiritual…

The older I get, the more I realize how true it is that God truly is in control. I have no control over so many countless things in this life. The one thing that I do have control over is me. My thoughts, my actions, my words. That's it. This is why it is vital that I trust in the ONE who created all things...including me! The Lord may bring sunshine and roses into my life and he may allow clouds and rain. When stormy weather comes, if I trust in Him, I can walk through it with peace, and joy, knowing all is well with my soul. Philippians 4: 6-7 tells us, "Do not be anxious about anything, but in every situation, by prayer and petition, with thanksgiving, present your requests to God. And the peace of God, which transcends all understanding, will guard your hearts and your minds in Christ Jesus." Thank you Lord for this wonderful reminder that you are in control. Help me to remember that I need only to trust you! In Jesus' name! Amen!

NOVEMBER 9

Yesterday, I noticed that all of the last remaining leaves had fallen from our trees. The branches were bare, and the ground was covered with a thick layer of color. I decided to take some time and get out my mower to mulch them and blow them underneath our pines along the edge of the yard. As I think about the approaching winter season, I am strangely comforted by the knowledge that one more chore is complete for this season. As I think about this, the Lord whispers...

As it is in the natural, so is it in the spiritual...

Completing tasks in the natural gives us a sense of accomplishment. However, in the spiritual realm we are told to put aside our chore list and be comforted by the work of Jesus Christ for he has completed the task required for our salvation. Yes, we are told to keep the faith, and we are told not to be weary in well-doing, but these are spiritual tasks, not physical chores. Hebrew's 4:11 explains, "Let us labour therefore to enter into that rest, lest any man fall after the same example of unbelief" (KJV). We must exert our efforts in the spiritual rather than the natural. We must remember that there is no work left for us to do other than trust in Christ's finished work on the Cross and seek to obey His holy word. Dear Lord, help me to remember that my salvation is complete in your finished work. Help me to rest in that knowledge, while yet being diligent to nurture my faith through prayer, bible study and being unashamed to share what I believe with others. In Jesus' name! Amen!

NOVEMBER 10

Today, we attended a funeral of a dear departed elderly woman from my childhood church. She was my Sunday School teacher and neighbor and one of the kindest, most caring souls I have ever known. She attended sporting events with her late husband until they were unable to do so. When I would see her, she always asked about each of my children and grandchildren individually and specifically. It was so moving to hear the words of her children and grandchildren as they fondly memorialized this beautiful lady and her love for the Lord and her family. She was a Godly example to each one who attended and countless others! As I thought about this, the Lord whispered to me...

As it is in the natural, so is it in the spiritual...

This family is a picture of the family of God. My heavenly Father has sent His Son, Jesus Christ to be a living example for us to follow. I have a deep desire to create a spiritual legacy for my children and grandchildren to follow. Proverbs 31 tells of this virtuous woman: Verse 28 "Her children arise up, and call her blessed; her husband also, and he praiseth her. 29 Many daughters have done virtuously, but thou excellest them all. 30 Favour is deceitful, and beauty is vain: but a woman that feareth the Lord, she shall be praised" (KJV). When I leave this world, I won't be taking worldly possessions; It won't matter how clean my house was or how much money I have when I stand before the Lord. Dear Lord, I want more than anything for my loved ones to say of me, "She loved the Lord Jesus and shared her faith with those who would listen." Dear Lord, I know that I am far from perfect and that I daily fall short in my endeavors to be the woman of God I desire to be. Help me to live each day to please You and be an example to my loved ones. In Jesus' name! Amen!

NOVEMBER 11

On our many treks to the woods we have noticed vines climbing our trees and creating havoc. We could see that they were actually growing to the tops of the trees and pulling the full-grown tree over into an arch. After doing a bit of research I found out that a small vine in the woods, if left alone, can kill a tree by taking over the canopy and stealing the sunlight. The vine will attach itself to a tree and climb it in a very short time, and then begin pulling the tree over until the tree is completely bent and unable to stretch up and receive sunlight. As I researched this issue, the Lord quietly pointed out that...

As it is in the natural, so is it in the spiritual...

We are much like a tree in this sense. II Peter 2:20 warns us: "If indeed they have escaped the corruption of the world through the knowledge of our Lord and Savior Jesus Christ, only to be entangled and overcome by it again, their final condition is worse than it was at first" (BSB). A strong and healthy Christian who is not careful to remove entanglements of this world can allow a small intruder to grow within their heart and this 'vine' can attach itself and begin warping and bending our once upright heart until it prevents us from receiving the Light we so desperately need. Lord, help us to carefully eradicate intruders from our life so that we can continue to stretch forth and receive "light" from our "SON." In Jesus' name! AMEN!

NOVEMBER 12

A favorite story of mine in II Kings tells of a poor widow whose husband had died owing money to a man. The man was demanding that her children work as servants to repay their father's debt. She pleaded with Elisha to help her. Elisha asked her what she had in her house, and she said she had nothing other than one jar of oil. He bid her to run to her neighbors and gather as many empty jars as she could. He instructed her to begin pouring her oil into the empty containers. She must have had doubts but obeyed the prophet and miraculously, she poured oil from her small jar to fill many empty jars! When there were no more jars available, the oil stopped. The widow was able to sell the jars of oil to spare her children from a life of slavery. As I read this the Lord was lovingly showing me...

As it is in the natural, so is it in the spiritual...

Many of us have very busy lives filled with jobs, family, church, daily chores, entertainments and etc. Our 'jar' is full! But notice: Elisha instructed the widow to go find empty vessels, and only after pouring into these empty containers, was she able to free herself and her children from their debilitating debt. This precious, valuable oil is symbolic of the Holy Spirit; the Spirit of Christ, which was poured out on all mankind (Acts 2:17) for any who would receive (Acts 2:39). Jesus proclaimed in Luke 4:18, "The Spirit of the Lord is on Me, because He has anointed Me to preach good news to the poor. He has sent Me to proclaim freedom to the captives and recovery of sight to the blind, to set free the oppressed..." (HCSB). How true this is! "Where the Spirit of the Lord is there is freedom" (II Corinthians 3:17). Dear Lord, help us to tap into the 'jar' of your Holy Spirit and pour it into the lives of others, bringing freedom, joy, and power to otherwise empty hearts. In Jesus' name! Amen.

NOVEMBER 13

I woke up this morning to a thick fog pressing upon the windows of our home. It was so foggy, I could not see the woods across the road. Fog this thick really impedes one's travels. It is the guiding force which determines how a person must move. It keeps drivers in check as they cautiously proceed down the road. As I thought on this the Lord broke through the fog and whispered...

As it is in the natural, so is it in the spiritual...

The presence of God is often referred to as a thick cloud in the old testament. In Exodus chapter 13, the Lord went before the children of Israel in a thick pillar of clouds by day to lead them through the wilderness. In the tabernacle and later in the temple, the Presence of God filled the house of the Lord so that the priests could not stand to minister because of the cloud (I Kings 8:10-12). Just as a thick foggy morning affects our every movement, forces one to slow down and forces one to acknowledge our limitations, so too did the miraculous presence of God affect the children of Israel and the priests in the temple. The presence of the Lord is still available today to all who are born again. Lord, I want your presence to be that guiding force, affecting my every movement, causing me to slow down, and acknowledge my limitations, and wait upon you for direction. Thank you for loving us and leading us! In Jesus' name! Amen!

NOVEMBER 14

Another foggy morning! Somehow this element of nature creates a quiet, muffled blanket of protection, shutting out all external sounds. This morning as I did my devotions, the fog was providing this type of quiet, with the exception of one Whippoorwill calling in the distance. As I read and prayed, the bird's voice was the only sound rising above the quiet of the fog. The Lord nudged me to the awareness that...

As it is in the natural, so is it in the spiritual…

So many of us seek to hear God speak into our lives and yet, there are so many other things competing for our attention that it is difficult to discern His voice. The bible tells us to "Be still and know I am God (Psalms 46:10, KJV). Jesus told us, "He that hath ears to hear, let him hear" (Matthew 11:15, KJV). We must find a place of peaceful quiet in order to shut out all external sounds so we can hear that sweet voice of the Lord calling in the distance. We must allow his voice to rise above the quiet and penetrate our world, our thoughts, our agenda, our bustling activity. Lord, help me to find that place of quiet each day, where the only sound rising in my heart is your word and your voice. Thank you for calling me. Thank you for giving me ears to hear. In Jesus' name! Amen!

NOVEMBER 15

Today is opening firearm season here in Michigan. Our trail camera captured many pictures of a beautiful buck I call "Pretty Boy's Son," and I have been claiming him as 'mine.' I even told our neighbors that I would be seeing him step out at 7:15 and he'd be down by 7:30 a.m. Walking and praying during the hike to my blind, I told the Lord if it was his will that I harvest this buck, he'd send him to me, let me know for sure it was him and help me get a good kill shot on him. Incredibly, at 7:15 am, after facing south watching all of the deer come out of the woods, the Lord prompted me to peek out of the north window of my blind... and there he stood! His silhouette against the dawning sky startled me. As crazy as it sounds, the words I had spoken the night before, came true, and I succeeded in harvesting this amazing buck! As I sit and think about all of this, the Lord illuminates to me that…

As it is in the natural, so is it in the spiritual…

In Mark 11, 22-24 Jesus is teaching the disciples about the power of speaking in faith "Have faith in God. Truly, I say to you, whoever says to this mountain, 'Be taken up and thrown into the sea,' and does not doubt in his heart, but believes that what he says will come to pass, it will be done for him. Therefore, I tell you, whatever you ask in prayer, believe that you have received it, and it will be yours." Mark 11:22-24. Dear Lord, you are the creator of this universe and the author of the miraculous. Help me to put my faith in your power to do the impossible in my life, and I will direct all the glory to you! In Jesus' name! Amen!

NOVEMBER 16

I have mentioned that we burn wood in an outdoor woodstove to keep our house nice and warm in the cold weather. It takes a lot of sweat and labor to keep that thing filled, and it takes continual tending to keep the fire burning hot enough to heat our home. My husband works hard cutting and hauling wood and feeding the wood stove every day all winter. I try to help out occasionally, but he is the main provider of our warmth and I appreciate all that he does. As I thought about this, it became clear to me that...

As it is in the natural, so is it in the spiritual...

Most of us have felt the warm sparks of faith at some point in our lives. We have either tended it into a burning flame or allowed it to fizzle out. Just as our woodstove needs continual care and feeding, so too does our faith. The Lord is the source where that spiritual spark began but I must be the firekeeper of my heart and the caretaker of that flame. Daily word, worship and prayer are the key elements I must tend this fire with, lest it ceases to burn. II Timothy 1:6 encourages us, "Therefore, I remind you to keep ablaze the gift of God that is in you through the laying on of my hands. 7. For God has not given us a spirit of fearfulness, [cowardice, timidity] but one of power, love, and sound judgment" (HCSB). Lord, help me be fearless and bold in a world so eager to extinguish any flames of faith towards Christ Jesus. In Jesus' name! Amen!

NOVEMBER 17

Poachers can be quite nervy. In our area if you own woodland property, it is a given that you will have a hunting blind set up in or on the edge of that woods. Most people abide by the laws and go find public land to hunt, but others seem to think it is ok to access private property without permission in order to bag their buck. Some folks like to drive around and road hunt or squat on the edge of someone else's woods and find nothing wrong with shooting at a deer in a field they do not have permission to hunt on. As I thought on this, the Lord revealed to me...

As it is in the natural, so is it in the spiritual...

In the same way that unscrupulous hunters trespass and hunt on property they have no right to be on, so too must we realize that the devil" sits on the edge of his legal boundary and take shots at God's children. He can launch bullets toward us and he can inflict much harm if we are not careful and watchful! He will push his limitations as far as he can to undermine our spiritual authority, injure our testimony, maim our joy and mortally wound our faith. Psalms 7:13 reminds us: "He has prepared His deadly weapons; He ordains His arrows with fire" (BSB). So how do we protect ourselves? Ephesians 6 lists the armor of God as our weapons of warfare! The belt of truth, the breastplate of righteousness, our feed shod with the gospel of peace. Then verse16 emphasizes: "Above all, taking the shield of faith, wherewith ye shall be able to quench all the fiery darts of the wicked. 17 And take the helmet of salvation, and the sword of the Spirit, which is the word of God: 18 Praying always with all prayer and supplication in the Spirit, and watching thereunto with all perseverance and supplication for all saints;" (KJV). This powerful passage truly provides all of the insight, wisdom and protection we need in order to contend with the enemy the devil who prowls about like a roaring lion, seeking whom he may devour! (1 Peter 5:8). Thank you Lord for your word, which gives us answers for every problem, solutions for every tactic of the enemy! Victory is ours when we follow your word! Amen!

NOVEMBER 18

Sipping my coffee early this morning I was overtaken by a series of sneezes. Let me tell you, a sneeze is a bodily function that can totally disrupt a quiet moment. One minute you are in deep reflection, enjoying the quiet, and the next minute your entire body is reacting to some external stimuli and off you go! AAAAACHHOOOO! Usually they come in multiples. And they are difficult to suppress. It usually takes a tissue and a good nose blowing to expel the foreign particle tickling your nose. As I thought about this the Lord kindly pointed out...

As it is in the natural, so is it in the spiritual...

Just as a sneeze can disrupt a peaceful moment, so too does the enemy come to disrupt your peace. And as it takes multiple sneezes and a tissue to be rid of the irritant, so too it may take multiple efforts to expel our foe from those areas of our life he has invaded. Psalms 44:5 reminds us, "Through you, we repel our foes; through your name we trample our enemies" (Berean Study Bible). Oh Lord, help me to be ever mindful of the attempts of the enemy to invade my thoughts and interrupt my peacefulness. Help me to repel his efforts through your mighty name! In Jesus name, Amen!

NOVEMBER 19

My dog Jewel is not shy about demanding attention. When I am writing, she will often jump up on the sofa and start batting at my hand or the laptop with her paw. She is relentless in her pursuit of getting attention from the one she loves. She will only stop once I reach out with my hand to pet her. As I thought on this, the Lord spoke to me...

As it is in the natural, so is it in the spiritual...

Just as my sweet pup demands my attention and I willingly give it to her with a smile, so too will the Lord give his hand to us, his children, when we ask. If only we were more relentless in our pursuit of His Love.

He is always willing and just waiting for us to draw near and ask for his affection, but we are often too busy or distracted to spend time with our Father. James 4:8 tells us to "Come close to God, and God will come close to you. Wash your hands, you sinners; purify your hearts, for your loyalty is divided between God and the world (NLT). Dear Lord, help me to remember that you are waiting with open arms for us to come to you. Help me not to get so busy with my life that I fail to spend time with the One who loves me most. In Jesus' name! AMEN!

NOVEMBER 20

Sitting in the deer blind, trees, branches and brush can be obstacles to our view. It is very frustrating to have our vision blocked and be unable to see clearly and sometimes we must rise up and move to gain a clearer sight line. As I thought about this, the Lord revealed...

As it is in the natural, so is it in the spiritual...

Just as trees, branches and brush can block our field of vision, so too can the busyness of our day and the problems of this life become obstacles that block our sight of God. Sometimes, we must rise up and move to gain a clearer sight like to Him. Keeping our focus on our target is vital to the Christian. Colossians 3:2 reminds us: "Set your sight on things above, not on things on the earth" (Jubilee). Lord, help me to keep my focus on you. Help me to know when to move so that I do not lose sight of my most precious goal, which is Heaven. In Jesus' name! Amen!

NOVEMBER 21

A foggy day on land can be quite disconcerting. For water travelers, it is even more so! The captain of a vessel can rely on their radar and navigation systems as they travel blindly through the fog, but when they reach their destination, they are looking for that lighthouse which will guide them safely home. As I thought on this the Lord nudged me and whispered…

As it is in the natural, so is it in the spiritual…

He gently reminded me that HE is that that lighthouse! He wants us to know that when we are in a storm and lost, we can look to him and find our way back to safety. In John 8, Jesus said, "I am the light of this world. He that followeth me shall not walk in darkness, but shall have the light of life." Lord, help us to remember that when we need guidance through the dark and foggy night, we can turn our eyes toward you…and you will show us the way. In Jesus' name! Amen!

NOVEMBER 22

As we approach Thanksgiving day, many of us are consumed with the menu, the guest list, the house cleaning, the football games, and of course, how to survive and stay sane with the busyness the holidays can bring. We focus on many tasks in preparation for that one amazing Turkey dinner. We look up new recipes, we clean under the beds, we shop for a new tablecloth and place settings, we fuss and fret over many details so that when we sit down to carve that perfectly golden brown turkey, we will have fulfilled our dream role as the host or hostess with the most! As I think about all of the fuss and bother we go through for this one amazing meal, the Lord nudges me…

As it is in the natural, so is it in the spiritual…

Or perhaps I should say as it is in the natural so it should be in the spiritual. You know where I am going with this! We spend much time, money, energy and stress on this one meal each year, and when it is over, we might have some lovely family memories, photos for the album, and a few extra pounds. However, let us ask ourselves, how much more important is it to make preparations for that great and awesome day when we are invited to feast with the King of Kings and Lord of Lords? Jesus tells his faithful followers, "You are the ones who have stood by Me in My trials. 29 And I bestow on you a kingdom, just as My Father has bestowed one on Me, 30 so that you may eat and drink at My table in My kingdom, and sit on thrones, judging the twelve tribes of Israel" (Luke 22, BSB). Lord, we know that your invitation is open for all who would come so as we enter this time of holiday preparation, help us also to remember to prepare our hearts for that great and mighty day when we will feast with YOU! Amen!

NOVEMBER 23

As we age, we inevitably discover changes in our bodies; many of which we do not like. Wrinkles are one such change. Looking in the mirror can shed light on the facial expression most frequently residing on one's mug. Wrinkles do not lie. If you purse your lips frequently, you will see lines there. If you furrow your brow, that's where the lines appear. If you smile, you will see the effects of that expression. Thinking about this, the Lord revealed to me…

As it is in the natural, so is it in the spiritual…

Just as our face takes on the lines and pathways of our most common emotions, so too our spiritual self takes on that which has been most commonly impressed upon us. If we allow anger, jealousy, and general negativity to invade our heart and soul, we will surely emit a sour spirit. If we, on the other hand, resist these negatives and allow God's spirit to be the prevailing influence on our heart and mind, then inevitably, we will likewise emit love, joy, peace, kindness, and other traits of the Lord Jesus. Proverbs 4:23 tells us, "Above everything else, guard your heart, because from it flow the springs of life" (ISV). Lord, we know that our thought life is the basis for our attitudes, our moods, our misery or our joy. It truly does determine the outcome of each moment of each day for all of our lives. Please help me to turn my thoughts to you each morning. To submit my mind and heart to your influence every moment. Lord guard my heart and help me to rid myself of any negativity, that I might live free in your joy, your peace, your purpose. In Jesus' name! Amen!

NOVEMBER 24

My hubby was talking to me about those old vehicles that are discovered in barns when perhaps an elderly resident goes to sell the property. The vehicle was put away and has accumulated much dirt, cobwebs and general filth. It is anything but clean and shiny. The engine may be seized up with no life left in it. But, despite appearances, when the right person discovers it, they pull it out, clean it up, restore the broken parts, tune up the engine, add fuel and vvrrooooom! Off it goes! The Lord revealed as we talked…

As it is in the natural, so is it in the spiritual…

In the same way, we might find ourselves shut up in a dusty old place, unproductive, not in working order, covered with the dirt and dust of a life apart from our maker. But just as these old vehicles can be restored back to what they were made to be, so too can we be restored back to what the Lord has created us to be. He pulls us out of our dusty dwelling, removes the filth from our life, washes us with his cleansing blood, fixes our broken parts, tunes up our heart and mind, adds his Holy Spirit and VVRROOOOOM! Off we go! Restored to the what the Lord created us for with His joy, His peace and His love shining forth from us! David writes in Psalms 51:12: "Restore to me the joy of thy salvation and uphold me with thy free spirit" (KJV). Lord, we all need restoration at times in our life. Thank you for your love and tender care which transforms me into that which you created me to be. In Jesus' name! Amen!

NOVEMBER 25

Have you ever experienced something such as a delicious food or amazing sunset and tried to describe it to someone…only to end your statement with the popular catch phrase, "I guess you just had to be there." As I thought about this, the Lord reminded me…

As it is in the natural, so is it in the spiritual…

Just as we are unable to fully relay beauty and awe in the natural world, we are also not able to adequately share our heavenly experiences with others. People must respond to Jesus on their own, for He promises that He will draw all men to Himself (John 12:32). Romans 1:19-21 is clear: "19 For what may be known about God is plain to them, because God has made it plain to them. 20 For since the creation of the world God's invisible qualities, His eternal power and divine nature, have been clearly seen, being understood from His workmanship, so that men are without excuse. 21 For although they knew God, they neither glorified Him as God nor gave thanks to Him, but they became futile in their thinking and darkened in their foolish hearts" (BSB). Dear Lord, as Ephesians 1:18 says "I pray that the eyes of your heart may be enlightened so that you will know what is the hope of His calling, what are the riches of the glory of His inheritance in the saints." Thank you for giving all mankind a promise and an opportunity to, 'O taste and see that the Lord is good: blessed is the man that trusteth in him" (KJV). In Jesus' name! Amen!

NOVEMBER 26

One day a pastor went out to visit a member of the church. The elderly gentleman had once been an active member of the congregation and had a flame burning strong for Christ, but due to a series of events, he had been missing church several weeks in a row. The pastor sat with him in his warm kitchen where the fireplace was burning. He chatted with the man for a time and then became quiet. After a few moments passed, the pastor got up, picked up tongs and moved a log from the midst of the burning pile and set it to one side of the fireplace, then resumed sitting in the quiet, watching the crackling fire. Soon, the log that he had set aside lost its red flame and began to smolder and finally the log lost all signs of life. After a few moments, the pastor got up and moved the log back into the center with the other logs and within seconds the flames sparked to life and the log was burning brightly once again. The pastor left a short time later and as he bid his parishner goodbye, the man thanked him for his 'fiery' sermon. As I read this story, the Lord whispered...

As it is in the natural, so is it in the spiritual...

The implication is obvious...Just as that log needed to be near the other logs that were on fire in order to keep burning, so too must a believer do if we want to keep our flame alive. If we isolate ourselves from spiritual things and other believers, we may soon find our hearts cold and our flame of faith extinguished. Hebrews 10:22-25 reminds us, "22 let us draw near with a true heart in full assurance of faith, our hearts sprinkled clean from an evil conscience and our bodies washed in pure water. 23 Let us hold on to the confession of our hope without wavering, for He who promised is faithful 24 And let us be concerned about one another in order to promote love and good works, 25 not staying away from our worship meetings, as some habitually do, but encouraging each other and all the more as you see the day drawing near" (HCSB). Dear Lord, help us understand the importance of worshipping with fellow believers, and gathering together to encourage, strengthen and keep our hearts aflame for YOU. In Jesus' name! Amen!

NOVEMBER 27

As I get older, I am understanding the need to adopt a healthy nutrition and exercise lifestyle to feel good and to work out my muscles to maintain the level of strength I have always taken for granted. Being active is no longer enough. I can't just read about healthy living or talk about it with friends. I must actually do something! I must discipline myself. I must set aside time to plan meals and set aside time to work out in order to keep things in proper working order. If I fail to take care of this body, I will end up fatigued, overweight, and unhealthy. As I thought on this the Lord whispered…

As it is in the natural, so is it in the spiritual…

If I am to maintain a healthy spiritual relationship with the Lord, I cannot rely simply on hearing or reading His word. I must actually do something! I must discipline myself, and plan for prayer time and fasting. I must allow the Power of God to fill me before I can walk in this world and still remain spiritually healthy. Throughout scripture we see examples of what happens when people attempt to do things without God's power: Moses disobeyed the Lord and because of his act of defiance (striking the rock) he did not get to enter the promised land. King David fell into adultery and murder because he wasn't walking in the power of God. Peter denied Jesus because he was not walking in the power of God; Judas sold out for thirty pieces of silver and committed suicide…and the list goes on. These are just a few examples of what happens when we do not strengthen our spiritual self on a daily basis. Our weakness can be costly. Lord, help me to daily draw my spiritual strength from you and walk in your power that I may do what is pleasing in your sight. In Jesus' name! Amen!

NOVEMBER 28

Sunday, our associate pastor began his message with a detailed description of the preparations that go into a banquet held by the Queen of England at Buckingham Palace. The planning begins a year in advance. Each glass set upon the table was made in 1953 for her coronation and bears the Queen's cipher. The 4000 pieces of cutlery, tableware, salvers, and centerpieces were part of the Grand Service bought by King George IV 200 years ago. The only way a guest would ever be allowed to partake of such a grand affair is to be personally invited by the Queen. He made the connection for us...

As it is in the natural, so is it in the spiritual...

As prestigious as it is to be invited to such a glorious banquet at the Royal Palace, how much more amazing is it that each of us, are personally bidden to come and partake of all of the spiritual blessings prepared for us by the King of Kings, and Lord of Lords. We have immediate access to come and sup at table in the glorious Kingdom of Jesus Christ. His wares are not made by human hands but rather by the hand of the Almighty Creator of the Heavens and the Earth. Jesus told the crowd who followed him, "But don't be so concerned about perishable things like food. Spend your energy seeking the eternal life that the Son of Man can give you. For God the Father has given me the seal of his approval." (John 6:26 NLT). We humans are consumed with fulfilling our earthly wants and needs, but do we spend time and energy seeking after that which truly matters when our days here on earth are done? Lord, help me to daily seek after you and that heavenly manna which fills the spirit and soul with food that will not perish. Thank you for providing for my every need. In Jesus' name! Amen!

NOVEMBER 29

Yesterday, my husband was working on the woodstove outside. I watched as he stood up and smacked his head on the flue handle. YEOOOCH! Later when he showed me the bruise, I said, "You gotta look up before you make a move dear!" As the words came out of my mouth, the Lord said...

As it is in the natural, so is it in the spiritual...

Wow. How true is this? Whatever the situation, you can apply those words. We ought to always be looking to the Lord before we make decisions for even the smallest things. My favorite author, Corrie Ten Boom, is notorious for this type of relationship with the Lord. Each move she makes is precipitated by a bequest to the Lord on where to go, what to say, what to do. She looks up before she moves! Psalms 121:1-2 is a reminder, "I will life mine eyes up to the hills, from whence cometh my help? My help cometh from the Lord which made heaven and earth" (KJV). Dear Lord, thank you for reminding me that you are the one we can always look up to in every situation to find help, direction, wisdom, for you are the creator of heaven and earth and you formed me out of that dust and know the beginning from the end. Hallelujah! In Jesus' name! Amen!

NOVEMBER 30

The snow has blanketed the ground and trees, and suddenly, autumn has turned to winter. The beauty of sparkling snow is a drastic change from drab and dreary browns and grays. As much as I prefer the beauty of snow, I am aware of the fact that it could all be gone with forty-degrees and a little rain. It is truly a delicate dichotomy! As I thought about this the Lord prompted me to realize...

As it is in the natural, so is it in the spiritual...

Our faith can be as fleeting as the snow. We can be beautifully dazzling with the Love of God, affecting others with our sparkling faith one minute, and be full of frustration, impatience or anger the next. When we allow our circumstances or interactions with others to affect our behavior, we are like the fleeting snow: here today and gone tomorrow. James 1:12 says: "God blesses those who patiently endure testing and temptation. Afterward they will receive the crown of life that God has promised to those who love him." Verse 19 gives further instruction: "Understand this, my dear brothers and sisters: You must all be quick to listen, slow to speak, and slow to get angry" (NLT). Dear Lord Jesus, help me to exercise the fruit of the spirit each moment of my day so that my beautiful, sparkling faith is now blown away by the elements that surround me! In Jesus' name. Amen!

DECEMBER 1

Driving to work today I was surprised to find that the seemingly insignificant snowfall we received in the night time had become quite troublesome. Some roads had blown in to the point where they were nearly unrecognizable and impassable. I saw a child attempting to navigate down his drifted driveway to his school bus. As I thought about this, the Lord reminded me that...

As it is in the natural, so is it in the spiritual...

Just as those roads can quickly be filled in with just a little bit of precipitation, so too, can our spiritual path can be blocked by life's problems, sin and other distractions. A path that was so clear and distinct today, can be completely covered over and concealed by things we might think of as insignificant. We need to continually rely on God's guidance because he knows what to watch for and he can make our paths clearly visible once again. Proverbs 3:5-6 says "Trust in the Lord with all your heart; and lean not unto your own understanding. 6 In all your ways acknowledge him, and he shall make your paths straight" (NIV). The Message says: "Listen for God's voice in everything you do, everywhere you go; he's the one who will keep you on track." Lord, please help me continually look to you for guidance in all of my life. Thank you for keeping my path clear! Amen!

DECEMBER 2

Driving on ice for the first time this winter reminded me that experience is the best teacher. I know that if I hit my brakes on ice, my car will not stop quickly. I know that I need to beware of chatter bumps on ice or I will end up sideways. I know that icy, snowy roads are perilous and could be dangerous if I do not proceed with caution. I know all of these things but just because I know them, doesn't mean I practice them the first time it snows. I sometimes have to do a little slipping and sliding before I exercise that caution. As I thought about this, the Lord nudged me and reminded me that...

As it is in the natural, so is it in the spiritual...

Our spiritual path is also one we must navigate with care. It can quickly become a slippery one if we allow certain things to come into our path. For each of us, it may be something different that can cause our wheels to spin and for us to lose control of our direction. In an instant, a life can be turned around and we can end up in a spiritual ditch or worse. Psalms 121:3 promises, "He will not let your foot slip. He who watches over you will not slumber" (NIV). Lord help me to be aware of my own spiritual weather map and navigate this road cautiously so I can stay on that path you have set before me! Amen

DECEMBER 3

This has been a strange winter here in Michigan's Thumb. Typically, we have had several snowstorms and there is a base of white on the ground, but this year we have no snow on the ground as I write this. I always say, "If it's gonna be cold, we may as well have snow to beautify our world! Snow covers what otherwise would be a bleak, gray, lifeless landscape. As I thought about this the Lord nudged me...

As it is in the natural, so is it in the spiritual...

In the same way that the snow provides a covering of beauty over the brown and gray landscape, so too are our sins covered by LOVE. I Peter 4:8 says, "And above all things have fervent love for one another, for love will cover a multitude of sins" (NKJV). The Lord gave us an example of how to love one another sacrificially when he robed Himself in flesh to walk this earth and die for us. He became that perfect lamb who shed his blood to cleanse us from our sins. Lord Jesus, I thank you for the sacrifice you made on the cross. Your precious love covers my sins and makes me white as snow! I thank you and give you all of my praise! In Jesus' name! Amen!

DECEMBER 4

Driving to work this very frosty morning, a semi-truck pulled out and nearly clipped me on my driver's side as he proceeded without stopping. Gripping the steering wheel a bit more tightly and swerving to avoid him, I prayed my daily prayer of safety for my family and friends traveling. The truck quickly caught up with me, due to my cautious traveling, and was soon tailgating me at a distance that I was not comfortable with. I touched my taillights to signal him to back off, but instead at the next opportunity, he zoomed past me and cut me off! I felt so disrespected and angry! As I ponder that moment in time, I am suddenly aware that…

As it is in the natural, so is it in the spiritual…

Our loving heavenly Father gives us signals each time we come too close to some source of danger. Today after this near incident with the truck, I was forced to ask myself how He must feel when I disregard those little 'brake light taps' he sends me as warnings. Am I so caught up in getting to my own destination that I cannot take a moment to respond to his signals? Acts 28:27 relays God's heart: "For this people's heart has grown callous; they hardly hear with their ears, and they have closed their eyes. Otherwise they might see with their eyes, hear with their ears, understand with their hearts, and turn, and I would heal them" (BSB).

Dear Lord, please help me be ever so watchful and attentive to your warnings and signals. Help my heart to be soft and not callous. Help me see and hear YOU and never turn away from your voice so that I may proceed along my path and follow YOU. In Jesus' name! Amen!

DECEMBER 5

I have been keenly aware of the matters of life and death lately. A friend and neighbor recently lost her battle with cancer after traditional treatments failed. Another dear friend is currently battling cancer with faith, prayer, a clean diet and alternative treatments. My husband's friend is fighting for his life after a heart transplant, while yet another very close friend is with her daughter and their preemie baby after a scary labor and delivery. As I whisper prayers for these and more, the Lord whispers...

As it is in the natural, so is it in the spiritual...

Just as we battle against death of this body, there is most certainly another battle going on. That great and vital battle for our soul. So many of us cling to what is seen and disregard what is unseen. The sad truth is that the unseen is far more important for it determines where we will spend eternity. We spend far too much energy, time and money trying to cling to and enjoy life here on earth when it is truly just a blink of the eye when compared to eternity. The Lord reminded me that we ought to "Store up for yourselves treasures in heaven where moth and rust do not destroy and where thieves do not break in and steal, for where your treasure is, there also shall your heart be (Matthew 6:20-21). Thank you Lord for reminding me that the most important battle we can fight here is the one that brings us to eternity with YOU! Amen!

DECEMBER 6

Many times, when I am writing on my laptop, my little dog Jewel attempts to gain my attention by grabbing my moving fingers (softly) with her teeth in an attempt to engage me in some play time. She is relentless no matter how often I shoo her away she comes back barking and grabbing and then darting out of reach to avoid my grasp. It is as if my affections are her greatest need! As I thought about how this scenario is actually more humorous than annoying, the Lord nudged me...

As it is in the natural, so is it in the spiritual...

When we are in need of affection and attention, the Lord is waiting on us to come to Him. I am reminded of Jesus' parable in Luke 11 of a man who went to his friend's home at midnight asking for bread. The friend finally gave in due to his neighbor's persistence. The contrast between the unwilling friend and Jesus is apparent in the following verses. "And I say unto you, ask and it shall be given you; seek and ye shall find; knock and it shall be opened unto you." Just as my dog Jewel fails not to seek my attentions and affections, we must be bold and unafraid to seek out the Lord. The Amplified version of Matthew 7:7 highlights this principle: "Keep on asking and it will be given you; keep on seeking and you will find; keep on knocking [reverently] and [the door] will be opened."ABear Lord, help me to remember that You are daily waiting for me to ask and seek your presence so that you may lavish your love and affection upon me. In Jesus' name! Amen!

DECEMBER 7

Winter weather in Michigan can change drastically from one day to the next. Just a couple of days ago, we had a lush covering of fresh, fluffy, white snow covering our world and with the sunshine, it was blindingly brilliant and beautiful; today, we have foggy, gray, dark day with drizzle, and our snow base has diminished quite a bit. How quickly things can change with just a bit of precipitation! As I pondered this, the Lord quickened to me that...

As it is in the natural, so is it in the spiritual...

I know I wrote about a similar principal a few weeks ago, but this has a different slant so please bear with me! The Lord wants us to see that just as the landscape outside of our window can change quickly depending on the weather, so too can the landscape of our soul change quickly if we allow certain 'precipitation' to enter our therein. Seeking happiness in our human ways can be momentarily satisfying but things can turn dreadfully dark and gray quickly when conditions change. The beauty and joy that exists in the heart of a believer is there because we are embracing God's purpose for our life; this will not fade when the drizzle of daily trials falls upon us. Romans 14:7 tells us; "For the kingdom of God is not meat and drink; but righteousness, and peace, and joy in the Holy Ghost" (KJV). Lord, help me to remember that the temporal things of this world will never truly improve a dreary gray landscape within a human soul. Only showers from heaven will bring beauty, peace and joy! Amen!

DECEMBER 8

I was reading a friend's Facebook post about her son's experience with a popular online video site. Apparently, he had searched for a children's cartoon and was sitting quietly next to her watching it. At least that's what she thought...until she looked at the screen. She was appalled and horrified at what she saw. The "cartoon" was a dupe that had been uploaded by some evil, twisted person who created a video with graphic violent and sexual images with the cartoon title. The cartoon voiceover was playing so the parent who is not directly watching would think their child is simply watching a cartoon. As I thought about this the Lord pointed out...

As it is in the natural, so is it in the spiritual...

Satan has been a liar and deceiver ever since he tricked Adam and Eve in the Garden of Eden. The bible says that he disguises himself as an angel of light (II Corinthians 11:14). Jesus says this of evil people: "Ye are of your father the devil, and the lusts of your father ye will do. He was a murderer from the beginning, and abode not in the truth, because there is no truth in him. When he speaketh a lie, he speaketh of his own: for he is a liar, and the father of it" (John 8:44). It is shocking to discover that such individuals exist in a world where we want to trust others. But the truth is, we must be on our toes. We are warned in I Peter 5:8, "Be on your guard and stay awake. Your enemy, the devil, is like a roaring lion, sneaking around to find someone to attack" (CEV). Lord, help me to daily come to you for wisdom, discernment and spiritual direction. Guard me and my loved ones against the wiles and schemes of the enemy of our soul. In Jesus' Name! Amen!

DECEMBER 9

Once the leaves have fallen, the crops are harvested, and the temperatures turn cold, the scenery around us turns brown and bleak here in Michigan. It is as if everything living has died and the scenery can be quite gloomy. What was once green and lush is now colorless and dried up. As I look around feeling a bit saddened, the Lord revealed to me...

As it is in the natural, so is it in the spiritual...

In the same way that winter is the season in the natural that reflects the dying of leaves and plants, so too can we enter those wintry spiritual seasons. If we allow our hearts to grow cold to the Lord, then our spirit will begin to die and we can end up with bleakness and hopelessness. In order to ward this off, we must refresh and renew our hearts and minds, turning daily back to God in prayer. Acts 3:19 tells us, "Therefore repent and return, so that your sins may be wiped away, in order that times of refreshing may come from the presence of the Lord; 20 and that He may send Jesus, the Christ appointed for you, 21 whom heaven must receive until the period of restoration of all things about which God spoke by the mouth of His holy prophets from ancient time" (NASB). Lord I pray you will lead me in daily repentance and renewal that newness of life and a passion to serve you will spring up in my heart. In Jesus' name! Amen!

DECEMBER 10

Today, my school is having their first snow day of the year. As the free time looms before me, I begin checking off the possible 'To-do' items in my mind. I even put them down on paper. There are dozens of tasks that I could focus on today but I soon realize I haven't got time for them all...so I need to prioritize my list! As I thought about this, it the Lord tapped my proverbial shoulder and reminded me that...

As it is in the natural, so is it in the spiritual...

Our Lord Jesus Christ has taught us that we not to be so concerned over daily tasks as we are about seeking after Him. Yes, there are things we want to accomplish in this lifetime, but we ought not allow our 'list' crowd out the more important things. In Matthew 6:25 Jesus tells us, "Take no thought for your life, what ye shall eat, or what ye shall drink; nor yet for your body, what ye shall put on. Is not the life more than meat, and the body than rainment?" and he further exhorts us in verse 33 to "Seek ye first the kingdom of God and His righteousness; and all these things shall be added unto you" (KJV). Lord, help me to prioritize my life by focusing on my spiritual life and help me understand that by seeking after your kingdom and your righteousness, I can find true fulfillment in you and then everything else will not seem so pressing!

DECEMBER 11

Thinking back to a time when we got a new puppy. It takes time and patience when you are in the process of training them. She was very attached to us very quickly and we realize that she is totally dependent on us for her very life...food, water, shelter and love. It truly reminds me of an infant and how helpless and in need of vigilant parents they are. As I think of this, the lord reminds me that...

As it is in the natural, so is it in the spiritual...

In the same way that infants and puppies are so dependent upon us, so too do I realize how dependent I am upon the Lord for my spiritual survival! The nourishment for my soul comes from being in His presence, feeding on his word, and discovering His love, shelter and protection in my times of prayer. Deuteronomy 8:3 tells us, "So He humbled you, allowed you to hunger, and fed you with manna which you did not know nor did your fathers know, that He might make you know that man shall not live by bread alone; but man lives by every word that proceeds from the mouth of the LORD" (NKJV). Luke 12:24 also reminds us, "Consider the ravens: they neither sow nor reap, they have neither storehouse nor barn, and yet God feeds them. Of how much more value are you than the birds!" (ESV). Thank you Lord, for your promises are true! He is the provider for our every need! Amen!

DECEMBER 12

This week, the multi Billionaire founder of Facebook is involved in senate hearings regarding data privacy. To put it plainly, the social media kingpin is accused of manipulating the information that shows up on some 87 million users news feed. By censoring what comes across the news feed they can essentially change the truth into a lie. They can push the agenda of one group, while squelching the voice of another. By presenting 'Fake News' they manipulate the thought lives of millions of people. Oddly (but not oddly if we believe the Lord is alive and working in our lives when we allow!) today during my morning devotions, I was reading about how the enemy speaks into our lives and then sends other voices to support his cause. I'm not gonna lie! This is a bit disturbing! My husband he likened it to what is going on with Facebook this week and the Lord reminded me that…

As it is in the natural, so is it in the spiritual…

Just as social media giants have the power to infiltrate our thoughts by pushing a certain agenda, so too does the enemy of our soul infiltrate our minds. He is crafting his news reel each day in order to entice us away from God's purpose for our lives. By using 'Fake News' the enemy will strive to send lies and false information into our lives. He stirs up doubt and fear and seeks to destroy our faith in Jesus Christ. He is a thief and a liar and we must daily protect our stream of information by going to His Word. John 17:17 says, "Sanctify them through thy truth; Thy word is truth.' The psalmist wrote, "Thy word is a lamp unto my feet and a light unto my path." Lord help me to daily turn to your word first and let it be the filter through which I view all of the issues and matters of life. In Jesus' Name…Amen.

DECEMBER 13

I like my social media site; in fact, I try to scroll through it for a few minutes each day to check for birthdays and just see what's happening out there! I also use online shopping sights and do most of my Christmas shopping online. Recently I have noticed that on my social media site, the ads that pop up are for those items I have been shopping for. I realize that we can control the settings for which sites can leave cookies so I will need to make that adjustment if I want these pestering little ads to go away. As I was thinking about this somewhat creepy, big brotherish, circumstance of retail tracking that is so common in the internet age in which we live, the Lord clarified to me that

As it is in the natural, so is it in the spiritual...

Just as my shopping site tracks my shopping habits and eerily sends ads my way on other sites, so too does the enemy of our soul track our habits. He stalks us. He listens to what we say, and watches what we do and takes note of where we go. He then plans his attack. He attacks our thought life by infiltrating our minds with his agenda. He exploits our weaknesses and sends 'ads' and enticements into our lives to draw us away from our indented path. Wow. I Peter 5:8 says "Be sober, be vigilant; because your adversary the devil, as a roaring lion, walketh about, seeking whom he may devour..." (KJV). Lord, help me to be daily aware that the enemy of my soul is watching me and waiting for me to make a false move so he can consume me. Keep my mind fixed on YOU, oh Lord Jesus. In your mighty name, Amen.

DECEMBER 14

We are experiencing a very serious ice storm this weekend. We lost power yesterday afternoon as did many others. I reported it about ten minutes after it went out. I've been checking my app periodically and even resubmitting the distress call! I just want to know for sure that they have a plan and a timeline for restoring my power! I am trying to be patient. My circumstances are out of my control. Another ice storm has now arrived. So, we wait. And now, the same message is being displayed even this morning: "DTE Energy is aware of the problem. However, a restoration estimate is not currently available." As I read this message again for the umpteenth time, the Lord whispered...

As it is in the natural, so is it in the spiritual...

Many times, we are in need of something and we take it to the Lord in prayer. Once we do this, we must believe that the Lord is aware of the problem. We must now trust that He has received our cry of distress, but sometimes, there is no immediate answer. Sometimes we must wait. Our patience is tried, our circumstances are out of our control. Psalms 130:5 reminds me, "I wait for the Lord, my soul doth wait, and in his word, do I hope" (KJV). Lord help us to trust you enough to wait upon you for answers. When situations are out of our control, help me to be patient in knowing that you know my every need. In Jesus' name! Amen!

DECEMBER 15

Time is a precious commodity in this life and I admit that I struggle with making decisions on how to spend unplanned time off. I have a snow day today and the opportunity to just be at home and catch up on housework, and bills, and later on today, I have a massage appointment. However, because the snow day called last night wasn't as bad as predicted, my daughter and two grandkiddos who live near me are going to Bay City to visit my younger daughter and her one- month old baby. Even though I always have a "To Do" list, I never regret spending time with my kids and grandkids. I need to grasp those moments when they present themselves. Seize the day! Carpe Diem! As I thought about this, the Lord nudged me...

As it is in the natural, so is it in the spiritual...

We often fail to recognize that we really do not know how many days, months or years we have left here on this earth! Time is a gift from the Lord, and it would behoove us to check with him before we make decisions on how to spend it! Yes, family is of utmost importance as is church attendance and time spent building our own personal relationship with Jesus through prayer, bible study and ministering to others. As we give of our time for the things of God, we will never know the impact until we get to heaven! Ephesians 5:15-17 says, "15 Pay careful attention, then, to how you walk, not as unwise but as wise, 16 redeeming the time, because the days are evil. 17 Therefore do not be foolish, but understand what the Lord's will is" (BSB). Lord, help me seek your will and then obey you, so I may spend my time wisely as you would have me to. In Jesus' name! Amen!

DECEMBER 16

Watching a baby grow and learn never ceases to amaze me. Their health and well-being are completely dependent upon the care they receive from parents or caregivers. They are sustained with their mother's milk for many months until they reach the age when soft foods, fruits and vegetables are added and finally, a more substantial diet including proteins and complex carbohydrates are necessary to sustain a healthy, growing person. Yes, indeed, food is a vital element in the health and well-being of a growing human! As I thought on this, the Lord reminded me that...

As it is in the natural, so is it in the spiritual...

Just as our dietary needs evolve as we grow in to adults, so must our spiritual diet change. But this is dependent on how well we have put to use what was already fed to us! Paul talks about this in Hebrews 5: "For when for the time ye ought to be teachers, ye have need that one teach you again which be the first principles of the oracles of God; and are become such as have need of milk, and not of strong meat" (KJV). In I Corinthians chapter 3, Paul also writes, "1 Brothers, I could not address you as spiritual, but as worldly as infants in Christ. 2 I gave you milk, not solid food, for you were not yet ready for solid food. In fact, you are still not ready, 3 for you are still worldly. For since there is jealousy and dissension among you, are you not worldly? Are you not walking in the way of man?" (BSB). The key here is that God desires for us to grow spiritually by first digesting his word - the Bible. I Peter 2 states: "2. As newborn babes, desire the sincere milk of the word, that ye may grow thereby: 3 If so be ye have tasted that the Lord is gracious" (KJV). Lord help me to crave the pure milk of your word so I may grow spiritually stronger that I may be a teacher of your word, strong and mighty through you! In Jesus' name! Amen!

DECEMBER 17

Today is the birthday of our amazing grandson, Levi, Kristin and Nick's firstborn baby. This little guy made his appearance on a snowy day, three weeks early. Despite his early arrival, he was healthy and strong. Levi has always had a big, infectious smile and a laugh that makes my heart sing! He is kind and tender-hearted, and as he grows, we see his athletic gifts coming forth. Thinking about the love I have for this grandson of mine, the Lord whispers...

As it is in the natural, so is it in the spiritual...

Each child and grandchild that we are blessed with is so precious, unique, and loved! Likewise, the Lord wants us to each realize how precious, unique and loved we are to Him. John 3:16 reminds us, "For God so loved the world that he gave his one and only son, that whoever believes in him shall not perish but have eternal life" (NIV). It is very difficult to put my love for my family into words. I can only say that God's love for us is the best comparison I can make! Dear Lord, thank you for your unbelievable unconditional love. Thank you for my children and grandchildren, who were given to me by you, and help me to be able to show them not only my love for them, but also to teach them how great the love of Christ is for each of them! In Jesus' name! Amen!

DECEMBER 18

We had another snow day yesterday, but the main roads were fine so I decided to make a quick trip to Port Huron for craft supplies for Christmas. Our snowy road had tracks in it where previous vehicles had passed prior to the hard freeze overnight. The result was a very deeply carved path in the road, which demanded that you stay in those tracks. However, some of those tracks seemed to be leading me straight to the ditch!! I was fighting my vehicle to maintain control and stay on the road! As I thought about this the Lord quickened to me that...

As it is in the natural, so is it in the spiritual...

Those frozen ruts in my road were a result of someone else's driving, and yet I felt helpless to get out of that rut and into my own safe lane. Likewise, in life, we have to make choices about the path we are on. Just because someone else made a path, does not mean it's the one we ought to be on! We need to prayerfully consider our purpose and God's plan for our life, and we then need to follow His paths if we want true joy and peace. David writes in Psalms 16:11, "You make known to me the path of life; you will fill me with joy in your presence, with eternal pleasures at your right hand" (NIV).

DECEMBER 19

We had a little snowstorm pass through Michigan again yesterday, and although we did not get a bunch of snow, many in our area closed schools today. My husband had to go in, so I have the entire day to do with whatever I wish. As I have mentioned, times this can be a dilemma for me as I am that type A person who wants to get everything in order, but just never seem to have the time to do it all! Even with extra time off, I find myself becoming frustrated and overwhelmed! As I thought on this, the Lord reminded me...

As it is in the natural, so is it in the spiritual...

Just as many of us have the desire to get everything in order in our daily lives and we run from this to that and end up frustrated, so too can we become frustrated in our spiritual lives when we attempt to accomplish too much on our own strength. We are not supposed to undertake the concerns of this life on our own, but rather, in Luke 22 Jesus tells us "Therefore I say to you, do not worry about your life, what you will eat; nor about the body, what you will put on. 23 Life is more than food, and the body is more than clothing..." and he goes on to say that we need to "Seek ye first the Kingdom of God and His righteousness and these things shall be added unto you" (KJV). Help me today Lord, to see those things which are eternal and not be so focused on the things that are visible. Thank you for showing me your path! Amen!

DECEMBER 20

We had a big ice storm this week and it brought to mind a few truths of nature and life. When a storm such as this one hits, we suddenly realize that we often take for granted things like electricity and mobility. The beauty and the fierceness of winter is simultaneously and suddenly etched across the canvas of our lives in the form of sparkling snow crystals and icicles hanging from every inch of every branch of every tree. Even the most-dreary landscape on a typical day is transformed into a breathtaking scene. The view can paralyze us and mesmerize us all at once. The world becomes an extravaganza reflecting beauty and brilliance at every angle and when the sun shines, the effect is blinding. As I thought on this, I realized...

As it is in the natural, so is it in the spiritual...

My wintery visual experience can be compared to that moment when we come into the presence of God. Our breath is taken away and we are blinded to anything dreary or dark because the light of the world has overcome darkness. Beauty takes the place of dullness. Life takes our breath away once again and we cannot find words to express the majesty of the Lord. Psalms 96:9 proclaims, "Worship the LORD in the splendor of His holiness; tremble before Him, all the earth" (BSB). Lord, thank you for your marvelous creation, the work of your hands! You have designed such a beautiful world for us to live in and marvel at! Help us to remember that YOU are the author of all of this creation, so that we may worship you accordingly! Amen!

DECEMBER 21

This Christmas, for our whole family gathering, we decided to adopt a family rather than buying gifts for each other. While there are many in need, I selected two children from my school who often wear clothes that don't fit and shoes with holes in them. They don't have proper winter coats, hats and mittens. They come in without baths or showers, with ratted hair and unwashed faces, and we just know that these kids need a helping hand. As I thought about this the Lord quickened to me that ...

As it is in the natural, so is it in the spiritual...

Many of us need to strip down our lives to the bare minimum before we can even begin to understand 'need' or 'want', and if we are never in want of anything in the physical realm, it is very difficult for us to feel needy in the spiritual realm. When we clutter ourselves up with so many other activities, concerns, and worries of this world, it becomes difficult to understand the desperate spiritual deficit that we have. We must strip ourselves down through self-denial, and serving others, especially the needy if we want to honor God. Proverbs 14:31 addresses this: "Whoever oppresses the poor shows contempt for their Maker, but whoever is kind to the needy honors God" (NIV). Jesus said in Matthew 5:6, "Blessed are those who hunger and thirst after righteousness for they shall be filled" (KJV). Thank you Lord for all of the blessings we have and for giving us a heart to share and a hunger to honor YOU! Amen!

DECEMBER 22

I wrote this in 2018: Every Christmas for the past several years, a popular new story is told to children everywhere about the Elf on the Shelf. His arrival in their homes creates a bit of an uproar. Elf is a controversial and somewhat hypocritical character: he gets into mischief at night, but yet spies on the kids and reports their behavior to Santa. This little dude dwells in the homes of millions of people who hope his presence will help children behave. Children give him a special name, and he is a social media star as parents tweet and snap the shenanigans this nocturnal tattletale gets into while the children are nestled all snug in their beds. He is either loved or hated, cherished or rejected. Psychologists analyze his influence on children, parents pray he brings a peaceful home, children either dread or adore him. He truly is a fellow with a mixed following. His presence and power in our children's lives is temporary, for one day they will know he is just a toy. As I thought about this the Lord pointed out...

As it is in the natural, so is it in the spiritual...

Each Christmas for the past several millennia, a story is told to children everywhere about the birth of Jesus Christ. His arrival brought a tremendous uproar. He is a controversial character, accepted and adored by some, rejected and hated by others. He dwells in the hearts of countless people who have put their hope in His presence to change their lives. His name is above all names on the earth and He is the bright and morning star. Psychologists analyze his effect on mankind, people pray for His peace to fill the earth, and He is either loved or hated, cherished or rejected. He truly is a fellow with a mixed following. Jesus' presence and power in our children's lives is eternal, and one day they will discover he is real. While Elf 'reports' to Santa, Jesus advocates for us. Elf exposes children's mistakes, while Jesus covers our sins with his blood and forgives us of each and every one! He is our ever-present help in times of trouble! Dear Lord, as we enter this Christmas week, may we remember to place you first in our lives and in the lives of our children. Let us remember to teach our children the greatest story of all...the one of Your birth. Isaiah 9:6 says it well: "For unto us a child is born, unto us a son is given: and the government shall be upon his shoulder: and his name shall be called Wonderful, Counselor, The mighty God, The everlasting Father, The Prince of Peace" (KJV). May we look to Jesus to bring love, joy and peace into our homes! Amen!

DECEMBER 23

At Christmas last year, my sister gave me and my sisters in law a beautiful 'Sisters' bracelet. It was so sweet and thoughtful, and I felt bad that I had nothing to give in return! I began to brainstorm what to get for her, but I realized that a gift reciprocated after the fact just isn't the same as one given with planning and forethought. As I thought about this, the Lord reminded me that...

As it is in the natural, so is it in the spiritual...

The feeling I had that day is a glimpse of how we should feel when we think about the amazing, life changing gift that can never, ever be reciprocated: God's gift of Salvation to us. The Lord made a plan from the beginning of time to redeem mankind with an unfathomable gift. He gave himself! YES! He robed himself in flesh, and came down from heaven to walk this earth and shed his blood to cover our sins. Ephesians 2:8 says, "For it is by his grace that we have been saved through faith, and this faith was not from you, but it is the gift of God" (ABPE). What a gift! We could never, ever reciprocate what God has done for us and yet, we somehow feel we must try and try to earn his love. Rest easy my friends. His gift has already been placed in your hands. Receive it. Cherish it and accept it as with a thankful heart. In Jesus' name! Amen!

DECEMBER 24

As we make our final preparations for tomorrow, I am making lists, checking them twice, playing Christmas music, touching up the tree decorations and baking yummy treats. I am excited to be together with my family. My mom is running out of space to host these get togethers in her home as our family continues to grow, and each year she says, "This is the last time I'm doing this! I don't have room for everyone!" But every year, we make it happen. We set up tables in the garage and extend the dining space by one more card table! With Christmas being tomorrow, I can't help but think of the night Jesus was born. The little town of Bethlehem was overflowing with people who were there to pay their taxes, so there were no rooms left for a very pregnant Mary and her husband Joseph. Finally, an innkeeper gave them permission to stay in his stable. As I think about the incredible circumstances that surrounded the birth of the King of Kings and Lord of Lords it struck me...

As it is in the natural, so is it in the spiritual...

Much like that little town, so many have filled our lives to overflowing with busyness that we have no room for Jesus. Perhaps it's work, or play, or running kids to and from sports or school activities or other extracurricular things. Perhaps it is church that keeps us too busy to actually make room for a relationship with our Savior! Whatever the reason, we all must take time to evaluate how we spend our time and what we have made room for. Ephesians 5 says, "15 Therefore be careful how you walk, not as unwise men but as wise, 16 making the most of your time, because the days are evil. 17 So then do not be foolish, but understand what the will of the Lord is" (NASB). Lord, Jesus, I thank you for this little reminder. Help me to make room first and foremost for You and keep a proper perspective on what is important in my life. Help me to scale back on things that keep me from living for Your kingdom, Your power, and Your glory. Amen!

DECEMBER 25

This was written in 2015 on Christmas Day. I pray you have a blessed day rejoicing in the truth of what this day truly commemorates!

> We've got dasher and dancer and all Santa's reindeer
> Bright decorations and hopes for the New Year
> Holiday parties where joy does abound
> Sweet little treats, yummy food all around

Too many nice gifts wrapped and under the tree
Something for everyone including me!
Waiting, excited for Christmas to come
Then all too suddenly, wow…it's all done!

Sitting and pondering this season of wonder
God whispers something…"Did you remember..?
Did you remember the widow next door?
Did you remember the soldier at war?

Did you bring joy to the lost and the hurting?
Did you take time to give what costs nothing?
I came to seek and save those who are lost
This you can share, not a dime it will cost"

Friend, do you remember the reason for joy?
Do you remember that one special boy?
Immanuel - God incarnate - was born
The Glory from heaven that first Christmas morn

Born in a manger, no room at the inn…
The Lord of Creation came down as a man
The purpose was simple, to save all mankind
Bring hope for the hopeless, give sight to the blind

Rejected and scorned, but no hate in his heart
"Forgive them" he urged just before he'd depart
The world still rejects Him, they don't understand
He is our Savior, fully God, yet a man

Take time this Christmas, and read that old story
Of Lord of Creation, who came down from Glory
Whisper his name out of worship or need
Whenever it's spoken tis promised, he'll heed

A peace like a river did flood my own soul
And He is the reason that I am now whole
He ran to me, as I whispered His name
And for each one of us He'll do the same

Blessings to you, Merry Christmas my friends
With love in my heart, till I see you again!

DECEMBER 26

The day after Christmas can be one filled with leftovers. Some foods are great warmed up or chilled for a day or two, but have you ever bitten into something that is well past its freshness? YUCK! I tried to eat some fruit today that had turned to mush and it was nasty! Fruit that is ripe and fresh is wonderful! But if it is not used at the proper time, it is wasted and just needs to be discarded into the compost pile. As I thought about this, the Lord quickened to me that...

As it is in the natural, so is it in the spiritual...

Our spiritual being is much like fruit. We must allow God to use us in our season of maturity. If we set ourselves on a shelf, we will surely grow soft, mushy and moldy. Matthew 7 likens people to trees which bear good fruit and bad fruit. It is a stern reminder that those not bearing good fruit will be cut down and cast into the fire! Jesus emphasizes obedience as a vital part of being used by Him: "Not everyone who says to me "Lord, Lord" will enter the kingdom of heaven but only the one who does the will of My Father who is in heaven" (NIV). Dear Lord, I pray that I can be the kind of fruit that is pleasing to You...not easily bruised by external pressures, but firm in my faith, obediently fulfilling your will for my life. May I be used of You in this season of my life to bring something sweet and good into the life of others. In Jesus' name! Amen!

DECEMBER 27

Today we watched one of my favorite preachers, Brother JH Osborne. He was talking about leprosy and the stages of this disease. It is known that Leprosy begins internally, so there is an incubation period where the person isn't aware they've contracted it. It begins to manifest in various ways including numbness, weakness or even paralysis, blindness and finally disfiguration and in extreme cases it may lead to loss of limbs and other body parts. As he spoke, the Lord quickened to me exactly where Brother Osborne was leading us...

As it is in the natural, so is it in the spiritual...

Sin is like leprosy in so many ways. It begins internally in our thoughts and desires (lust of the flesh, lust of the eyes and pride of life). This is the incubation period where the person isn't manifesting any real sinful symptoms, for it is still in the thoughts. But if let go untreated, it begins to show itself in various ways. We become numb to the things of God. We are too weak to resist temptation. We are paralyzed to defend our Christian beliefs to those who might oppose us. Finally, our sins begin to seep into our outward being, disfiguring our countenance, causing us to lose sight of the Lord, our purpose and calling. Finally, and tragically it leads to death which is separation from God, who only wants to bring us Life everlasting. James 1:14 says, "Temptation comes from our own desires, which entice us and drag us away. 15. These desires give birth to sinful actions. And when sin is allowed to grow, it gives birth to death" (NLT). Lord, help me to identify the disease of sin before I allow it to enter my spirit. Help me to remain immunized by your mighty hand and come daily to you for cleansing. In Jesus' name! Amen!

DECEMBER 28

Visiting our kids here in Iowa overlooking their lake, the signs of the season are evident. There was ice on the lake one day then after a couple days of warm weather it was melted! When we went to bed last night, there was no ice but this morning there is a layer of ice with snow on top. In just a matter of hours, the lake can be transformed from one form to another. As I thought about this phenomenon, the Lord reminded me...

As it is in the natural, so is it in the spiritual...

The transformation of water to ice and ice to water on a lake is very comparable to the transformation of one's heart when it comes in contact with the presence of God. In His presence, the icy heart is warmed and melted. A person whose heart is warmed and softened will have a mind that is willing and ready for change. They can be transformed into an entirely different person in a very short time! Romans 12:2 tells us, "And be not conformed to this world; But be ye transformed by the renewing of your mind, that ye may prove what is that good, and acceptable, and perfect, will of God" (KJV). Dear Lord, thank you for the miracle of your presence. Thank you for warming my heart, transforming and renewing my mind so that I may do what is pleasing to you! In Jesus' name! Amen!

DECEMBER 29

As I look outside this morning, I see the effects of this year's El-Niño weather. The snow barely is covering the ground and I think about how this winter thus far has been so bleak and so mild. Many people love mild winters. Many complain when there is too much snow or it's too cold. This mild weather may appeal to us in some ways, but there is something to be said for a blanket of snow. There is a reason why farmers want a good old-fashioned solid covering of snow over their fields. It is so much better that the ground be protected in the winter rather than exposed to the elements. Not only does it look better, but the snow protects the soil from losing the precious nutrients that will be the bed for next year's crop. As I ponder this, the Lord reminds me that...

As it is in the natural, so is it in the spiritual...

Just as the ground needs that solid covering of snow to hold the nutrients in for the next year, so too our hearts, minds and spirits need the solid covering of the Lord in order to protect us. We need the blanket of his hand to protect us from the elements of this world that seek to destroy us and wash away that which is precious. When we go through our El-Niño season, we may experience loss. Psalms 5:11 reminds us, "But let all who take refuge in you be glad; let them ever sing for joy. Spread your protection over them, that those who love your name may rejoice in you" (NIV). Dear Lord, let us seek your covering, protection and benefits, so that we can bring forth a harvest for Your kingdom! In Jesus' name! Amen!

DECEMBER 30

As the new year is approaching, I can't help but to think about making a list of resolutions. Eat better, lose weight, exercise more, clean my closets, stay organized...you get the picture. I always feel like this time of the year is the perfect time to do things like clean the closets, (out with the old, in with the new!) adopt a healthier lifestyle by eating better foods, make things look better by perhaps putting up new curtains up in our bedroom or laying down fluffy new rugs for the bathroom so when I am getting ready my feet are warm and so on! As I ponder what that might look like this New Year season, the Lord drops this thought into my heart...

As it is in the natural, so is it in the spiritual...

Just as cleaning a closet, eating healthier meals, or buying curtains and rugs can spark a little zest for life, so too must we consider how to add a spark to our spiritual lives. Start by cleaning out old grudges and getting rid of old attitudes we are weary of. Then remove the old dusty curtains that keep us from seeing things from God's point of view. Next, we need to consume more of God's word on a daily basis for spiritual well-being and exercise self-control and other attributes that will build our faith. Finally lay down a foundation of principles upon which we can stand each morning as we prepare for what God has for us today! Dear Lord, thank you for showing me how to prepare for another new year by renewing my spiritual self, casting out the old and bringing in the new and amazing things you have in store for me! In Jesus' name! Amen!

DECEMBER 31

New Year's Eve is here. Each new year provides an opportunity to reflect on the past year and assess where we can make changes to improve for the year to come. Many people are in the mindset of 'out with the old and in with the new.' The New Year's Baby is a symbol newness of life! These past few days, there were pictures of the little tot everywhere, reminding us that the New Year is approaching. As I thought on this the Lord reminded me that…

As it is in the natural, so is it in the spiritual…

A new baby brings hope for the future and excitement into one's life as well as the desire to share this news with everyone around us. Likewise, so too does a new life in Christ Jesus. With Christ, our hope is an eternal one, and our dreams and thoughts become centered on helping others find true peace, joy and salvation through Him. Let us begin this year by casting out the old doubts, fears and unbelief, and ringing in a celebration of our life in Christ, so that we can joyfully share the good news with all people. Romans 15:13 says it well: "Now the God of hope fill you with all joy and peace in believing, that ye may abound in hope, through the power of the Holy Ghost" (KJV). Lord, I thank you for dropping each of these thoughts into my heart. I give you all the praise and glory for any good thing that comes from theses writings! My prayer is that each one of you have enjoyed the many ways that God has expressed his GREAT love for us through these metaphors. In Jesus' name! Amen!

Credits

Prince, D. (2013). Pulling down strongholds.

Abbreviations for Bible Versions Used
ABPE Aramaic Bible in Plain English
BSB Berean Study Bible
CSB Christian Standard Bible
DBT Darby Bible Translation
ERV easy to read version
ESV English Standard Version
GNT Good News Translation
NASB New American standard Bible
HCSB Holman Christian Standard Bible
KJV King James Version
NIRV New International Readers Version
NIV New international Version
NLV new living testament
WEB World English Bible